Animating Facial Features and Expressions

Animating Facial Features and Expressions

Bill Fleming

and

Darris Dobbs

CHARLES RIVER MEDIA, INC.
Rockland, Massachusetts

Executive Editor: Jenifer L. Niles
Production: Publishers' Design and Production Services, Inc.
Cover Design: Sherry Stinson
Cover Art: Bill Fleming
Printer: InterCity Press, Rockland, MA

CHARLES RIVER MEDIA, Inc.
P.O. Box 417, 403 VFW Drive
Rockland, MA 02370
781-871-4184
781-871-4376(FAX)
chrivmedia@aol.com
http://www.charlesriver.com

This book is printed on acid-free paper

Animating Facial Features and Expressions
by Bill Fleming and Darris Dobbs
ISBN 1-886801-81-9
Printed in the United States of America

00 7 6 5 4 3

CHARLES RIVER MEDIA titles are available for site license or bulk purchase by institutions, user groups, corporations, etc. For additional information, please contact the Special Sales Department at 781-871-4184.

Contents

Introduction

There are many aspects to 3D graphics but none more fascinating and complicated than facial animation and expression. Creating emotion can be challenging, but the reward clearly outweighs the effort. Of course, it can be very daunting if you don't fully understand the nature of facial expression. This is evident by the lack of truly inspiring facial expression on 3D characters. We have been bombarded with a plethora of 3D characters over the last several years, but they all seem to have the same blank expression on their faces.

There are many possibilities for facial animation. They aren't simply limited to human heads. You can animate cartoon characters, animals, alien creatures, and talking trees if you get the urge. No matter what character you are animating, facial expression becomes a critical part of the project. Nothing is quite as disappointing as a wonderfully modeled and surfaced character that appears lifeless because it has poorly animated expressions. Creating believable and expressive facial expressions brings your character to life, no matter how cartoony it may appear.

This book is designed to provide you with a wealth of resource material for facial animation and expression. Actually, when you get right down to it, facial animation is the easy part. Creating the inspiring and engaging expressions is the real challenge. In the coming chapters we will explore a number of facial animation and expression issues. Here is a brief overview of what we will be discussing in this book.

Overview of the Book and Technology

New technology is steadily being developed that expands the capabilities of 3D products. Even the most basic 3D programs possess many of the essential tools for creating killer facial expressions and animations. While the capabilities of 3D programs will continue to grow, the principles of 3D facial expression and animation will always remain constant. This book covers countless universal techniques for creating inspirational facial expression and animation. These techniques are not fixed to any one specific program, but rather apply to nearly every 3D program on the market.

If you use any of the following programs you should read this book: SoftImage, Alias, LightWave, 3D Studio MAX, 3D Studio, AnimationMaster, Strata Studio Pro, ElectricImage, Ray Dream Studio, trueSpace, Extreme 3D, Animation Master, Houdini, Imagine, Cinema 4D, Soft/FX, and even POV-RAY.

How This Book Is Organized

This book is divided into three parts that will take you logically through the process of developing facial expressions and animations. Each part is a complete concept, allowing you to reach closure at the end. You don't have to read one part to understand another. If you are only interested in how to animate your facial expressions with morph targets you can read Part II and skip the other parts of the book, though I do recommend that you read the entire book if you are interested in the complete process of developing awesome facial expressions and animations.

PART I—THE HUMAN HEAD
Chapter 1—Anatomy of the Head

We'll start by taking a look at the anatomy of the human head. To explore facial animation we must first start below the skin where all expression is created. Now, this is not a medical anatomy book, and I don't expect you to remember a myriad of Latin names, but what I do want is for you to gain a complete understanding of how the different muscles in the head affect particular regions of the face. The key to creating believable expressions is to first understand the mechanisms behind them. Once we have a handle on the skeletal structure of the human head, we'll take a look at one of the most daunting aspects of human head modeling—proportions.

Chapter 2—Proportions of the Head

Creating the proper proportions for the head is essential if we want the facial expressions and animation to appear convincing. There is no more difficult task than creating believable human facial animation and expressions. We see human expression every day in the world around us, on television, in the movies, and walking down our city streets. Therefore, we have an expectation of how a 3D human head should appear. Now we may not know exactly what is wrong with a model, but we will most certainly recognize that something is wrong. In our exploration of proportions, we will cover every detail of the perfect human head. The important thing to remember is that this discussion is merely to serve as a foundation for your own head modeling. Some variables of the head remain constant in most humans, making them a necessity to include in your model if you want the viewer to be convinced that it is alive.

Once we have a handle on the physical proportions of a human head, we'll take a look at the mechanism behind facial expression and animation—facial muscles.

Chapter 3—Facial Muscles

The facial muscles drive expression and animation. Knowing how each of the facial muscles works will give you a distinct advantage when creating facial expressions and animations. In this chapter we'll explore each of the facial muscles and view examples of them in action. You'll see many example images as well as animations that show the actual facial muscles moving.

After we've satisfied our craving for human head anatomy, we'll take a look at how facial expression is used to set the stage for an image or animation.

PART II—EXPRESSION
Chapter 4—Facial Features and Expression

A character's face tells the story. Nothing is more important than its facial expressions. Let's face it, we can spend days properly lighting the mood of a dark and eerie cemetery scene, then spend another several days littering it with dozen of creepy skeletons and an abundance of other evil characters, but if we don't develop the proper expression for our teenage kids running through the haunted cemetery we'll destroy an awful lot of effort. Your character's expression tells the story. A look of pure terror on the teenagers' faces puts the scene in perspective.

In this chapter we'll explore a few case studies of facial expression in 3D images to gain a better understanding of their impact on the message of the scene. Once we have had a little fun with expressions, we'll get our hands dirty in Part III—Animation.

PART III—ANIMATION
Chapter 5—Speech/Lip Synch

In this chapter the principles of lip synch will be introduced. We'll learn the phonemes necessary for lip synch, how to break down a sound file, and how to create a timing chart. We'll also explore straight morphing, the most common technique for creating lip synch animation. Then, using the straight morph technique, we'll walk through creating a short dialogue animation.

After we have a handle on straight morphing, we'll take a look at the advanced morphing system, weighted morph, which is used to integrate emotions with lip synched dialog.

Chapter 6—Weighted Morphing Animation

This is the chapter where you get your hands dirty. Morphing animation is the backbone of character facial animation. In this chapter we'll explore another common technique of facial animation: segmented morphing. After we get a handle on this method, we'll take a look at how the morph targets are used to create facial expressions.

Finally, we'll see how a facial animation is created using weighted morph targets, including an insightful section on changing facial expressions during the phoneme synching process.

Chapter 7—Lip Synch with Magpie

There are a number of programs on the market for analyzing a voice track. In this chapter we will discuss Magpie, a shareware program that is used to break down an audio track. It can be complicated at times to determine exactly where and when to use morph targets to facilitate facial animation. Magpie makes it easy to visualize the breakdown process and supplies you with lip synch data or a printed exposure sheet, which can be used as a reference when creating your characters' lip synch.

APPENDICES
Appendix A—Typical Human Expression Weighted Morph Targets

In this section you'll find a visual reference for the human expression morph targets used for the segmented morphing style described in Chapter 6. They may look a bit odd, but in Chapter 6 you'll see the reasoning behind the madness.

Appendix B—Typical Human Visual Phonemes

In this section you'll find a visual reference for common phoneme morph targets to be used with human models.

Appendix C—Typical Cartoon Expression Weighted Morph Targets

In this section you'll find a visual reference for cartoon character expression morph targets used for the segmented morphing style described in Chapter 6. They may look a bit odd, but in Chapter 6 you'll see the reasoning behind the madness.

Appendix D—Typical Cartoon Visual Phonemes

In this section you'll find a visual reference for common phoneme morph targets to be used with cartoon character models.

Appendix E—Facial Expression Examples

In this section you'll find reference material for 50 facial expressions, including front and profile images of each expression as well as a detailed description of the distinguishing aspects of the expression. Outlining how the four major parts of the face are changed: brow, eyes, mouth, and chin. You're provided with examples for both a human and a detailed cartoon character.

In addition to the expression descriptions, you'll be provided with a list of the common morph targets used for the expression and their rough morph percentages. While these may vary with your program, they will get you very close to the desired expression.

Appendix F—Just For Fun—Cartoon Expressions

In this section you'll find a number of examples for cartoon character expressions. A cartoon character has fewer emotional expressions, but it is more exaggerated than a human or detailed cartoon character.

Who Should Read This Book

This book is for any 3D artist who desires to take character facial expression and animation to the next level. If you are truly dedicated to making engaging images and animations, you should read this book. There seems to be little in the way of quality help for those who seek to wow viewers with interesting facial expressions and animation. Unfortunately, this is the backbone of any image featuring a character. If you want to create 3D killer facial expressions and animations that leave your viewers satisfied and entertained, then this book is for you.

If you fall into any of the categories below you should read this book:

- **Seeking a Career in 3D**: If you are seeking a career in 3D graphics, this book is a must. While there are literally thousands of 3D artists seeking work, only a handful are capable of generating detailed facial expressions and animations. A proficiency in these areas puts you at the top of the stack of resumes in the major studios. You should read the book cover to cover, because it will give you a distinct advantage in the job market.

- **Multimedia/Games:** If you are in the multimedia or game industry you are well acquainted with 3D graphics. 3D effects have permeated every aspect of your industry. Where it was once acceptable to use simple facial expressions and animation, it is now required that you create more complicated facial effects. Competition is fierce, forcing you to keep improving the quality of your 3D graphics. In this book you'll discover professional techniques for wowing your customers and clients with amazing character expressions and animations.

- **Film/Broadcast:** No industry is more particular about the quality of 3D work than yours and none requires more facial animation. Every form of visual media is being saturated with 3D graphics, whether it's needed or not. From virtual sets to animated stunt characters, 3D effects have become a part of nearly every film and broadcast production. On the leading edge of these 3D graphics is facial animation. It's the defining element of any animation. Traditional 2D animation is being replaced with digital effects. This book will provide you with the knowledge to create detailed and comprehensive facial animations for your next project or production.

- **Print Media:** Computer graphics have taken your industry by storm. More 3D graphics are popping up in print media every day. Your industry is probably the most challenging when it comes to photorealistic 3D. Unlike the film industry where most things move by you too fast to really get a good look, your work lies there motionless so even the smallest flaw can stand out like a beacon. This book will show you countless techniques for creating eye-popping facial expressions for your digital actors.

- **3D Modelers:** You are the foundation of every animation. It all starts with modeling. If you want to know the secrets of making incredible human heads for facial animation or possibly how to create morph targets for facial expressions, you should dive right into Part I. You'll discover proven techniques for creating human heads and defining facial expressions.

- **Hobbyists:** You've been experimenting with 3D and you really want to do something spectacular. Let's face it, you want to show the world what you're capable of doing. You want to leave everyone dumbfounded who looks at your 3D characters. Well, you're only 300 pages away from doing just that! Remember this: Facial expression and animation are more attention to detail than artistic talent. It's all about observation. Let everyone else be artistic while you create dazzling facial expressions and animations that knock their socks off!

Whether you are an amateur or a professional you will benefit from reading this book. In short, if you are a 3D artist who's interested in creating detailed facial expressions and animations, read this book!

Tools You Will Need

You will, of course, need a 3D program to take advantage of the information this book has to offer. Any 3D program is fine, the principles and techniques are not limited to any one program. I do recommended that you purchase SoftImage, Alias, LightWave, or 3D Studio MAX if you are interested in exploring all the resources described in this book. The lower-priced programs typically lack the detailed morphing features found in the higher-end program, although both RayDream Studio and trueSpace have excellent morphing plugins that compete with the big boys.

You will require a working knowledge of modeling to take advantage of most of the information found in this book. While we do cover modeling in Chapter 3, we won't go into great detail, since this book is more about expressions and animations. The main focus of this book is to illustrate the concepts behind facial expression and animation and the methods for producing animations. If you are just beginning to explore 3D, you should become more acquainted with your program before beginning to read this book.

The last item you need is dedication. You have to be dedicated to creating detailed facial animation and expressions. It doesn't happen overnight.

The face is a highly complex feature of the body and is most highly scrutinized by your viewers. It takes practice and experimentation to reach the level of awesome facial work. In time it will become second nature. You won't even have to think about doing it.

What's on the CD

Included with this book is a companion CD that contains a variety of support materials for each chapter. The support materials are provided in common formats that are compatible with all computers and 3D programs. Below you'll find a detailed description of the contents on the companion CD-ROM.

Here's what you'll find on the CD:

Chapter 1

Movies   jawmovement.mov: An example of jaw movement
                jawrotation.mov: An example of jaw rotation
                mandiblemove.mov: An example of mandible motion
                mandiblerotation.mov: An example of mandible rotation
                noselock.mov: An example of nose lock
                supraorbital.mov: An example of supraorbital motion

Chapter 2

DXF Models   A female skull, head modeling template
             A male skull, head modeling template

Chapter 3

Movies   QuickTime movies demonstrating movement of the following muscles: corrugator, depressor, frontalis, levator, masseter, mentalis, obicularis oris, obicularis oculi, platysma, triangularis, and zygomaticus

Chapter 4

Movie   An animation of Papagaio demonstrating facial expression and emotion

Chapter 5

Movies	Knuckles1.mov: The first pass at lip synching Knuckles
	KnucklesFix.mov: The improved Knuckles animation
Sound File	Knuckles.wav: Knuckles dialog

Chapter 6

Movies	2TargetMorph.mov: An example of weighted morphing
	Ptest1.mov: The first pass of lip synching Guido
	Guidofinal.mov: The second pass at lip synching Guido
Sound File	Youwant.wav: Guido's dialog

Chapter 7

Movie Files	Sweet.mov
	Sweetanm2.mov
	SweetFIX.mov
Sound Files	Sweet2.wav

Expression Templates

Modeling templates for forming facial expressions

Phoneme Templates

Modeling templates for forming basic phonemes

Getting Started

HARDWARE/SOFTWARE REQUIREMENTS

You'll need a QuickTime player for viewing the included QuickTime Movies. If you don't have a QuickTime player, you can download one from http:www.apple.com/quicktime/. You'll also need a sound player capable of playing WAV files to listen to the dialog examples. To view the color figures and modeling templates found on the companion CD-ROM you'll need an image viewer capable of viewing JPG files.

Facial animation and expression can be the most challenging task you'll undertake, but fortunately you have a wealth of help at your fingertips. While this book may not provide answers to every question you have, it will take you deep into the art of facial animation and expression.

Well, without further ado, let's get started by taking a look at skeletal and muscle anatomy.

The Human Head

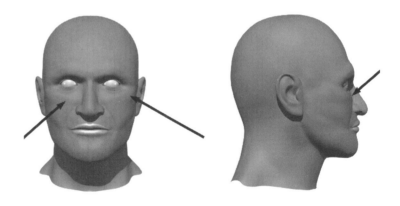

Before you can create stunning facial animation, you need to have a solid foundation. This means creating a detailed head model. Of course, creating a proper head requires a good amount of research. I've seen many 3D heads, but unfortunately most seem to fall prey to the common shortcoming of 3D heads—poor proportions and anatomy. The typical errors include eyelids that don't lie flat against the eye and mouths that are hollow inside, meaning the gums don't lie flush against the teeth. Additional common errors include poor placement of ears and general misalignment of the head details. While the human head is a very complex structure, we are surrounded with an overwhelming abundance of source material. If we are to create awesome 3D heads, we need to take advantage of this source material.

It's simply a matter of pulling out a mirror and taking a look at our own faces to have more than enough source material for creating our perfect 3D heads. The key to creating stunning human head models is to first understand the nature of the head structure then the placement of individual parts and their appropriate sizing. This is where it helps to have some reference material, since it can be awkward to measure our own faces.

This part of the book is dedicated to exploring the anatomy of the human head. We'll start with the skull, which is the foundation of our head. Many 3D artists overlook the skull, but if we want to create killer heads we need to start with an exploration of the skull's shape. The skull defines the general shape of the head. It's important to understand the foundation of the head before we can properly model it.

After we have a handle on the skull, we'll embark on a detailed study of proper proportions and placement of the head details. This is the most critical aspect of facial expression and animation, since a head with poorly placed details will completely undermine the impact of the expressions. We'll be carefully examining each minor detail of the head and mastering techniques for ensuring we have the proper proportions and placement of details.

Finally, we'll move on to the individual muscles of the head and how they affect facial expression. The key to creating proper facial expressions is to first understand how the muscles create the expressions. We'll be taking a look at each muscle group in the face and the particular nuance of expression that it affects.

The head described in this section is a perfect human head, meaning the placement of details and proportions are exact. Obviously not all humans are perfect, or any, for that matter, but you'd be surprised at how closely the average skull comes to being perfect. While they may be larger or smaller, taller or shorter, the proportion values remain fairly constant; they just change scale depending on the head.

Well, that's enough chatter. Let's get started with our exploration of cranial anatomy.

1 Anatomy of the Head

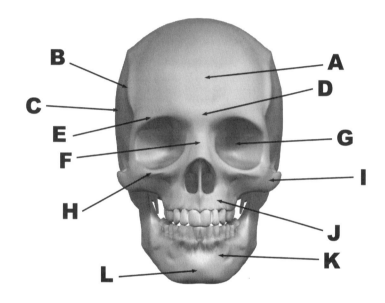

B

A

C

D

E

G

F

H

I

J

K

L

Basic Parts of the Skull

Creating a human head requires an understanding of the skull. It's the foundation of the human head and serves as the template for 3D heads. If you want to create a properly proportioned head, you must be aware of how the skull is formed. It provides you with the rough outline of the head's shape as well as the placement of the major facial features such as the nose, mouth, and eyes. Figure 1.1 shows several views of a 3D human skull.

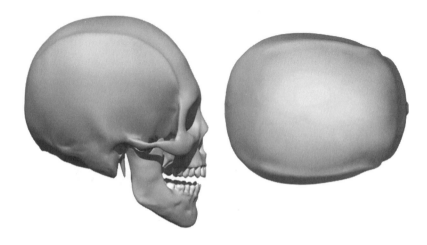

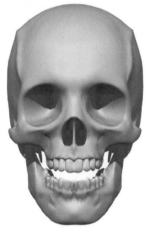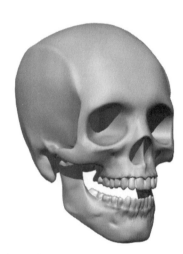

FIGURE *The human skull.*
1.1

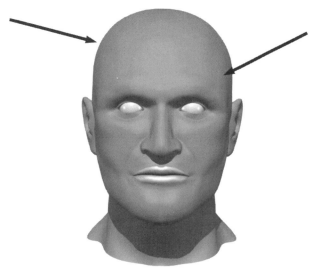

FIGURE   *The temporal ridge.*
1.2

As you can see, the skull has a number of distinct features, many of which are passed over by most 3D artists when they create their heads. For example, running along the side of the skull is the temporal ridge, which creates the block shape of the head, though we rarely see this distinct detail in 3D human heads as seen in Figure 1.2.

Notice the hard ridge running up the skull of Demon, a character from the Platinum 3D comic book. This temporal ridge makes him appear more intense and downright evil. It's a popular gimmick added by Hollywood FX people to make their creatures appear more intimidating. Naturally, it doesn't have the same effect on a normal human skull, but it does make a difference in the appearance of the head. It forces the head into a squared shape at the top, as seen in Figure 1.3.

While you can't actually see the ridge, you can see the effect. Notice how the sides of the head are somewhat flat until they approach the top of the head. The temporal ridge is what keeps the shape of the head linear until near the top. All too often we see 3D humans with rounded heads. While this is possible in reality, it's rather rare and should be avoided if you are attempting to create a realistic human head.

The temporal ridge is just one of the many cranial features that create the foundation for external details we can see. Let's take a moment to examine the features of the skull that are relevant to creating a detailed human head and the role they play in forming the facial features. Take a look at Figure 1.4.

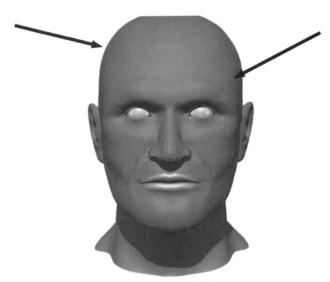

FIGURE *The temporal ridge on a human head.*
1.3

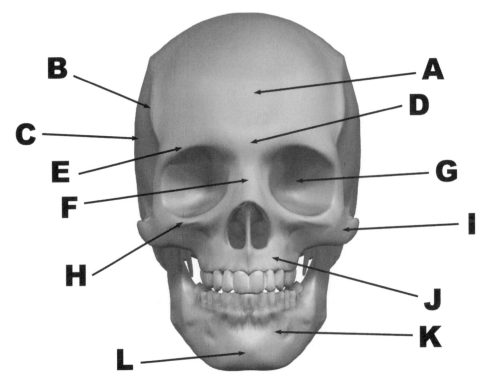

FIGURE *Major features of the skull.*
1.4

A. **Frontal bone:** The frontal bone constitutes the forehead structure. It's a rather thick bone that terminates at the brow, just above the nose.

B. **Temporal ridge:** The temporal ridge runs along the outer side of the upper skull. It's not very pronounced but is responsible for creating the square-shaped appearance of the upper skull.

C. **Parietal bone:** This is the side of the head. It's a smooth curved surface that extends outward until it lines up with the back of the jawbone.

D. **Nasion:** This is the point where the frontal bone meets the nasal bone. It's the curvature we see just above the nose as shown in Figure 1.5.

E. **Supraorbital margin:** The supraorbital is one of the most distinct bone masses of the face. It creates the ridge above the eyes shown in Figure 1.6.

The supraorbital lies directly under the eyebrows, hanging over the eyes like an awning, blocking the sunlight from directly hitting the eyes. When you animate your character facial expressions the skin moves over the supraorbital margin. A common mistake is to actually move the Supraorbital margin on the model, which tends to make the effect unre-

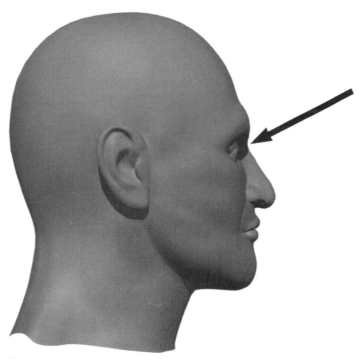

FIGURE *The nasion.*
1.5

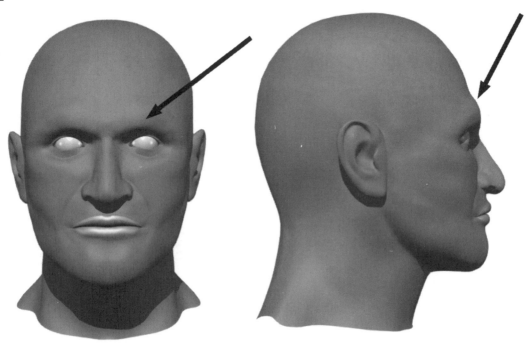

FIGURE *The supraorbital margin.*
1.6

alistic. The best approach is to move the physical tissue on the upper portion of the supraorbital margin, keeping the lower portion locked in place as shown in Figure 1.7.

Notice how the center of the eyebrow is moved but the sides stay locked. That is because they are resting on the supraorbital margin. To get a better feel for the movement of the eyebrow, take a look at the supraorbital.qtm movie file in the Chapter1 folder on the companion CD-ROM. Notice how the tissue just above the outside of the upper eyelid is pulled upward. This isn't the supraorbital margin moving but rather the sagging skin tissue that hangs underneath it. When you raise your eyebrows this tissue is pulled taught over the supraorbital margin. When you are animating facial expressions, you'll want to keep the sides of your supraorbital margin region fixed so your model doesn't look like a cartoon character.

F. **Nasal bone:** The nasal bone is the small bone structure at the top of the nose where it meets the nasion. It's the point where the nasal bone terminates, usually creating a small bump in the nose as seen in Figure 1.8.

The cartilage that forms the tip of the nose is connected to the nasal

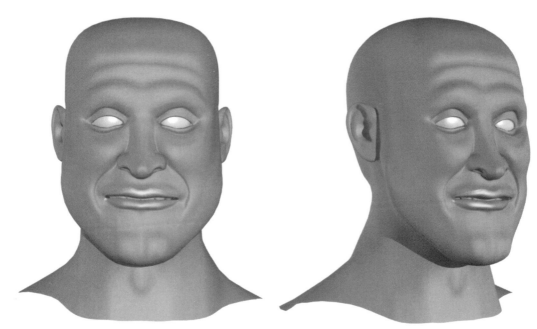

FIGURE
1.7 *Moving the eyebrows.*

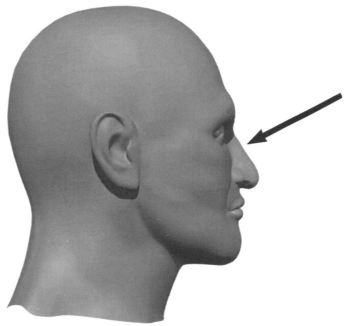

FIGURE
1.8 *The nasal bone.*

bone. A common mistake in facial animation is to move the tip of the nose during facial expression. This doesn't occur in reality because there are no tendons connected to the cartilage because it's a weak structure and far too flexible. You want to keep the tip of the nose fixed at all times, as shown in Figure 1.9.

As you can see, the tip of the nose has not moved but the surrounding tissue has changed dramatically. You can see this better in the nose-lock.qtm movie file located in the Chapter1 folder on the companion CD-ROM. In this animation you'll see the tissue surrounding the tip of the nose change shape without affecting it. You always want to lock the end of the nose, well, unless your character is being punched in the face, of course.

G. **Orbital cavity:** This is the large hole where the eyes are located. The orbital cavity is much larger than the actual eye, which sits rather high in the orbital cavity.

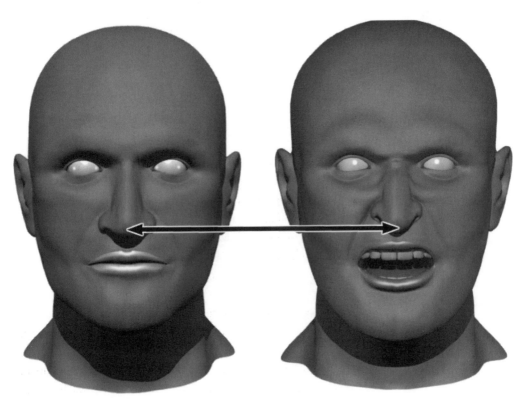

FIGURE *Locking the tip of the nose.*
1.9

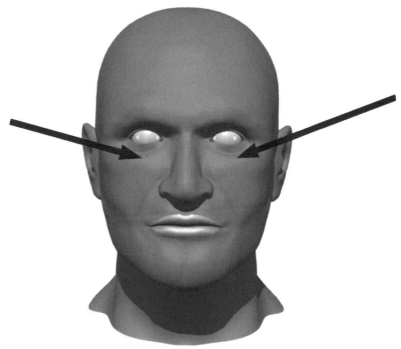

FIGURE   *The infraorbital margin.*
1.10

H. **Infraorbital margin:** The infraorbital margin is the lower portion of the orbital cavity and the upper portion of the cheekbone. It creates the ridge under the eye as shown in Figure 1.10.

    The infraorbital margin is directly responsible for the bags that collect under our eyes when we are tired or when we are older. It supports the excess fluids and tissue to create the bags. One of the common mistakes made in facial animation is to move the infraorbital margin. When the cheeks are raised, the tissue rides up and over the infraorbital margin, collecting under the lower eyelid, forcing it to puff up. Since the muscle tissue can't move over the infraorbital margin, it collects under it and creates the puffy cheeks as shown in Figure 1.11.

    When you animate your facial expressions, you'll want to move tissue up and over the infraorbital margin, but still keep the rise of the infraorbital margin intact. To get a better idea of how this works, load the Infraorbitalmargin.qtm movie file from the Chapter1 folder on the companion CD-ROM. You can see how the tissue moves up and collects under the lower eyelid while the muscle tissue collects under the infraor-

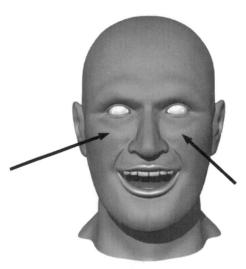

FIGURE   *Tissue collected under the infraorbital margin.*
1.11

bital margin. During the entire transition you can still see the infraorbital margin bulge.

I. **Zygomatic bone:** The zygomatic bone is the cheekbone that lies directly under the infraorbital margin as shown in Figure 1.12.

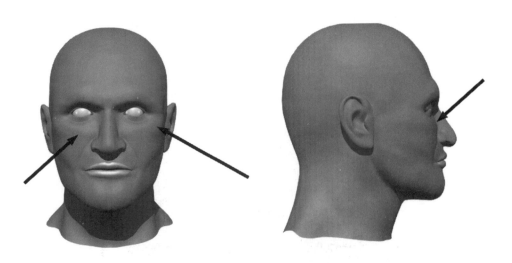

FIGURE   *The zygomatic bone.*
1.12

The Zygomatic bone is obscured by the infraorbital margin from the front view but is visible on the outer edge where it protrudes from the face, creating the common cheekbone. When you smile, the tissue collects in front of the zygomatic bone, which pushes it outward to create the puffy cheeks we saw in Figure 1.12.

J. **Maxilla:** The maxilla is the upper jawbone, directly under the nose, as shown in Figure 1.13.

K. **Mandible:** The mandible is the bulk of the lower jaw shown in Figure 1.14.

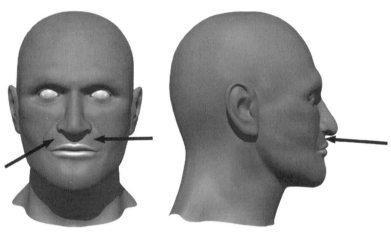

FIGURE *The maxilla.*
1.13

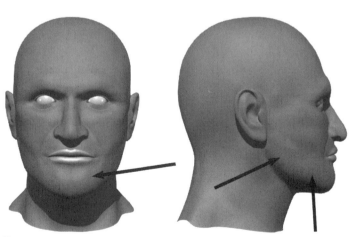

FIGURE *The mandible.*
1.14

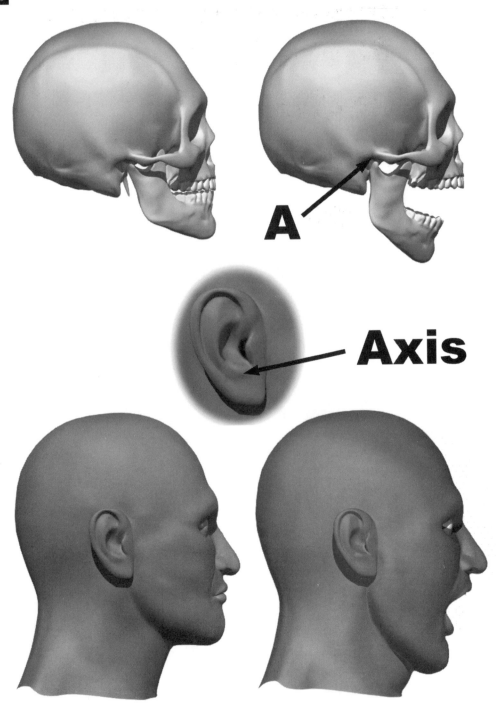

FIGURE   *The jaw rotation axis.*
1.15

The mandible is the complete lower jawbone that defines the contour of the face. It's the largest facial bone and is the only movable bone on the skull. Speaking of movement, the placement of the jawbone is crucial when working with facial animation and expression. All too often we see a 3D head where the jaw has been rotated from the wrong point. To understand the proper axis for jaw rotation you need to know the shape and placement of the mandible. This is one of the major reasons why an exploration of the human skull is necessary before you can properly animate the face. Figure 1.15 shows the axis for jaw rotation.

The axis for jaw rotation is located at the tip of the condyle (A), just behind the earlobe. A reference for an exterior axis would be base of the antihelix where it meets the lobule, as shown by the axis designation in Figure 1.15. When you rotate your jaw, you'll want to pick the center of this point in the ear for your axis. To get a better idea of how the jaw rotates load the jawrotation.qtm movie file from the Chapter1 folder on the companion CD-ROM. It illustrates the proper rotation of the lower jaw. You can also load the mandiblerotation.qtm file, which illustrates the proper movement of the jawbone.

In addition to vertical movement the jaw also moves from side to side. It doesn't rotate from side to side but actually shifts its position horizontally as shown in Figure 1.16.

The movement of the jaw seems quite dramatic in the skeletal model but not so dramatic in the actual head because there is an abundance of tissue covering the movement. Figure 1.17 shows the extent of the jaw movement limits.

The teeth provide an easy guide to determining the movement limits. At the jaw's maximum movement the gap between the two lower front teeth lines up with the outside edge of the incisor. This applies to movement in both directions. Of course, if your character is toothless, you'll need to use the gums as the guide. The gum tissue raised up between the two lower teeth will serve as the guide. To see the jaw movement in action, load the jawmovement.qtm and mandiblemovement.qtm movie files from the Chapter1 folder on the companion CD-ROM. The movement will look rather odd because we aren't used to seeing such an obvious movement, but you will find cases where this movement is necessary to achieve certain facial expressions, such as dumbfounded, confused, and chewing.

L. **Mental protuberance:** The mental protuberance is the very tip of the lower jawbone. This bone forms the chin of the human head shown in Figure 1.18.

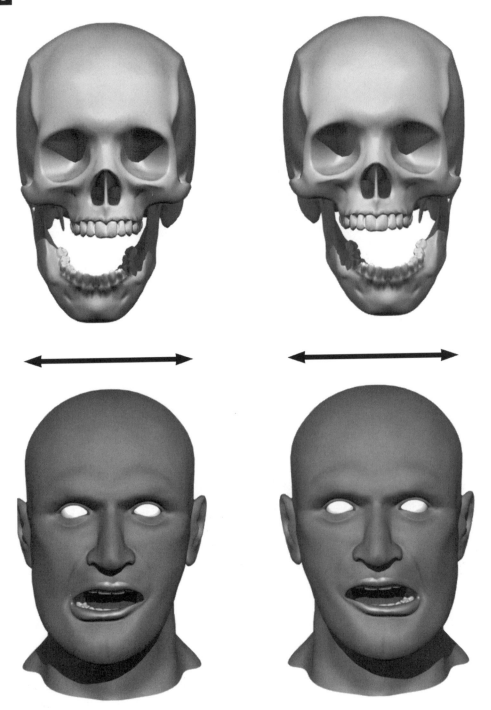

FIGURE *Horizontal jaw movement.*
1.16

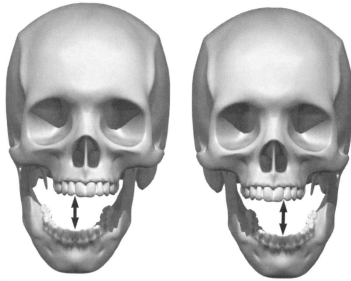

FIGURE *Jaw movement limits.*
1.17

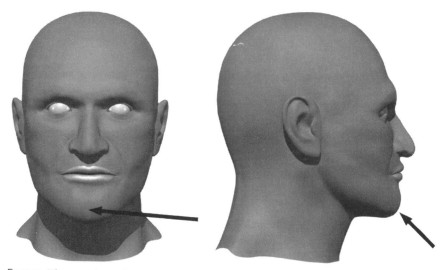

FIGURE *The mental protuberance.*
1.18

As you can see, there are a number of skull features that define the visible facial features, as well as how they animate. When modeling a human head, you need to take into consideration the proper proportions and placement of the skull features so you can properly animate the face. Let's take a moment to examine the proportions of a human skull.

Skull Proportions

It's very critical that you properly proportion the head of your model so the facial animation looks appropriate. To create a properly proportioned head we need to understand how the foundation, the skull, is shaped. Figure 1.19 shows the distribution of skull mass.

The skull is divided into two main masses, cranial and facial. The cranial mass, indicated by the "A," occupies two-thirds of the total skull mass. It's the least detailed portion of the head, but it constitutes the top and back of the skull. The facial mass, indicated by "B," is the most detailed portion of the skull, yet it occupies only one-third of the total mass. The facial mass is the most critical element when creating human heads. It contains all of the details, though we can't neglect the cranial mass, which gives the head its shape.

Speaking of shape, from the side view a human skull fits perfectly in a square. Its height is the same value as its depth, as shown in Figure 1.20.

The distance from the chin to the top of the head is equal to that of the brow to the back of the head. This is a very important correlation since most 3D heads tend to be rather shallow. We tend to make the head shorter from front to back because it looks so awkwardly large otherwise. We don't notice this problem in real humans because they have hair that balances out the shape of the head.

When modeling your human heads, you should have a square in the background for proportioning the model, as shown in Figure 1.21. It's a simple technique but it will ensure you have created the proper proportions from the

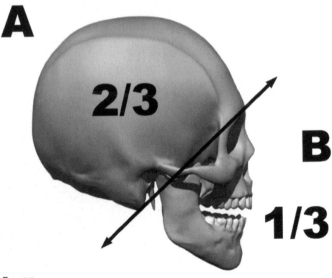

FIGURE
1.19　*Skull mass distribution.*

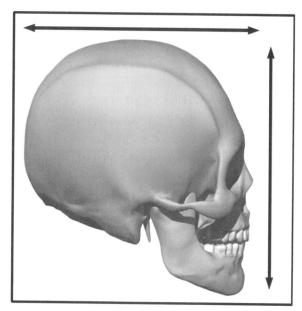

FIGURE   *The skull proportions.*
1.20

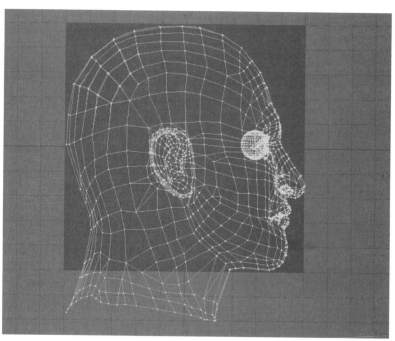

FIGURE   *Proportioning the head.*
1.21

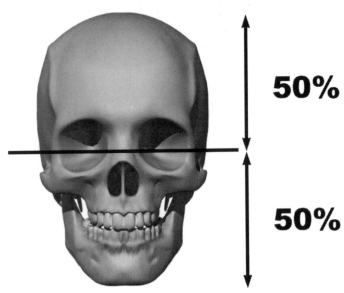

50%

50%

FIGURE *The frontal mass proportions.*
1.22

side view of the head. Proportioning the model from the front is a bit more complicated, but we'll get into that in a moment when we move on to Chapter 2. Right now let's finish our exploration of skull proportions.

Another proportion to consider is the front of the facial mass. The head can be evenly divided by drawing a line through the orbital cavity as shown in Figure 1.22.

The distance from the chin to the center of the orbital cavity is identical to the distance from the center of the orbital cavity to the top of the skull. With this measurement and the skull proportions measurement, you can accurately develop the general shape of the head so it's proportional to a human head.

Wrap Up

Understanding cranial anatomy gives us the knowledge we need to properly model and animate a human head. Even though we may never create a skull for our characters, it's the most important element in the creation of 3D heads. Once we have a firm handle on the foundation of the human head we can begin to build realistic faces.

In fact, that's exactly what a forensic anthropologist does—determine how a creature or human would appear based on the proportions and details of the skull. Speaking of reconstructing a head, let's jump over to Chapter 2 and take a look at how the features of a human head are proportioned.

CHAPTER

2 Proportions of the Head

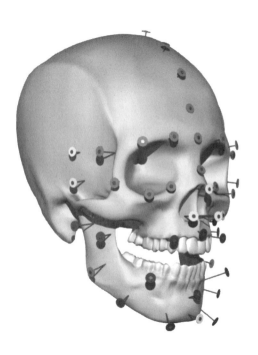

To properly proportion a human head you need to think like a forensic anthropologist. OK, so what is forensic anthropology? On a basic level forensic anthropologists are physical anthropologists, meaning they investigate the development of the physical and skeletal characteristics and the genetic makeup of humans. Forensic anthropology is the application of the science of physical/biological anthropology to the legal process. Forensic anthropologists work to identify skeletal and other decomposed human remains. They suggest the age, sex, ancestry, stature, and unique features from the skeleton. A great deal of information can be derived from a simple skull. For example, the sex of the skull can be determined by the shape of the cranial features, as shown in Figure 2.1.

There are a number of differences between male and female skulls. Let's take a moment to examine those differences.

A. **Cranial mass:** The male cranial mass is more robust than the female. It tends to be more blocky while the female is more rounded and tapers at the top.

B. **Supraorbital margin:** The supraorbital margin of a female skull is sharp on the underside while the male's is rather round and dull.

C. **Zygomatic muscle attachments:** The muscle attachments on the zygomatic bone are more pronounced on a male skull. Males have more muscular faces as a result of our evolution. The male of the human species is the warrior and hunter, so stronger jaw muscles are required for combat, hunting, and devouring prey. Yes, we have evolved to the point of shopping at the local supermarket, but it will take thousands of years of evolution before we shed our primitive traits.

D. **Mandible:** The mandible of a female is rounded while a male mandible is squared. Males require a strong jawbone for hunting and fighting.

E. **Cranial mass depth:** The male skull has a deeper cranial mass, which is meant to provide more protection for the skull.

F. **Superciliary arch:** The superciliary arch on a male is large and pronounced. It overhangs the ocular cavity more to provide protection for the eyes and shade them from the sun. Back in our earlier days men spent a great deal of time hunting for food, so they needed more protection from the elements, particularly the rays of the sun. It's hard to catch your prey when blinded by the sun. The female superciliary arch is less pronounced because women were smart enough to stay in the shade.

G. **Canines:** The canines on the male skull are significantly larger to provide them with a weapon and to help them eat. Males tend to eat more aggressively so they formed larger canines.

Male   Female

FIGURE *Determining sex through skull features.*
2.1

As you can see, there are a number of differences between male and female skulls that help the forensic anthropologist to narrow down the appearance of the head they are rebuilding. These are also important issues to consider when we build our 3D human heads. The structure of a male head is significantly different than that of a female. To properly construct out heads we must ensure they conform to the features of the specific sex we are modeling.

The science of recreating a person's appearance from a skull is called forensic craniofacial reconstruction. Using fossil fragments, plaster, clay, and epoxy putty, the anthropologist creates a lifelike reconstruction of the head. The process begins by creating a plaster cast of the skull and placing depth markers in strategic locations, as seen in Figure 2.2.

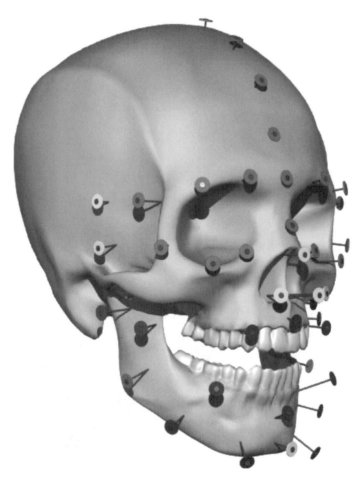

FIGURE *Placing depth markers.*
2.2

The depth markers are color coded to give the anthropologist an idea of how deep the tissue is in that region. The tissue depth is determined by a number of factors. One of the main factors is the shape of the skull features. We know that the skin is very thin over the bony ridges such as the supraorbital and infraorbital margins. It's also rather thin along the frontal bone. Also, the shape of the mental protuberance tells them how much of a chin the person had, while the size of the nasal bone suggests the size of the nose and the distinguishing bump on the middle of the nose. In addition to cranial evidence, the anthropologists use bone analysis to determine the age of the person, which helps them to identify the proper tissue depth. Our tissue depth changes with age.

Once they have gathered all the appropriate information and have placed the depth markers on the model, they begin to place the clay on the skull as shown in Figure 2.3.

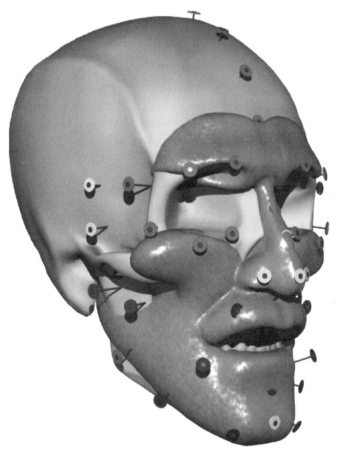

FIGURE   *Adding clay to the skull.*
2.3

They keep adding clay, using the depth pins to direct the depth of the tissue until they have the completed head, like the one shown in Figure 2.4.

Of course, now that we have entered the age of 3D graphics, forensic anthropologists are starting to use 3D software to reconstruct the heads. They start by digitizing a clay cast of the skull. Then they use software to place virtual depth indicators that define the outer surface of the facial mesh. These depth indicators basically represent control points for splines to be wrapped around the skull. The process is really very fascinating.

OK, so why all the discussion on forensic craniofacial reconstruction? Well, creating a 3D model isn't that much different. Actually, it's a great idea to start your 3D models with a skull. The 3D skull is used as a template for ensuring the proportions and features of the head are accurate. I'm not saying that you should build a skull for every head you create, but you should use a single skull or possibly a male and female skull as a template for your head model. For example, take a look the images in Figure 2.5.

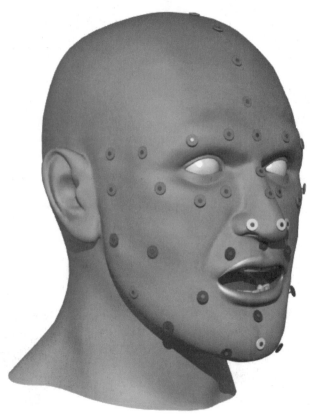

FIGURE *The reconstructed head.*
2.4

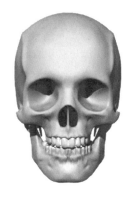
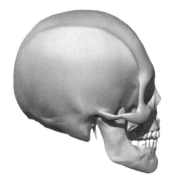

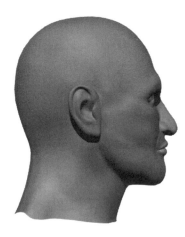

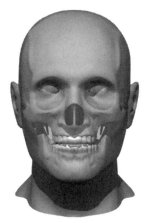
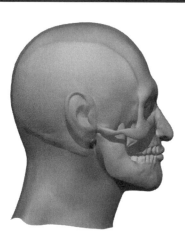

FIGURE   *Using a skull template.*
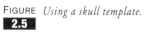
2.5

Here we see a male skull and its corresponding head. On the bottom of the image you can see the skull superimposed over the head. The skull was modeled first, then the head was modeled to take the shape of the skull. It can be very challenging to properly shape a 3D head without a template. Using a 3D skull is an awesome way to ensure you have a properly shaped head. I've provided low-resolution (10,000 point) male and female skulls in the Chapter2 folder on the companion CD-ROM. They are named maleskull.dxf and femaleskull.dxf. I strongly suggest you use these skulls as a template for shaping your head and placing the details. I typically start by building the basic head shape then I load the skull template in the background and fine-tune the shape of the head as shown in Figure 2.6.

As you can see, a 3D skull template really makes a significant difference in shaping the head. Without it you could spend hours trying to get the right

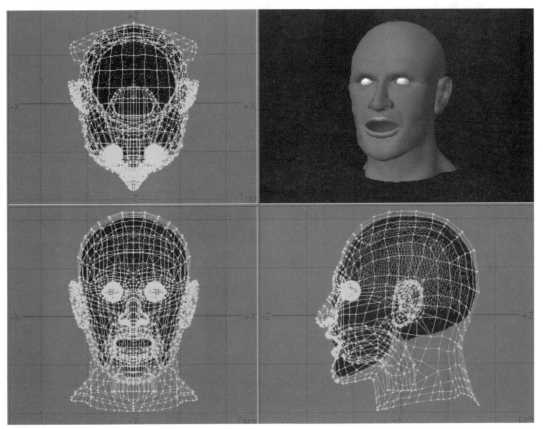

FIGURE *Using a 3D skull template.*
2.6

shape, and you may never get it perfect. Eyeballing is fine for fantasy creature heads that aren't exacting, but if you want to create a realistic human head, you'll need to be as precise as possible, meaning you should take advantage of everything you can find that will make the job easier.

Of course, not all heads are shaped the same, but the template skulls provided will get you 90% of the way home and save you countless hours of tweaking your model. Speaking of creating properly proportioned heads, let's move on to the real meat of this chapter—determining facial feature proportions and placement.

The External Facial Features

Creating properly proportioned facial features is a must if you want your head to be convincing and not look like a cartoon character when it's animated. There are eight major facial features to consider when creating your heads:

1. Brow ridge
2. Eyes
3. Nose
4. Cheekbones
5. Mouth
6. Chin
7. Lower jaw
8. Ear

In this part we'll be taking a look at each of these facial features and the method for determining its proper proportions and placement. The techniques outlined are very simple and don't take any experience to apply; they can be used to ensure the success of creating a perfect human head.

Let's start with the brow ridge.

THE BROW RIDGE

The brow ridge is the midpoint of the face. A common technique for determining the size of the brow ridge is to use eye lengths. The head width along the brow ridge is five eye lengths wide as shown in Figure 2.7.

The brow itself is four eye lengths wide, which can be seen in Figure 2.8.

Another thing to note when creating your brow ridge is to dip the center of the brow where it lies over the glabella, just above the nasion. Quite often you'll see a 3D model where the brow runs straight across the forehead, which tends to make the character look like a troglodyte.

The next facial feature to consider is the eyes, which can be one of the most complicated features on the face.

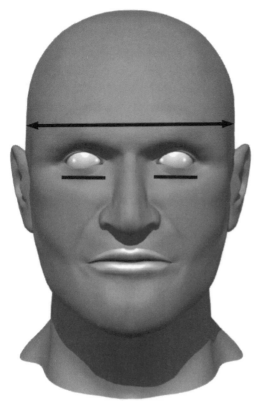

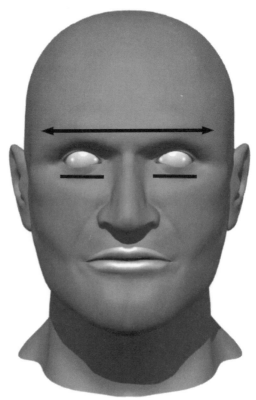

FIGURE *Determining the width of the head.*
2.7

FIGURE *Determining the brow ridge size.*
2.8

THE EYES

The eye socket, or ocular cavity, extends halfway down the length of the nose, terminating at the top of the cheekbone (zygomatic bone). The eye itself is roughly one and a quarter inches in diameter and nearly perfectly round, with the exception of the conjunctiva and cornea, which form the bulge in front of the iris. The shape of the eye mass is very important since it's the center of our focus when we view the face. Poorly modeled eyes are a common problem found in 3D human head models. They suffer from many problems, such as exposed upper eyelids as shown in Figure 2.9.

Notice how the eyelid is clearly visible. This is nearly impossible on a human head because the supraorbital margin hangs over the upper eye. It can happen in rare cases, but it doesn't look attractive. The proper formation of the upper eyelid has the tissue under the supraorbital margin covering the upper eyelid as seen in Figure 2.10.

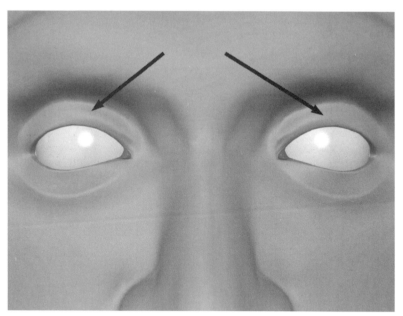

FIGURE   *The exposed eyelids of a poorly modeled 3D head.*
2.9

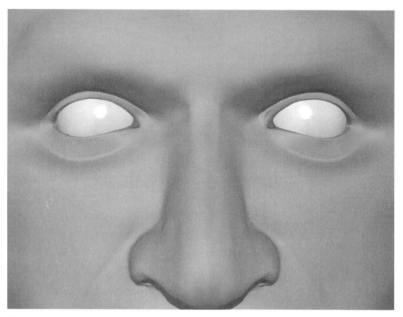

FIGURE   *A properly modeled upper eyelid.*
2.10

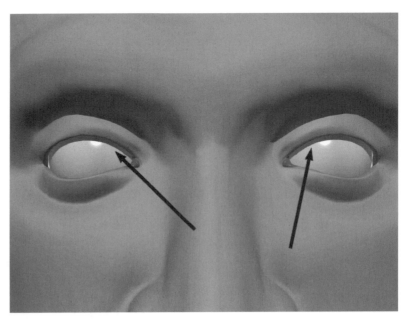

FIGURE *Floating eyelids.*
2.11

Another common problem in 3D human head models is floating eyelids. There are many 3D heads running around out there with eyelids that float above the eye, casting shadows on the eye as seen in Figure 2.11. As you can see, this looks very strange. In reality the eyelids form an airtight seal over the eyes, so proper 3D eyelids should lay flush against the eye as seen back in Figure 2.9.

The last of the common eye trauma we see in 3D models is poor placement. All too often we see 3D heads with the eyes either too close together or too far apart. While these may not seem too noticeable at first, we are accustomed to seeing eyes, so we have a subconscious predisposition as to how they should be placed on the head. The proper placement of the eyes is one eye width apart as shown in Figure 2.12.

In addition to poor eyelid shape, there is another commonly overlooked aspect of the eye—the shape of the eye opening. Most 3D models tend to have an oval eye opening, which is close, but there are subtle nuances in the shape of the eyelids that make the eye more detailed and interesting. The eye opening is not a symmetrical oval, but rather oblique. The high point of the upper eyelid is close to the inside of the eye while the low point of the lower eyelid is close to the outside of the eye, as shown in Figure 2.13.

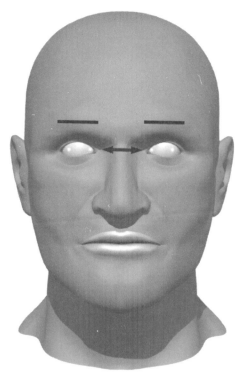

FIGURE *Proper eye placement.*
2.12

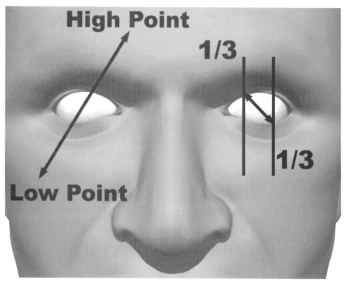

FIGURE *The proper shape of an eye opening.*
2.13

The arrow cutting through the eye on the left indicates the high and low points of the eye opening. On the right you'll see a simple method for determining the placement of the high and low points of the eye opening, which are both one-third of the eye opening width inward from the outside edge.

Now that we have a handle on the eye mass, let's take a look at the eye itself. The iris is the major feature of the eye and its placement is essential for proper facial expression. It appears to hang from the upper eyelid, hovering just above the lower eyelid, allowing a sliver of the eye white to be visible between the bottom of the iris and the lower eyelid as shown in Figure 2.14.

Many times you'll see a 3D model where the pupil is covered on both the top and bottom. This isn't the normal position of the iris but it does all depend on the head being created. The eyelids of older people tend to close around the iris more, covering both the top and bottom edge. On the other hand, younger people tend to be more bright-eyed, so they have a clear separation between the iris and the lower eyelid. The more the iris is covered, the more depressed the character will appear.

OK, the last detail of the eye is the size of the iris. This is an important measurement since a poorly sized iris will make the eye appear unnatural. The pupil is roughly one-half the width of the eye opening, as shown in Figure 2.15.

As you can see, the eye is quite elaborate and requires attention to detail to

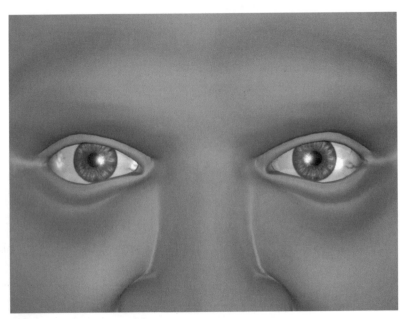

FIGURE *Proper placement of the iris.*
2.14

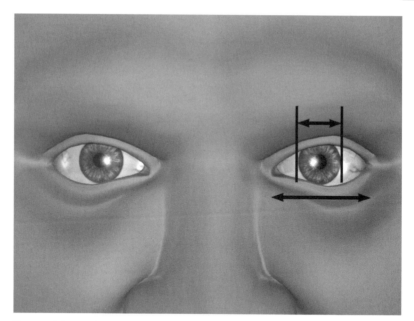

FIGURE *The pupil size.*
2.15

make it believable. In the scope of head modeling you should focus the majority of your time on the eyes because they will be the most critically judged by the viewer.

The next facial feature to consider is the nose.

THE NOSE

The nose divides the facial mass down the middle and its length covers half the vertical distance of the facial mass as shown in Figure 2.16.

The length of the nose from the bridge (nasion) to the tip is the same distance as the tip of the nose to the bottom of the chin (mental protuberance). The base of the nose is the same width as the eye, which is shown in Figure 2.17.

The upper nasal mass is divided in the middle where the Nasal bone terminates, thus creating the bulge. The reference for this measurement is shown in Figure 2.18.

The last measurement for the nose is the bridge between the eyes, which is one eye width across as shown in Figure 2.19.

Well, that does it for the nose proportions and placement. As you can see, creating properly proportioned facial features isn't terribly complicated. It just

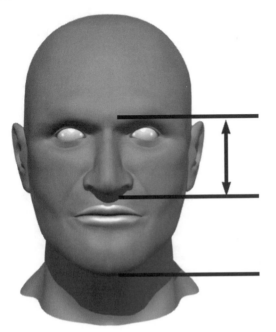

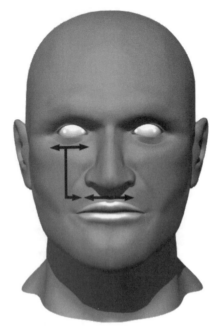

FIGURE *The length of the nose.*
2.16

FIGURE *The width of the lower nose.*
2.17

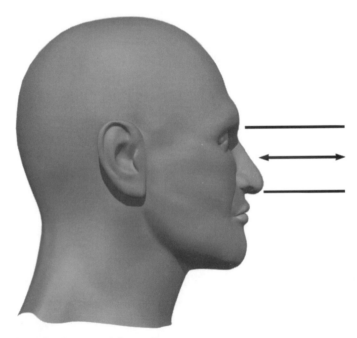

FIGURE *Placement of the nose bump.*
2.18

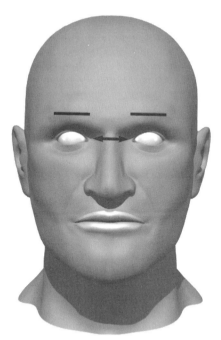

FIGURE   *The width of the nose bridge.*
2.19

requires an understanding of measurement techniques and a commitment to details.

OK, let's continue by looking at the cheekbones.

THE CHEEKBONES

The cheekbone is a vital part of the facial structure. It gives your head personality and character. Its placement is crucial for proper facial animation since the cheek muscles play a major role in facial expression. The baseline of the cheekbone lines up with the base of the nose as seen in Figure 2.20.

The cheekbone starts at the top of the nasal bone and runs 30 degrees diagonally from the corner of the eye socket to the angle of the jaw as shown in Figure 2.21.

The depression of the cheekbone is at the midpoint of this diagonal line. The last element of the cheekbone is the arch, or top, of the cheekbone. This starts at the infraorbital margin and lines up with the termination of the nasal bone, or midpoint of the nose, and ends roughly in the middle of the ear as shown in Figure 2.22.

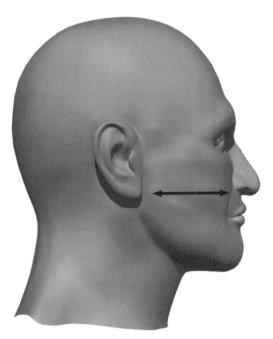

FIGURE *The baseline of the cheekbone.*
2.20

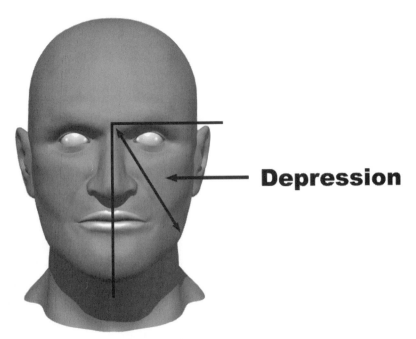

FIGURE *Placement of the cheekbone depression.*
2.21

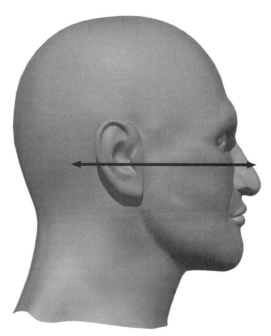

FIGURE *The cheekbone arch.*
2.22

Just below the cheekbone lies the mouth. Let's take a look at how we determine the proportions and alignment of mouth.

THE MOUTH

The mouth is one of the more complicated facial features. It has both an internal and external structure. We'll start by taking a look at the external features. The mouth itself occupies two-thirds of the space from the tip of the nose to the chin, as shown in Figure 2.23.

The corners of the mouth are typically aligned with the center of the ocular cavity, as shown in Figure 2.24.

From the side of the head, the corners of the mouth are aligned with the angle of the lower jaw as shown in Figure 2.25.

The lips are a common problem area for 3D models. Artists tend to make them flush, but they are actually angled as shown in Figure 2.26.

As you can see, the upper lip overhangs the lower lip slightly, forming a 7.5 degree angle. This is an important consideration because the upper teeth overlap the lower teeth in front, so the upper lip must do the same. In fact, why don't we take a trip inside the mouth and explore the interior details?

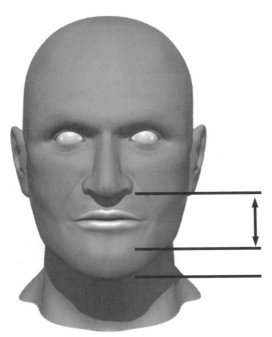

FIGURE   *The mass of the mouth.*
2.23

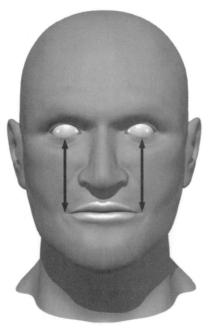

FIGURE   *Aligning the corners of the mouth.*
2.24

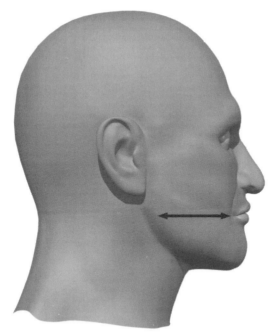

FIGURE *Side alignment of the jaw corner.*
2.25

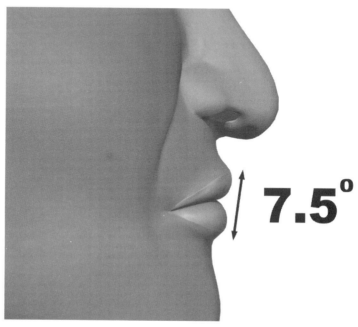

7.5°

FIGURE *The lip angle.*
2.26

The Mouth Interior

The interior of the mouth is significantly more complicated than the exterior; it's also one of the major problem areas seen in 3D human heads. One of the common problems is inflated cheek tissue as seen in Figure 2.27.

You can see how the cheek tissue is drawn away from the gums, making the mouth interior more like a balloon. In reality the cheek tissue is drawn tightly against the gums, as shown in Figure 2.28.

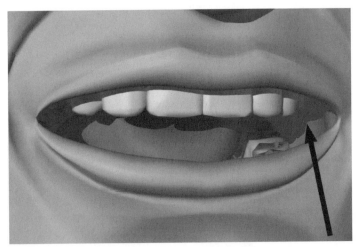

FIGURE *Inflated cheek tissue.*
2.27

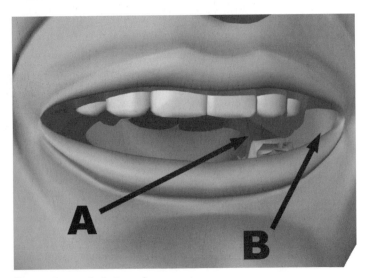

FIGURE *Proper cheek tissue placement.*
2.28

In fact, we quite often bite our cheek tissue because it tends to fold between the teeth. If we are not paying attention, we can shift our jaw slightly to the side and bite the soft cheek tissue, which tends to hurt a bit. The tissue should also fold in a bit just after the corner of the mouth as indicated by "B" in Figure 2.28. This also helps to prevent the "barrel mouth" effect.

Another common mistake is to make the lips too parallel as shown in Figure 2.29.

The lips should contour around the form of the gums, pulling the sides of the mouth back into the head as shown in Figure 2.30.

Speaking of gums, the placement of the gums and teeth is crucial. Two dental arches, the maxillary and the mandibular, form the substructure of the mouth. The maxillary arch holds the upper teeth while the mandibular arch holds the lower teeth. The point where the teeth meet in the middle is directly behind the seam between the lips as shown in Figure 2.31.

The gums are also pressed tightly up against the back of the lips, though they don't actually touch the lips. The teeth are more inclined to touch the lips. One of the more challenging aspects of creating teeth for 3D characters is selecting the proper size. If you make them too big, the character will look goofy, and if they are too small, the character appears very unrealistic. Sizing the teeth is relatively simple. The first measurement is the width of the dental structure.

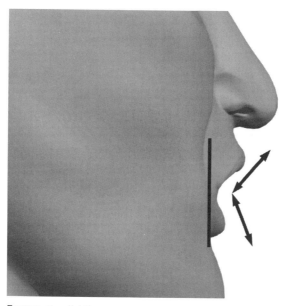

FIGURE *Parallel lips.*
2.29

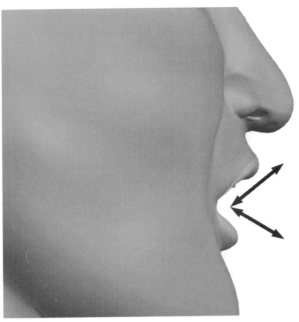

FIGURE   *The proper curvature of the mouth.*
2.30

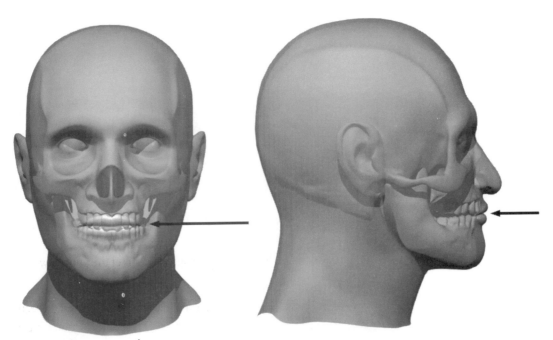

FIGURE   *The placement of the teeth.*
2.31

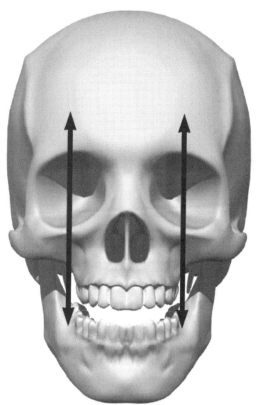

FIGURE   *Sizing the width of the dental structure.*
2.32

The sides of the teeth align with the center of the ocular cavity as shown in Figure 2.32.

Determining the size of the teeth is somewhat more complicated, but there is an easy reference for the front teeth, shown in Figure 2.33.

A. The four teeth in the center of the upper jaw are equal to the width of the lower nose.
B. The gaps between the upper and lower teeth in the center of the jaw are aligned.
C. The lower canines line up with the outer incisors of the upper jaw.

We have a total of 32 teeth by the time we are 20 years old, though the teeth in the front are the most relevant for facial animation. Directly behind the teeth is the tongue, which you obviously already know, but it does require a bit of study because most 3D heads seem to have rather flat tongues. The reality is that the tongue is quite fat, as shown in Figure 2.34.

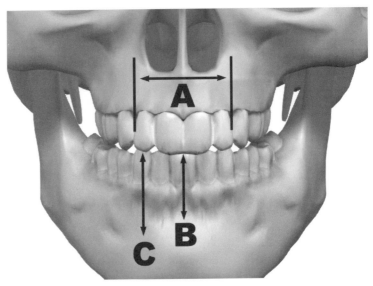

FIGURE *Sizing the teeth.*
2.33

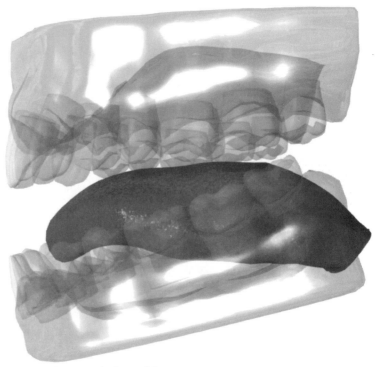

FIGURE *The proper thickness of the tongue.*
2.34

The tongue is a very flexible muscle that stretches quite a bit during facial animation. If you want to properly animate the face, you'll need to create a thick tongue for those times when the mouth is open and the tongue is resting on the lower pallet, such as during a yawn.

Another measurement to consider is the width of the tongue. In its resting position the tongue fills the lower gums, pressing up against the teeth as shown in Figure 2.35.

Creating the proper tongue dimensions will add a great deal of realism to your animations. Nothing is more unrealistic than a thin and narrow tongue in a human head.

OK, now we're ready to move on to the chin.

THE CHIN

The chin comprises one-third of the mass below the nose. At its widest point it aligns with the sides of the mouth as shown in Figure 2.36.

That's about all there is to chin proportions. Now let's move on to the lower jaw, which is very important facial feature because it defines the lower half of the face.

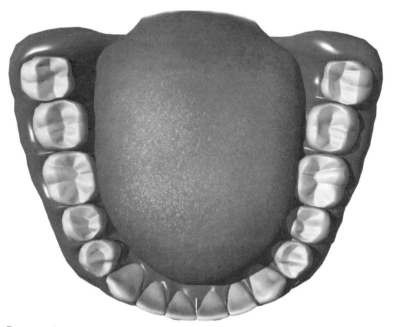

FIGURE *The proper width of the tongue.*
2.35

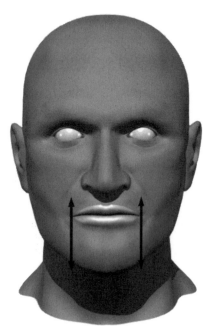

FIGURE *The proper chin width.*
2.36

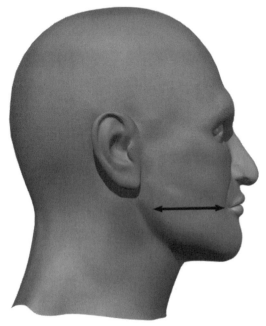

FIGURE *The angle of the lower jaw.*
2.37

THE LOWER JAW

The lower jaw defines the profile of the head. It's a very distinguishing element of the facial structure. The angle of the lower jaw aligns with the corner of the mouth, as seen in Figure 2.37.

From the front view, the widest point of the jaw is aligned with the outside edge of the supraorbital margin, as seen in Figure 2.38.

OK, now we are down to the last feature of facial expression, the ears.

THE EAR

The vertical placement of the ear lies between the eyebrow and the base of the nose as shown in Figure 2.39.

The horizontal placement of the ear is roughly in the middle of the head. Actually, the curved edge of the tragus is lined up with the vertical centerline of the head, as shown in Figure 2.40.

One common mistake made in 3D heads is to place the ear along a vertical line on the head. In reality, the rear is rotated back 15 degrees, as shown in Figure 2.41.

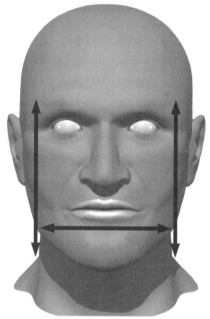

FIGURE
2.38   *The width of the lower jaw.*

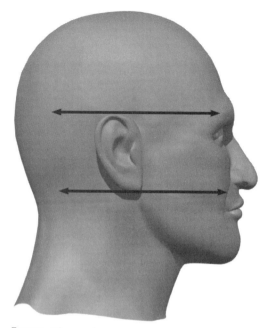

FIGURE
2.39   *The ear placement.*

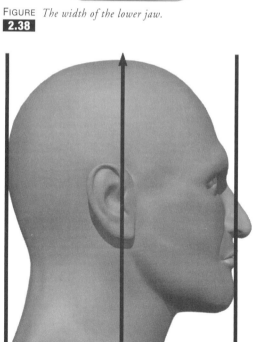

FIGURE
2.40   *The horizontal placement of the ear.*

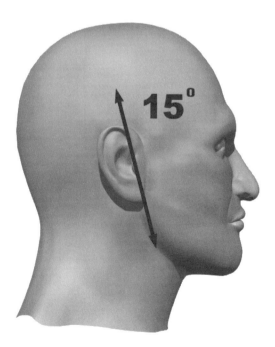

FIGURE
2.41   *The angle of the ear.*

The ear's angle is pretty much in alignment with the angle of the lower jaw. The ear itself requires a bit of thought since it's a rather complicated shape. An easy way to determine the size of the actual ear features is demonstrated in Figure 2.42.

The width of the ear is half its height. The widest point of the ear is across the outer rim of the helix. The concha, or hole in the ear, is equal to one-third the height of the ear and is centered vertically as shown in Figure 2.43.

The earlobe is one-third the height of the ear, as seen in Figure 2.44.

The width of the earlobe at its widest point is equal to half the width of the ear, as shown in Figure 2.45.

The last element of the ear is the antihelix, which is two-thirds the height of the ear and extends from the top of the earlobe to just under the helix as shown in Figure 2.46.

Well, that does it for the proportions and placement of human head features. I bet you thought it would never end. The process of creating realistic human heads can be daunting at first but after you've created a few heads it quickly becomes second nature.

Of course, no two human heads are alike, so you won't necessarily want to adhere strictly to these guidelines for every head you create. They are simple a foundation to build upon. You should take creative liberty when creating your human head, tweaking the details to give your head personality.

There are numerous forms of the human head. Some are tall, some are short, and others are wide. Then there's the ethnic nature of your head to con-

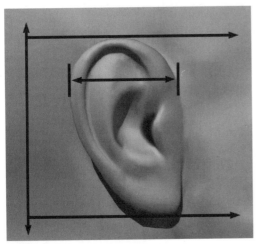

FIGURE *Sizing the ear details.*
2.42

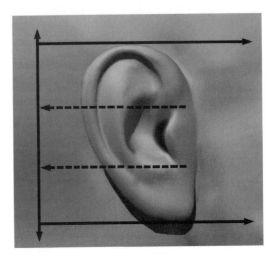

FIGURE *Placing the hole in the ear.*
2.43

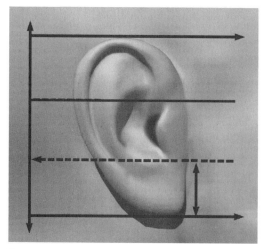

FIGURE **2.44** *The earlobe size.*

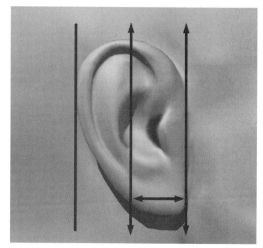

FIGURE **2.45** *The width of the earlobe.*

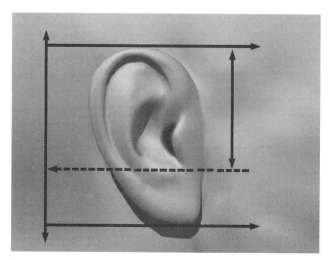

FIGURE **2.46** *The antihelix size and placement.*

sider. Heads change shape depending on race and geographic location. Before you create your next human head, you should spend some time comparing the heads of different people and races to give you some creative ideas for your head. Well, not "your head" but rather your 3D head. You won't want your 3D heads to be perfect every time or they'll end up being boring. What's important is that you have a firm understanding of the head's proportions and feature placement so you can properly build your heads.

Wrap Up

As you can see, there are a number of things to consider when creating a human head. Creating proper proportions and placement is paramount to the success of your head model. Taking care to ensure you have properly shaped the head will go a long way toward making your facial expressions and animation more believable.

Speaking of facial expression, now is a good time to take a look at the mechanism behind facial expression and animation – the muscles. Turn the page and we'll dive into Chapter 3, where we'll explore each of the facial muscles and the actions they perform.

3 Facial Muscles

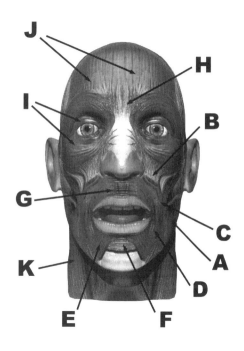

Now we're at the meat of facial animation and expression—the facial muscles. Before we can completely understand the process of facial animation, we need to gain a full understanding of the facial muscles. For example, if we didn't understand the movement of the cheek muscles, we would not realize that they collect under the zygomatic bone when raised, rather than traveling over it, which tends to be a common mistake made with 3D facial animation.

While facial muscle anatomy is a scientific topic, the movement of the facial muscles is paramount when creating facial animation. Don't worry, this chapter of the book is brief and short on words. The important thing to take away from this chapter is how muscle movement affects the facial tissue. If you have a handle on the facial muscle, you'll find creating facial expressions a great deal easier.

Let's dig right in and explore the eleven major facial muscles that control facial expression.

The Facial Muscles

Eleven facial muscles are responsible for facial animation. There are actually more than twenty facial muscles, but most of them tend to be supporting muscle rather than instigating muscles. The facial muscles are divided into four muscle masses: the jaw muscles, mouth muscles, eye muscles, and brow/neck muscles. Dividing the muscles into these four groups makes it easier to determine how they affect the facial movement. Figure 3.1 shows the different facial muscles.

Each facial muscle is indicated by a callout. We'll be taking a look at each individual muscle and exploring its involvement in facial expression and animation. Each of the muscles covered is featured in the plates at the end of this chapter. Each plate features a skinless head on the top with the muscle indicated in a light color and with arrows. On the bottom are heads showing the external effect of the muscle's movement. On the left is a neutral head with no muscle movement; on the right is the same head showing the result of muscle movement. We'll be referring to these plates frequently during our discussion.

OK, let's get started with the jaw muscle group.

JAW MUSCLES

A. Masseter—the clenching muscle

The jaw muscles actually include one major muscle and several smaller supporting muscles. The main muscle is the masseter, which is used to clench the teeth and raise the jaw. The masseter is located at the base of the jaw as shown in Plate 1 at the end of this chapter.

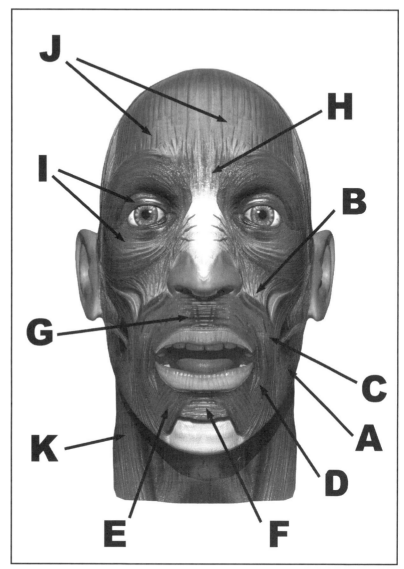

FIGURE   *The facial muscles.*
3.1

This muscle plays a major role in any movement where the lower jaw is dropped wide open. Some of the expressions created by the masseter muscle are fear and yawning, which are both shown in Figure 3.2. In both of these expressions the masseter muscle is used to raise the jaw to the neutral position. To see the masseter muscle in motion, load the Masseter.qtm movie file from the Chapter3 folder on the companion CD-ROM.

Yawn   Terror

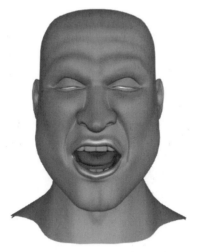 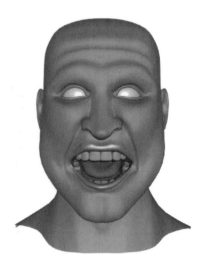

FIGURE *Expressions created with the masseter muscle.*
3.2

The masseter muscle is also used to clench the teeth together in a chewing action. It's used heavily when you eat food, particularly when it's something that requires a lot of grinding.

Well, that does it for the jaw muscles, the fewest number of any facial muscle group. The muscle group with the most muscle is the mouth, which we'll now examine.

MOUTH MUSCLES

B. **Levator labii superioris—the sneering muscle**

The levator labii superioris raises the upper lip beneath the nostrils. It's located around the upper and lower lips as shown in Plate 2. This muscle is one of the more limited mouth muscles, because very few expressions involve raising the upper lip under the nostrils. Of course, it plays a major role in creating the disgust and disdain facial expressions shown in Figure 3.3. In both of these expressions the levator labii superioris muscle is used to raise the upper lip. To see the levator labii superioris muscle in motion, load the Levator.qtm movie file from the Chapter3 folder on the companion CD-ROM.

C. **Zygomaticus major—the smiling muscle**

The zygomaticus major muscle raises the mouth upward and outward.

Disgust   Disdain

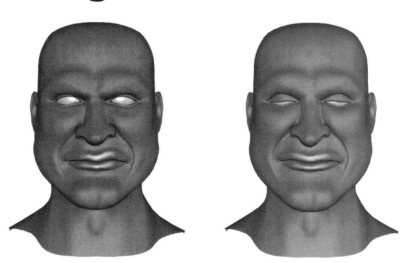

FIGURE *Expressions created with the levator labii superioris muscle.*
3.3

It's located around the upper and lower lips and attaches just before the ear as shown in Plate 3.

This muscle is one of the more frequently utilized, particularly if you have a sense of humor. It's used for any expression that requires the upper lip to be raised up and out, such as smiling and laughing shown in Figure 3.4.

In both of these expressions the zygomaticus major muscle is used to raise the upper lip, pulling it outward in the process. To see the zygomaticus major muscle in motion, load the Zygomaticus.qtm movie file from the Chapter3 folder on the companion CD-ROM.

D. **Triangularis—the facial shrug muscle**

The Triangularis muscle pulls the corner of the mouth downward. It's located around the upper and lower lips and attaches just before the ear and to the mandible as shown in Plate 4.

This muscle is not one of the more frequently used, but it is a crucial muscle for creating sadness miserable demeanors shown in Figure 3.5.

In these expressions the triangularis muscle is used to pull the corners of the mouth. To see the triangularis muscle in motion, load the Triangularis.qtm movie file from the Chapter3 folder on the companion CD-ROM.

Laughter

Smiling

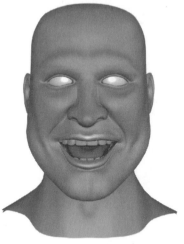
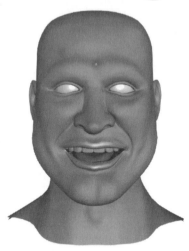

FIGURE *Expressions created with the zygomaticus major muscle.*
3.4

Sad

Miserable

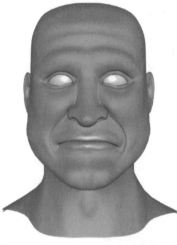
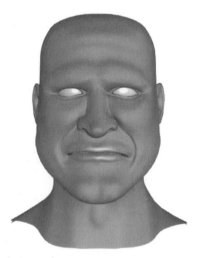

FIGURE *Expressions created with the triangularis muscle.*
3.5

E. **Depressor labii inferioris—the lower lip curl muscle**

The depressor labii inferioris muscle pulls the lower lip down and out. It's located around the upper and lower lips and attaches to the mandible as shown in Plate 5.

This muscle is not one of the more frequently used, but it is a crucial muscle for creating expressions like surprise, shown in Figure 3.6.

In this expression the depressor labii inferioris muscle is used to curl the lower lip out and down. To see the depressor labii inferioris muscle in use, load the Depressor.qtm movie file from the Chapter3 folder on the companion CD-ROM.

F. **Mentalis—the pouting muscle**

The mentalis muscle raises and tightens the chin. It also pushes the lower lip upward and outward. It's located on either side under the lower lip as shown in Plate 6.

This muscle is used to create expressions such as suppressed sadness and fear, which are shown in Figure 3.7.

In these expressions the mentalis muscle is used to push the lower lip upward and outward. Of course, as you can see in the "afraid" example, this doesn't always mean the mouth will be sealed tight. To see the mentalis muscle in action, load the Mentalis.qtm movie file from the Chapter3 folder on the companion CD-ROM.

Surprise

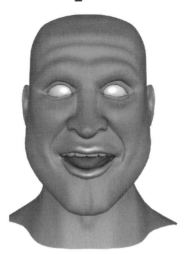

FIGURE   *An expression created with the depressor labii inferioris muscle.*
3.6

Suppressed Sadness

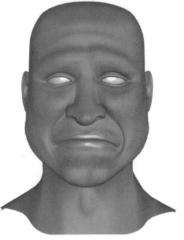

Afraid

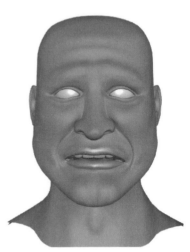

FIGURE *An expression created with the mentalis muscle.*
3.7

G. **Orbicularis oris—the lip tightener muscle**

The orbicularis oris is the last of the major muscles in the mouth muscle mass. It compresses and purses the lips. It circles the mouth as shown in Plate 7.

This muscle is used to create expressions such as disdain and repulsion, as shown in Figure 3.8.

In these expressions the orbicularis oris muscle is used to purse the lips. In both cases the orbicularis oris is used in conjunction with the levator labii superioris, which is used to lift the upper lip. You'll find that many muscles will often work in conjunction to move the facial tissue. To see the orbicularis oris muscle in action, load the Orbicularis.qtm movie file from the Chapter3 folder on the companion CD-ROM.

OK, that does it for the mouth muscle. As you can see, the mouth requires a greater number of muscles, because it can take on a variety of shapes. The mouth is the most expressive element of the face. I know you've probably heard that the eyes were the most expressive, but this just isn't true. The eyes have fewer muscles, meaning they can't achieve as many variations as the mouth. We'll get into this topic in more detail in Chapter 4. For now let's continue our exploration of the facial muscles.

Disdain   Repulsion

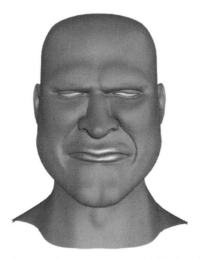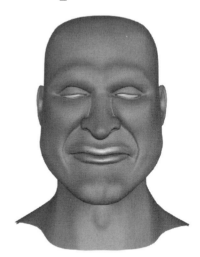

FIGURE *An expression created with the orbicularis oris muscle.*
3.8

EYE MUSCLES

H. **Corrugator—the frown muscle**

The corrugator muscle compresses the skin between the eyebrows, creating a frown. It's located directly between the eyes as shown in Plate 8.

The corrugator muscle is used to create expressions such as intense concentration and disgust, which are shown in Figure 3.9.

In these expressions the corrugator muscle is used to compress the skin between the eyebrows, making the character appear angered. To see the corrugator muscle in motion, load the Corrugator.qtm movie file from the Chapter3 folder on the companion CD-ROM.

I. **Orbicularis oculi—the squinting muscle**

The orbicularis oculi muscle closes the eyelids and compresses the eye opening. It encircles the eye as shown in Plate 9.

The orbicularis oculi muscle is used to close the eyes and make the character wink or squint. Common expressions using the orbicularis oculi muscle would be asleep or drowsy/tired, as shown in Figure 3.10.

In these expressions the orbicularis oculi muscle is used to compress the eyelids and even close them. This is probably the most relevant muscle in facial animation. It doesn't play a major role in expressions, but it does add that hint of realism by making the character blink occasionally.

Intense Concentration

Disgust

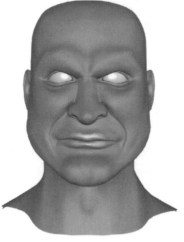
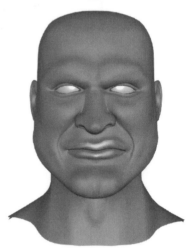

FIGURE **3.9** *An expression created with the corrugator muscle.*

Asleep

Tired

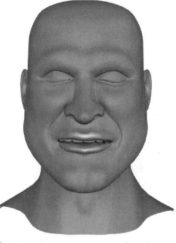
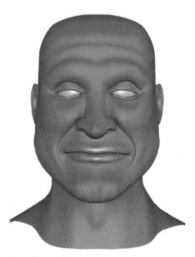

FIGURE **3.10** *An expression created with the orbicularis oculi muscle.*

To see the orbicularis oculi muscle in motion, load the Orbicularis.qtm movie file from the Chapter3 folder on the companion CD-ROM.

SCALP AND NECK MUSCLES

J. **Frontalis—the brow lifting muscle**

The frontalis muscle draws the scalp down and up, wrinkling the forehead skin. It covers the forehead as shown in Plate 10.

The corrugator muscle is actually two distinct muscles, one on either side of the head, which makes it possible to move the eyebrows independently as Spock used to do in the old StarTrek series. The frontalis is one of the most frequently used facial muscles. It's a part of nearly every facial expression. Some common expressions that use the frontalis are fear and a charming smile, both of which are shown in Figure 3.11.

In these expressions the frontalis muscle is used to pull the forehead skin upward, creating wrinkles. To see the frontalis muscle in motion, load the Frontalis.qtm movie file from the Chapter3 folder on the companion CD-ROM.

K. **Risorius/platysma—the lower lip stretching muscle**

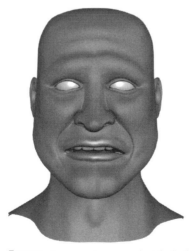
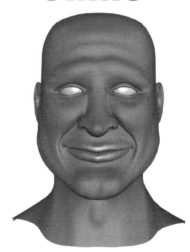

Afraid

Charming Smile

FIGURE *An expression created with the frontalis muscle.*
3.11

The risorius/platysma muscle is a unique facial muscle because it's primarily a neck muscle, though it does draw the lower lip downward and outward. It covers the neck, mandible, and parts of the mouth as shown in Plate 11.

The risorius/platysma is one of the most frequently used facial muscles. It's a part of nearly every facial expression. Some common expressions that use the frontalis are terrified and crying, which are shown in Figure 3.12.

As you can see, the lower lip has been pulled downward in both expressions. To see the risorius/platysma muscle in action, load the Platysma.qtm movie file from the Chapter3 folder on the companion CD-ROM.

Well, that does it for the major muscles of the face. As you can see, they play a major role in facial animation and expression. To get a better idea of just how many muscles are involved in creating a facial expression, let's take a look at how the crying expression is created. Take a look at Figure 3.13.

Let's take a moment to identify each feature of the crying expression and the muscles that create it.

Terror   # Crying

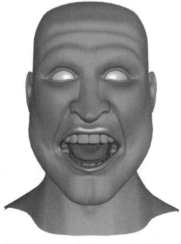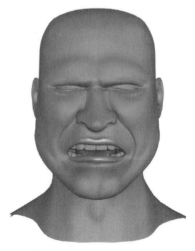

FIGURE *An expression created with the frontalis muscle.*
3.12

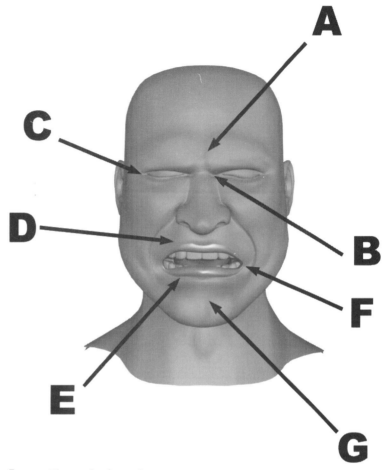

FIGURE *The muscles that make us cry.*
3.13

A. **Lowered brow:** The corrugator muscle lowers the inner eyebrow.
B. **Furrowed nose:** The procerus muscle assists the orbicularis oculi in tightening the inner eye.
C. **Tightly closed eyes:** The orbicularis oculi muscle tightly closes the eyes.
D. **Drawn Up Upper Lip:** The levator labii superioris pulls the upper lip upward.
E. **Curled Lower Lip:** The triangularis pulls the lower lip downward, curling it slightly.
F. **Stretched Out Mouth:** The risorius muscle pulls the corner of the mouth sideways.

G. **Crumpled Chin:** The mentalis muscle tightens the chin, creating a bulge.

As you can see, quite a few muscles were involved in create a single expression. You can also see how the facial expression can be quickly broken down into the muscles that create each detail. When you create your facial expression, you should consider the role of each facial muscle to determine how the facial tissue will be modified.

Wrap Up

The facial muscles drive our expressions and speech. Nothing is more important than understanding how they work. With a complete understanding of their motion we can develop accurate facial expressions and animations. It's critical to ensure that your muscles are traveling the right path during their motion. You don't want a muscle to move out of the normal motion or your character will look bizarre. The animations provided on the companion CD-ROM will give you a solid idea of how the facial muscles move so you can ensure you have created the proper animation targets.

OK, now that we have a thorough understanding of cranial anatomy, we're finally ready to take a detailed look at facial expression. Now would be a great time to take a break and clear you head before we move on. I know I could use a break. I don't want you to have a drowsy expression while you are reading the next chapter.

I'll see you in Chapter 4.

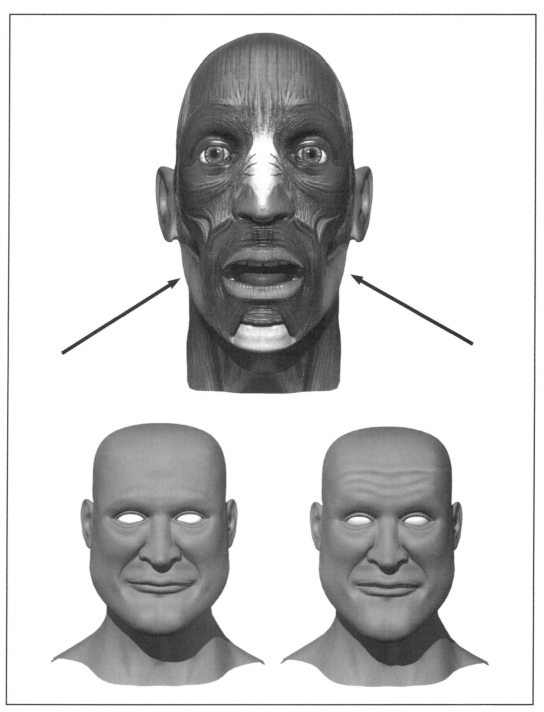

PLATE *Masseter.*
1

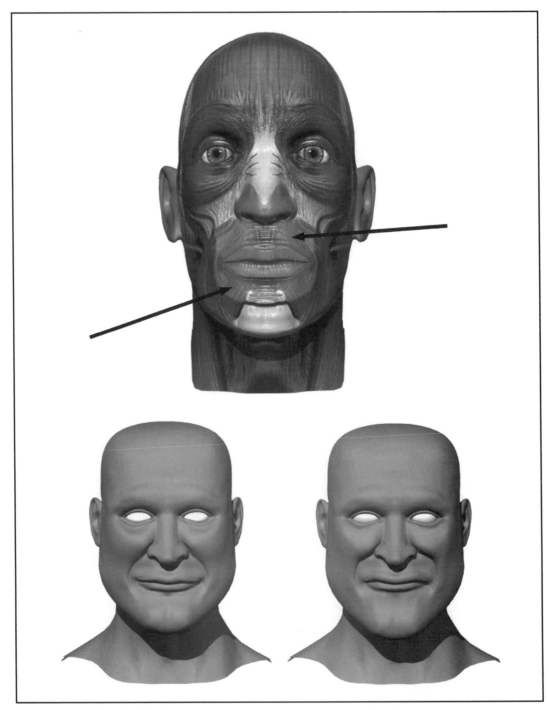

PLATE *Levator labii superioris.*

2

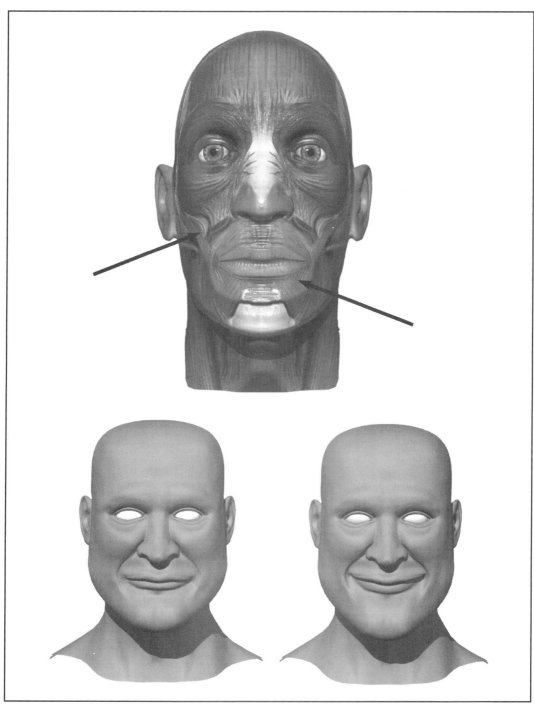

PLATE *Zygomaticus major.*
3

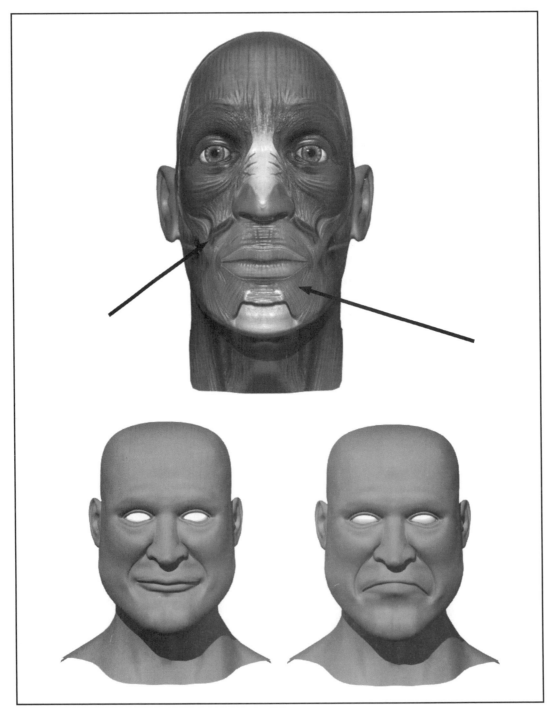

PLATE *Triangularis.*

4

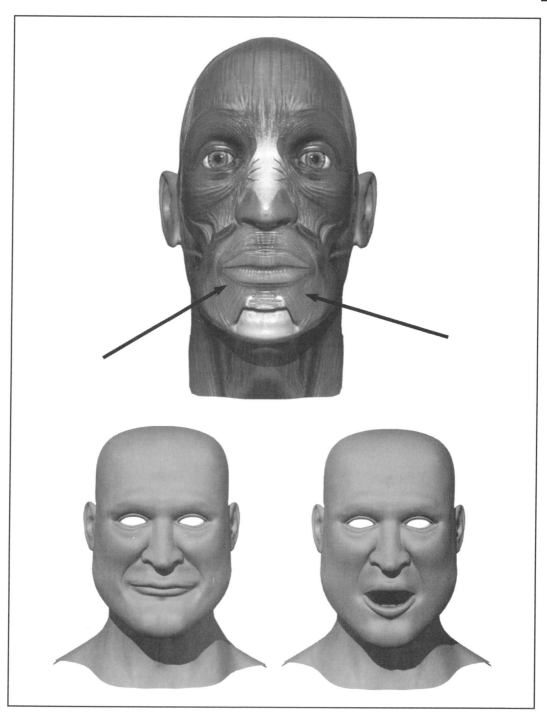

PLATE *Depressor labii inferioris.*
5

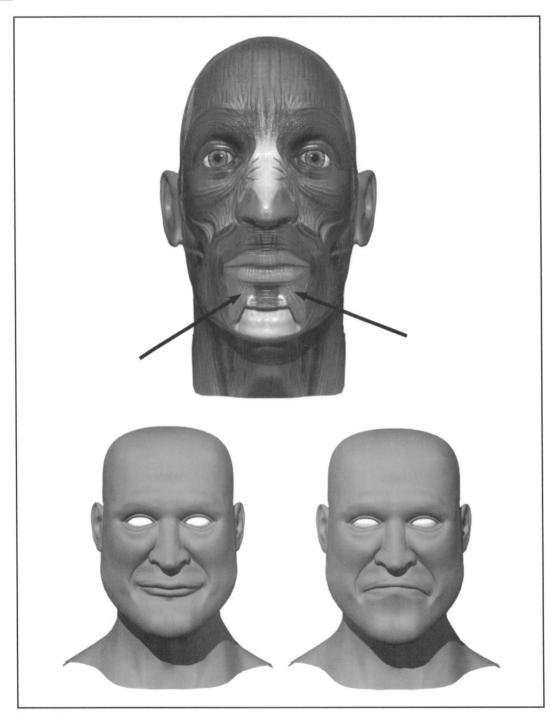

PLATE *Mentalis.*
6

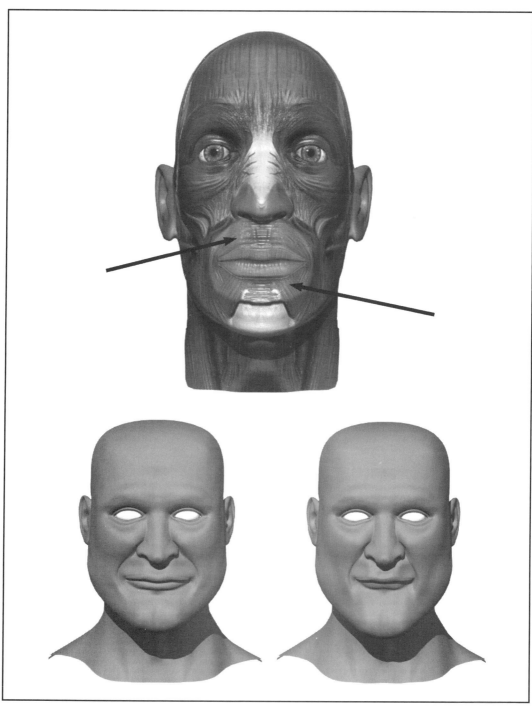

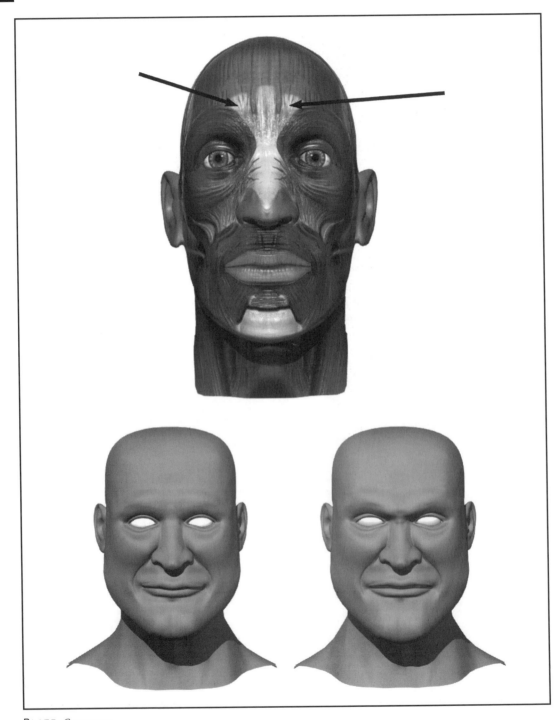

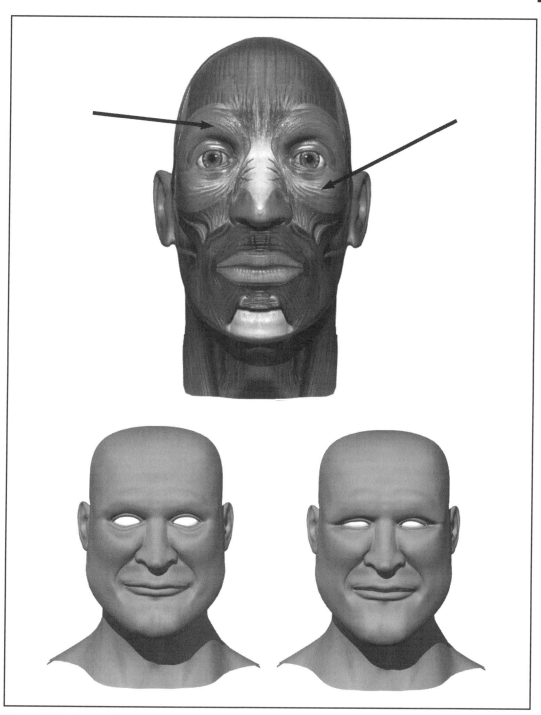

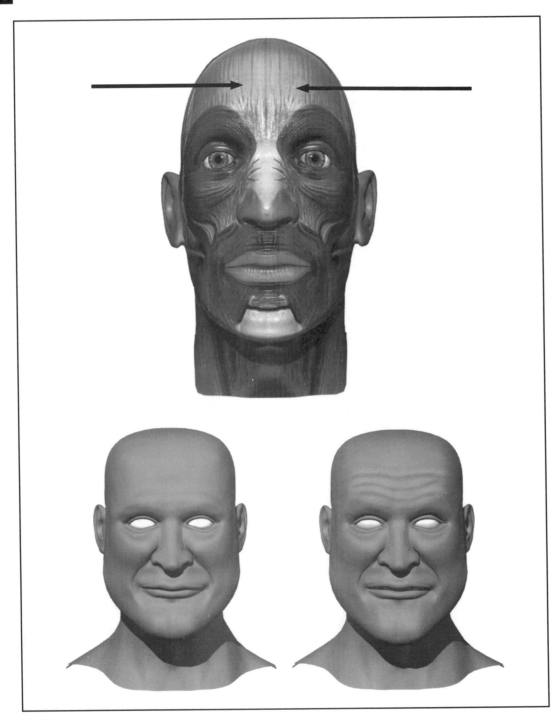

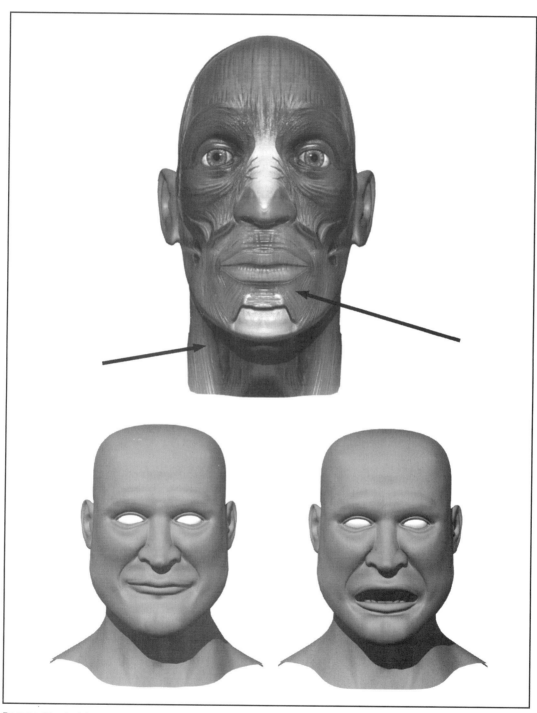

PLATE   *Risorius/platysma.*

11

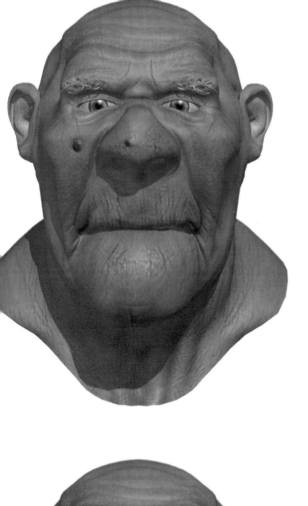

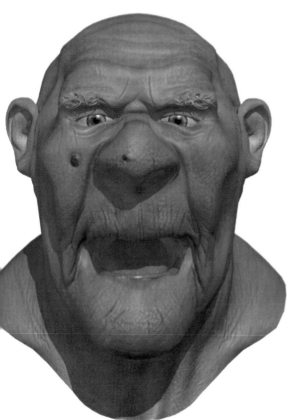
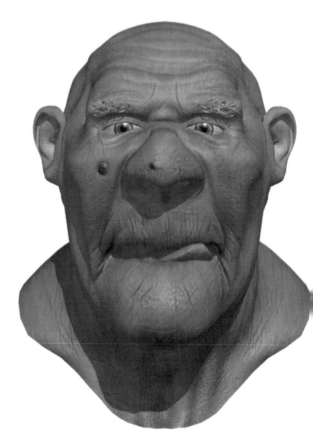

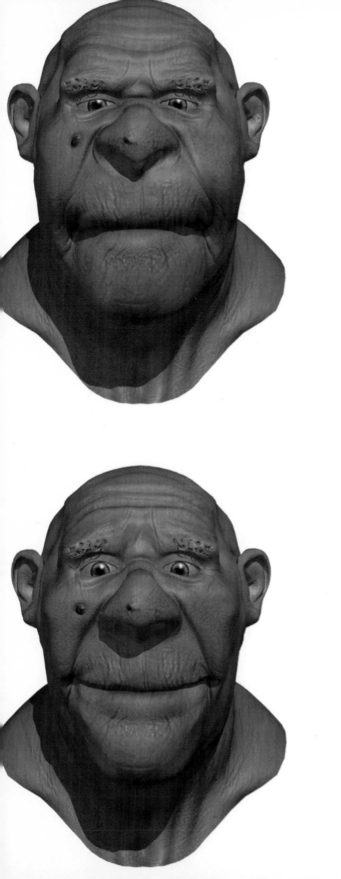

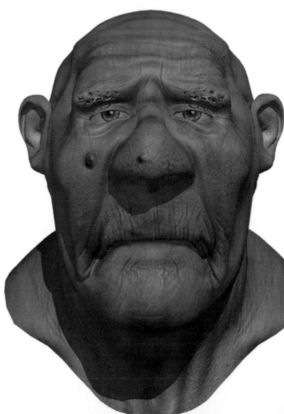

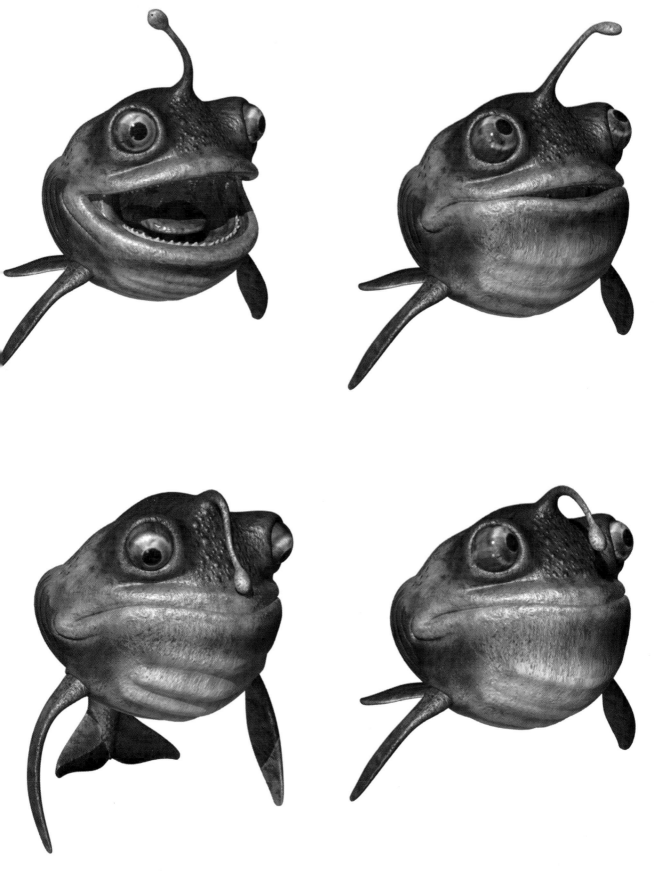

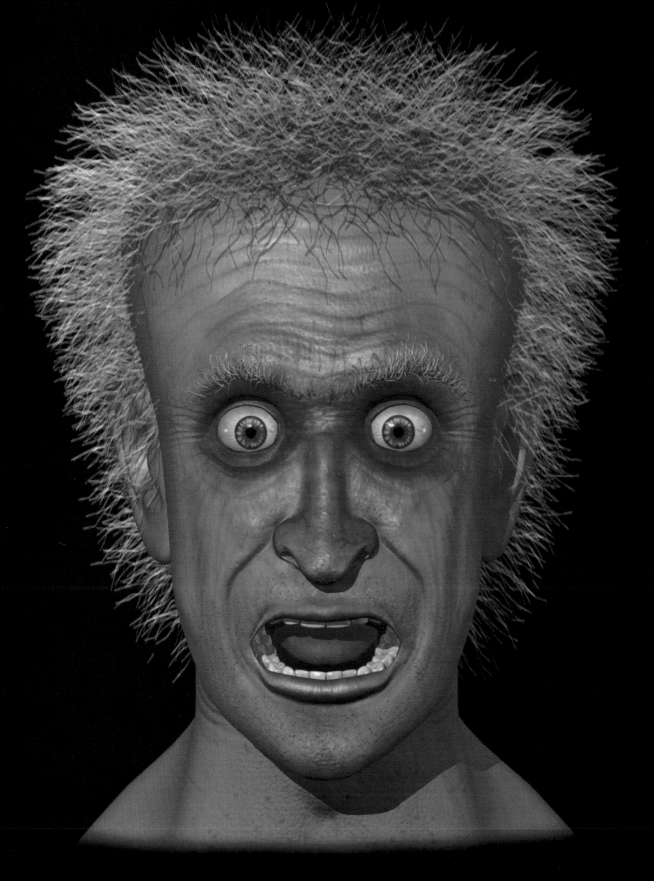

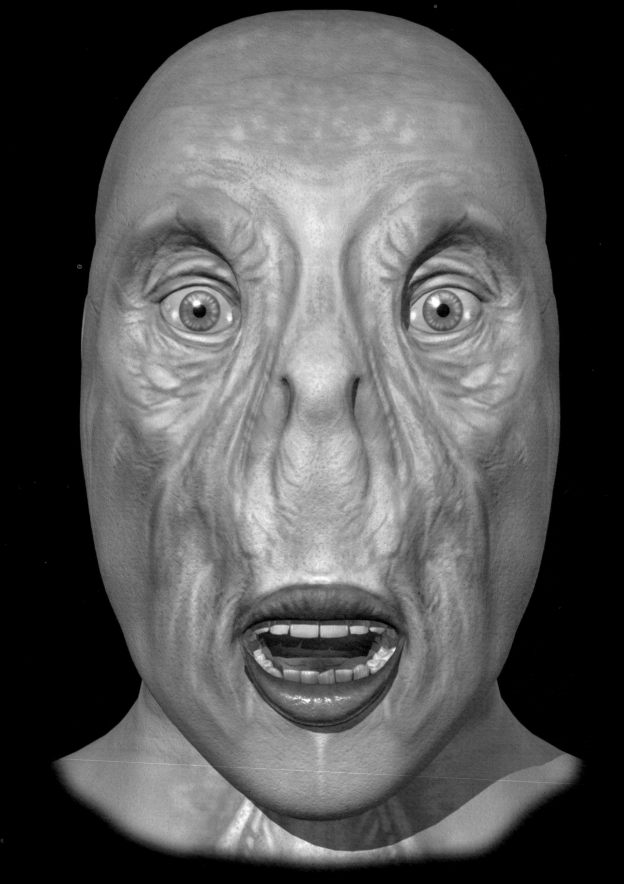

P A R T

II

Expression

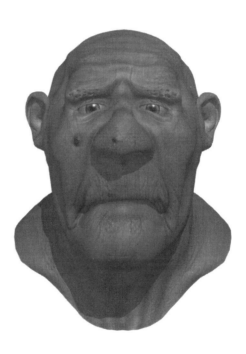

Your character's face tells a story. In fact, it says more than words can express. Creating dynamic facial expressions will set your work apart from the crowd. There are a number of 3D creatures and characters out there but, unfortunately, the majority have rather dry and lifeless expressions. If you want your characters to capture the imagination of the viewer, you need to show some emotions and break loose with the expressions. Nothing you will do with your character will be more important than its expression.

In this part we'll take a look at several key factors to consider when creating your character's facial expressions. There are certain elements of the face that define expressions, such as the brow, eyes, nose, cheeks, mouth, and jaw. We'll take a look at each of these areas and the role it plays in giving your character personality and bringing it to life in animation. We'll also explore some very simple techniques for giving your character unbelievable personality and character. Let's get started.

4 Facial Features and Expression

Terror   **Drowsy**

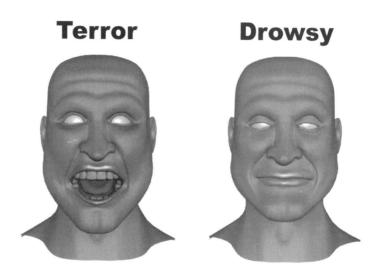

A good place to start when creating facial expressions for your characters is to determine the desired use. In short, you need to ensure that you are creating the right expression for the shot. This may seem relatively obvious, but there are countless subtle nuances that can make a huge difference in the outcome of your expression.

Before you start working on your facial expression, you should determine what type of expression it is. There are three types of facial expressions: questions, answers, and statements. The purpose of categorizing expressions is to make it easier to select the right expression for a particular situation. For example, you wouldn't use a statement expression when your character is questioning something. It just won't work. Categorizing the expressions into general groups makes it easier to quickly select the best choice.

Let's take a look at each of the types of expressions and the role they place in facial animation.

Question Expressions

Question expressions are typically those that show concern or concentration, as if to say "Is it safe?" or "what the heck is that?" Figures 4.1 and 4.2 show examples of concern and concentration.

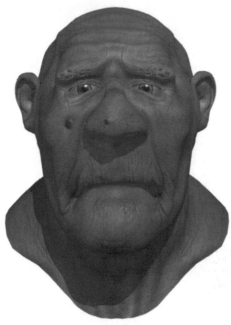

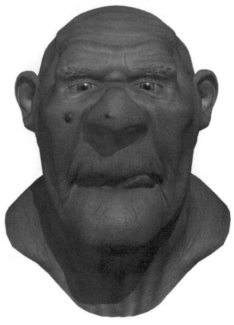

FIGURE *A concern question expression.*
4.1

FIGURE *A concentration question expression.*
4.2

Notice how both expressions seem to be posing a question to the viewer. They also cause the viewer to question what the character is thinking about. Another good example of a question expression would be a charming smile, which poses the question "Did I do something wrong?" Figure 4.3 shows a charming smile.

Notice how the eyes are wide open. This is a common trait of a question expression. Raised eyebrows denote confusion. The eyes play a major role in creating question expressions. We'll be talking about the significance of the eyes in creating facial expressions later in this chapter.

OK, so what makes an expression a question? Well, if the expression can't be used to make a statement or answer a question, then it's a question expression. For example, you may vocally state that you are confused but a confused look on your face posed a question, a pondering of that which boggles you. It would be unlikely that you would make a statement with a confused expression since the mere definition of confused indicates that you have a question.

It's important not to confuse what the character may be saying with what it is expressing with its face. While these may often go hand in hand, the face will quite often betray what is said by showing another thing. I may tell you that I know what you are talking about, but I might have a confused look on my face,

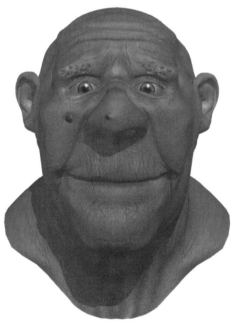

FIGURE *A charming smile.*
4.3

which is telling you I don't know what you are saying. The facial expressions of your character are the true honesty behind what it is saying. One of the most exciting and challenging aspects of facial expression is to have your character say one thing and express another. It makes for very intriguing animation.

Getting back to our discussion of question expressions, below is a list of common question expressions:

- Concentration
- Confusion
- Worry
- Fear
- Smirk
- Devious smile

Now it's important to note that these expressions are not always questions. For example, a smirk or devious smile can also be an answer, depending on the situation and how you use it. The purpose for providing this list is to give you a starting point for selecting an expression for your animation.

The next expression type is the statement.

Statement Expressions

Statement expressions are the instigators. They are used to tell the viewers or another character in the animation something of relevance about how the character feels. They tend to be more of the emotional category rather than ex-pressive, as with the question expressions. Common statement expressions would include *anger, misery,* and *joy.* Figures 4.4 and 4.5 show examples of anger and misery.

Notice Papagaio is telling you something with his expressions. He's telling you how he feels. Another great statement expression would be yawning, as shown in Figure 4.6.

Papagaio is definitely telling you he "feels" tired. The statement expressions are the feeling expressions. Like with any other expression they can betray the spoken word. For example, if you were to ask me how I felt right now, I'd prob-ably say fine, but my face would show that I was very sleepy since it's 2 am and I'm writing a book. My face has betrayed my dialog. Below is a list of common statement expressions:

- Rage
- Sternness
- Shouting
- Enthusiasm

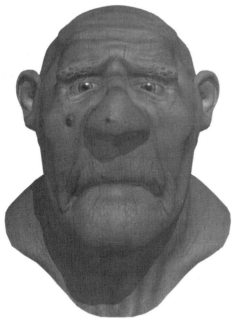

FIGURE
4.4

A misery statement expression.

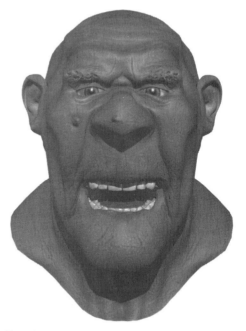

FIGURE
4.5

An anger statement expression.

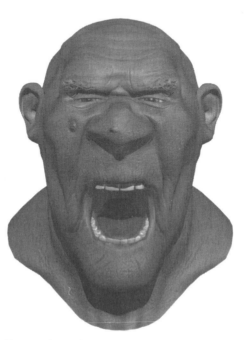

FIGURE
4.6

A yawning statement expression.

- Misery
- Exertion
- Drowsiness
- Yawn
- Sleep
- Passion
- Intensity
- Dazed
- Sadness

Of course, not all of the statement expressions are limited to being feelings. We obviously don't feel shouting, but it qualifies as a statement expression because, well, it's a form of making statements. It's also a variation of anger or rage, which are both statement expressions.

The last of the expression types is answer. Let's take a look at it now.

Answer Expressions

Answer expressions are just as they sound. They provide the viewer with a visual answer to a question posed, but the question doesn't have to be audible. For example, pain is an answer expression. While you wouldn't normally think of pain as an answer, if I hit you in the arm, your facial expression answer would be pain. Then, of course, it would probably turn to the statement expression anger as you popped me in the eye.

Common answer expressions would include laughter and crying, which are shown in Figures 4.7 and 4.8.

Laughter is a very common answer expression. When someone tells a joke, your face answers with a laugh. The same would apply to smiling and grinning, though a devious grin would be a statement or question. Repulsion is also a definitive answer expression. For example, if I asked you to eat a bucket of cockroaches, you would probably answer me facially with repulsion. Well, I certainly hope you would.

Common answer expression include:

- Crying
- Surprise
- Laughter
- Phony smile
- Exertion
- Phony laughter
- Pain
- Smiling

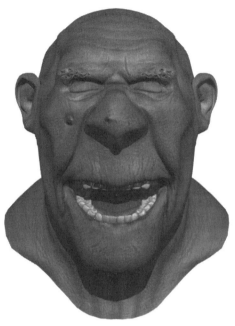

FIGURE **4.7**   *A laughter answer expression.*

FIGURE **4.8**   *A repulsion answer expression.*

- Terror
- Facial Shrug
- Repulsion
- Disgust
- Disdain

Answer expressions quite often follow question expressions. For example, the question expression afraid suggests that the person is concerned about some impending doom. He or she is questioning whether he or she will get through it OK. Of course, if doom does arrive the character will be using the answer expression terror.

OK, so how do these types of expressions come into play when we animate? When you are creating animations, or even a still, you want the faces of your characters to communicate the story. Basically, you know your facial animation is a success when you can turn off the sound and the viewers can still get the message you are trying to communicate. This, of course, doesn't apply to every situation, but it does when you are making a point to communicate and idea or concept. For example, let's consider the following scenario.

You have a mugger holding a gun on a victim, telling him to give up his wallet or die. The mugger would have a stern face, which is a statement question. The victim might refuse to surrender his wallet in a defiant manner. He would likely have an angered expression, which is another statement. Now the mugger gets hostile and pulls back the locking lever on the gun, stating that the victim has five seconds to surrender the wallet or die. Now the mugger is sporting an enraged shouting expression, but with eyebrows raised as if to say, "Do you really want to die over a few lousy dollars?" The mugger now has a question expression. Well, the victim now realizes the futility of his defiance and becomes fearful for his life. As he reaches for his wallet, he displays a frightened, wide-eyed expression, which is to say "OK, I'll give you the wallet, but please don't shoot." He has now shown an answer expression to the mugger's question expression.

As you can see the type of facial expression plays a major role in establishing effective communication with the viewing audience. While these expressions may seem obvious given the situation, it's the variations that sell the expressions. Let me explain. When the mugger stated his ultimatum with the enraged expression, he raised his brow at the same moment. The brow raising changed a "statement" expression into a question, revealing the fact that the mugger was intent on getting the wallet but really didn't want to shoot the victim. Now this wouldn't be so obvious to the now-frightened victim, but it's important for the viewer who is engaged in the story of the moment.

When you create facial animation, you should be keeping the viewer in mind, not just the characters in your scene. We are storytellers, so therefore we need to tell a story using the expressions on our characters' faces. A good example of storytelling with subtle gestures would be the hand gestures we see on TV shows and in the movies. The reality is that most people don't use large hand gestures, but actors do because they are communicating a story to the viewer. While the hand gestures are not relevant to the actual story, they are subtle clues, telling the viewer a little more about the story than what is being said by the actors.

The great thing about using contradictory expressions is that it makes the character multidimensional. All too often we see characters that lack any real emotional depth. When they have depth, it's merely two-dimensional, meaning they express exactly what they are speaking. In reality this rarely happens. We spend the majority of our time hiding how we really feel, but our faces always betray us. If you want to make truly stunning facial animation, you should invest some time in the exploration of facial expression types.

Now that we know the different types of expressions, let's take a look at what defines an expression. To be more precise, let's take a look at the individual elements of the face and the role they play in facial expression.

Expression Features

Each portion of the face plays a role in facial expression and some play greater roles than others. There are three major features of the face that influence the nature of facial expressions: the brow, eyes, and mouth. These features are broken into two categories, the *foundation* and the *modifiers*. The mouth is the foundation and the eyes and brows are the modifiers. This means the mouth sets the expression, while the eyes and brows modify it to achieve the wide number of facial expression variations that humans can create.

Let' stake a moment to examine each of these and the role they play in creating dynamic facial expressions.

THE MOUTH—FOUNDATION

The mouth is the defining element of facial expression. It's known as the foundation. I know you've probably heard it was the eyes, but that's simply not true. The mouth is the one feature of the face that never lies. The shapes it forms are always the same meaning, where the eyes are inconsistent with their meaning. Allow me to illustrate. Take a look at the heads in Figure 4.9.

Notice how the face has been separated into two segments, the eyes and the mouth. Now take a look at the eyes on the top and you'll see that by themselves they don't reveal the emotion of the character. In fact, the eyes are identical on both characters, but the emotions are different. Now take a look at the mouths on the bottom and you'll see that they are different. The mouths have accurately portrayed the expression and the eyes have not. The closed eyes could mean a number of things, such as sleep or straining, which means they are incapable of reflecting the true facial expression by themselves.

Perhaps you are thinking that these are very similar expressions, so the eyes haven't betrayed the mouth. Well, that is true, but take a look at Figure 4.10 and you'll see how the eyes are an unreliable means for determining the emotion of the character.

Notice how the eyes have remained the same but the mouth has changed dramatically. If the eyes were the leading element in facial animation, the head on the right would have to be crying right now, or at least sad. The reality is that the eyes did not define the expression. The mouth is the definitive element of these facial expressions, and all others for that matter. A smiling mouth always depicts happiness. A drooped mouth always depicts sadness. These are immutable. To further reinforce the point, take a look at Figure 4.11.

As you can see, a smiling mouth will always depict happiness, in spite of what the eyes are doing. The mouth is the most consistently reliable facial feature. It has the most muscle groups and is capable of a wider range of movement than any other feature on the face. Therefore, it's the foundation of all

Crying Mouth Closed

Crying Mouth Open

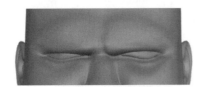

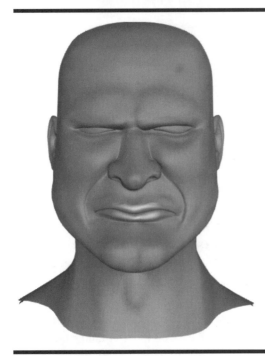
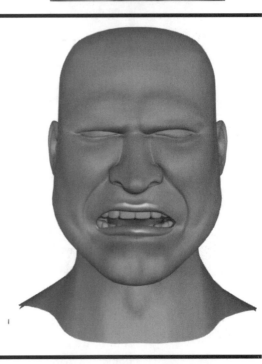

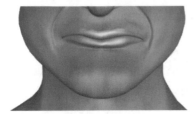
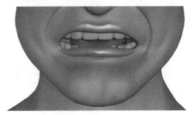

FIGURE *The inconsistency of eyes.*
4.9

Crying
Mouth Closed

Loud
Laughter

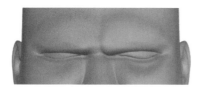
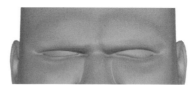

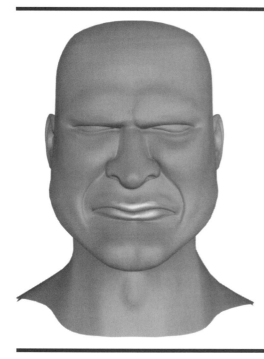
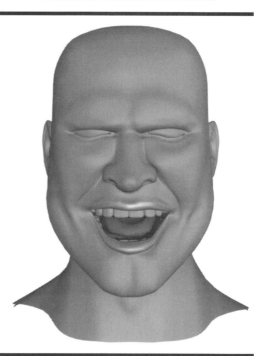

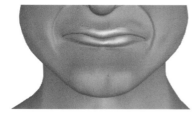
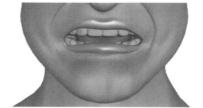

FIGURE *The eyes betraying the emotion.*
4.10

Laughter

Loud Laughter

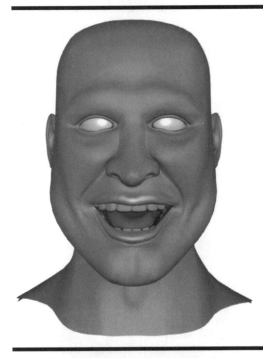

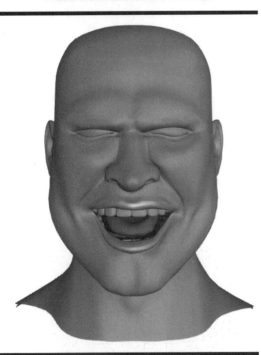

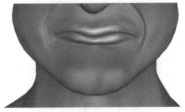

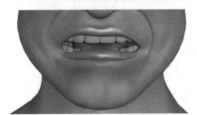

FIGURE *The honest mouth.*
4.11

facial expression. This doesn't discount the value of the eyes, but it does mean that mouth leads the expression.

Speaking of eyes, let's take a look at the role they play in facial expressions.

THE EYES AS MODIFIER

The eyes are the lead modifier and take a close second to the mouth in defining a facial expression. The eyes are used to reinforce, and in many cases modify, the facial expression created by the mouth. For example, in Figure 4.11 the mouths were the same, depicting laughter, but the eyes were different. The open eyes softened the laughter while the closed eyes amplified the effect. The eyes have a tremendous impact on the expression. Of course, the eyes are a great deal more than a ball and some lids. While the size of the ocular gap is relevant to the emotion of the character, it's the direction the eyes are looking that has the greatest impact on defining the expression. To get a better idea of the importance of eye direction, take a look at Figure 4.12.

Here we have Papagaio showing an expression of exhaustion. Notice how the eyes are hanging under the eyelids. This helps to reinforce the fact that he's tired. Now take a look at Figure 4.13.

FIGURE An exhausted Papagaio.
4.12

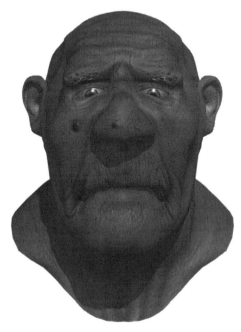

FIGURE A defeated Papagaio.
4.13

This is the identical facial expression, except the eyes are now focused downward. When the eyes look downward, they make a character appear depressed or defeated. While exhaustion and defeat are similar, they are used in unique contexts. By merely changing the rotation of the eyes we have created two different expressions.

The eyes are truly an essential element of facial expression. In fact, they are paramount when it comes to creating expressions for characters that aren't human. Take for example the challenge of giving an animal a facial expression. Well, for one thing, they aren't built for expressions. Their mouths aren't flexible enough to create most emotions so they must rely on their eyes to do the work. To get a better idea of how important the eyes are in creating creature expressions, take a look at Figure 4.14.

Here we have the Munch character from the Komodo Empire film, "Dwellers." In this particular image Munch is feeling rather stern. His mouth is clenched and he's looking right at us, defiantly. Now take a look at Figure 4.15.

FIGURE *A stern Munch.*
4.14

FIGURE *A pouting Munch.*
4.15

Here we have a very similar pose but this time the eyes are focused away from us. Now Munch looks like he's pouting, yet the only significant difference is the eye rotation. OK, now for one last variation. Take a look at Figure 4.16.

In this image Munch's eyes have been rotated upward, making him appear mischievous. We know he's done something wrong, but he's playing it cool. As you can see, the eyes are a significant factor in creating facial expressions for creatures, as well as humans.

When you are developing your facial expression you should put plenty of emphasis and thought on where the eyes will be looking. It will have a dramatic impact on the success of your expression.

The last element of facial expression is the brows.

THE BROWS AS MODIFIER

The brows have a tremendous impact on the facial expression. While they don't play a role in every expression like the mouth and eyes, when they do participate they have a great impact on the outcome of the expression. The brow suffers the same fate as the eyes in that it doesn't define the emotion. Figure 4.17 shows a great example of how the brow has no control over the general emotion.

FIGURE *A mischievous Munch.*
4.16

Terror

Drowsy

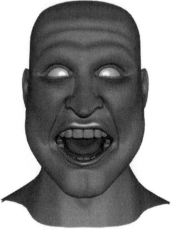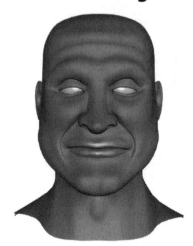

FIGURE *The impact of the brow.*
4.17

Here we have two distinctly different facial expressions but they both have identical brows. These emotions couldn't be any farther apart on the emotional spectrum, yet they both have the same brow details. This shows that the brow doesn't define the expression but definitely plays a major role in modifying it.

The brow works in conjunction with the eyes to create variations of the expression started by the mouth. The wonderful thing about the brow is that it can create numerous subtle variations that really add diversity to your expressions and can completely change their emphasis. For example, take a look at Figures 4.18 and 4.19.

Here we have two rather similar expression for Papagaio. The first, Figure 4.18, is Papagaio yawning. Notice how the brows are lowered over the eyes and are relatively parallel. Now take a look at the angry expression in Figure 4.19, and you'll see that there is a very subtle difference between the two sets of brows. The angry brows are turned upward in the middle, which makes Papagaio look irritated. This little detail has transformed his expression from a potential yawn into anger. The brows are a paramount element in facial expression and animation.

Speaking of animation. Let's take a look at the role these features play in facial animation.

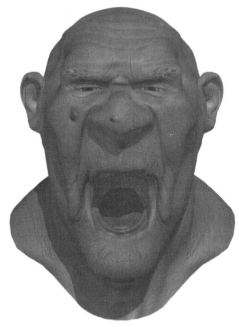

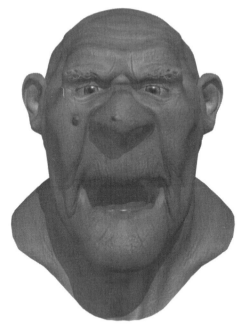

FIGURE *Papagaio yawning.*
4.18

FIGURE *Papagaio angry.*
4.19

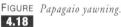

Animating Facial Expressions

Animating facial expression is the most challenging aspect of facial animation. It's also the most rewarding. When you animate the facial expressions of your characters, you need to take several factors into consideration. One would be their personalities and the other would be motion. Let's start by taking a look at personality. The personality of a character dramatically influences its expressions. For example, take a look at the character in Figure 4.20.

Here we have Knuckles, another character from the "Dwellers" film. Knuckles is a rather gruff brute who spends most of his time with a relatively stern expression. This has a great impact on the expression he makes. While he can achieve a wide range of expressions, most of them will be jaded by the factor that his features make him look angry. The large chin, heavy brow, missing teeth, and small ears combine to make him an intimidating character. When creating expressions of joy, we are fighting the physical characteristics for the character's head. He's inclined to look irritated no matter what we do. To get a better feel for how his physical structure affects his emotions, take a look at Appendix C, which features Knuckles posed in forty common expressions. You'll see that he tends to look irritated in nearly every pose. This, of course, is acceptable because that's his personality. When you are creating facial expressions

FIGURE   *The irritable Knuckles.*
4.20

you need to consider the personality of the character since it will both define and limit the flexibility of your emotions.

Of course, not all grumpy characters are resigned to looking mean in every expression. Take for example Papagaio, the character we've seen a number of times already in this chapter. Papagaio is a grumpy old man, but he is capable of very pleasant and endearing expressions, as you can see in Figure 4.21.

Doesn't he look inviting with that enormous smile and those soft eyes? He's normally a rather gruff character, but with the proper attention to expression detail he can become very pleasant, if not darn right adorable. When you are animating characters, you want to be able to take them from one emotional extreme to another without their personality remaining constant. This requires a great deal of attention to detail, but the payoff is well worth it, as you can see in the Papagaio.mov animation in the Chapter4 folder on the companion CD-ROM.

This animation features Papagaio making the transition through several facial expressions that cover a wide range of emotions. Pretty cool, isn't it? That's the power of facial expression. You can bring your 3D characters to life by properly applying them. Of course, when making facial animation there are some rules to consider that make the outcome a great deal more dynamic. Let's take a look at the rules of facial animation.

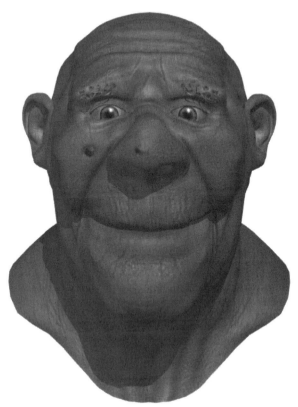

FIGURE *The warmth of Papagaio*
4.21

THE RULES OF FACIAL ANIMATION

1. **Keep the head moving.** One common mistake made in character animation is to keep the head still. In reality the head moves quite frequently. It's not always a dramatic movement but there is plenty of subtle movement. Incorporating this movement into your animations will add a tremendous amount of depth to the character, making it appear more believable.

   Take another look at the Papagaio animation and you'll see that his head moves frequently throughout the entire animation. This serves two purposes. It brings him to life and it keep the viewer from getting bored watching him. Now granted, the animation isn't meant to be typical dialog animation, but it does show how the movement really makes the animation awesome.

2. **Move the eyes.** Steady eyes are boring, not to mention eerie. You don't want your character to stare at the viewer. People's eyes are always looking about for something interesting to focus on. Your characters should do the same. The movement doesn't have to be dramatic, but it should be frequent and there must be times when the movement is severe, meaning they look to the side or even up and down. When people think, their eyes move up, to the side, and down, depending on the way they store information.

People store information in three ways: visually, audibly, and kinesthetically. A visual stores information as pictures, as in a photographic memory. An audible stores information with words, seeing everything in words when information is stored. Typically audibles are heavy readers. A kinesthetic stores information emotionally—feeling everything, which consequently makes information retrieval challenging.

When we search for information, we look for the information with our eyes. A visual will look up into his or her head for the information, an audible will look toward the ears, and a kinesthetic will look down toward the heart. These visual patterns are a necessary part of facial animation. If you take the time to watch an interview on TV, you'll see the eyes of the interviewee dart about searching for information. If you want your animation to be realistic, you'll need to incorporate this eye movement in your animation. Now this doesn't mean that the eyes will always be darting about, but they will move frequently during conversation.

To see an example of typical eye movement take a look at the Papagaio.mov file. Notice how his eyes spend a bit of time searching, then focus on the viewer, then go back to searching, and so on. This breaks the monotony of the animation. You'll also notice that the head is leading the eyes when he turns his head. There is a common misconception that the eyes lead the head. While the eyes may pick up on items in their peripheral vision, the head initiates the move before the eyes lock onto the target.

3. **Move the mouth.** While this doesn't seem like an obvious factor of facial animation, it's critical. Well, it's obvious the head moves for lip-synch, but what about the times when the character isn't speaking? Subtle mouth movements are very natural in humans, particularly when they think. They will quite often bite their tongues, lick their lips, roll their lips inward, press hard on them, and even chew on them. These are all nervous habits, which plague the majority of the world population. They may be undesirable nervous ticks, but they make awesome additions to animation.

Also, don't forget about saliva. We are constantly swallowing saliva but you'll never see a 3D character do it. Well, with the exception of Papagaio. If you take a look at the beginning of the animation you'll see him tighten his lips and the throat move upward. This is where he swallows. Then he goes on to chew a bit, like older people tend to do, and he licks his lips, too. These are all subtle details but they make a great impact on the animation. They really bring Papagaio to life and suck the viewer into the animation.

Well, there you have it, the three simple rules of facial animation. While it would seem like there would be many more rules, there really aren't that many. There are more rules regarding lip synch, but we'll get into those in the next chapter.

Wrap Up

The important thing to take away from this chapter is that there are many subtle nuances to facial animation. If you want your animation to wow the viewer, you'll need to pay strict attention to the details. It's more work than simply slapping a static expression on the face of your character. One look at Papagaio and you'll soon realize the reward for perseverance.

In the next part we'll be taking a look at lip synch and facial expression animation. This is where all your hard work creating the perfect character comes to life. Animation is very rewarding and isn't as hard as you might think. Let's flip the page and get to know lip synch animation.

P A R T

Animation

IY **IH, EY, EH, AE,** **AA, AO**
AH, AY, AW, AN, H

OW, UW, AX, **UH, ER** **Y**
OY, YU, W

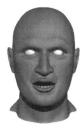

L, T, D **R**

Facial animation can be rather daunting since it appears complicated. The reality is that facial animation is very simple if you fully understand the power and proper application of facial expressions and phonemes. Nothing undermines character animation more than poorly animated facial expressions and dialog. We've seen far to many Hanna Barbara style 3D animations. While this style is great for cartoons, it lacks the depth we expect from a 3D character. Three-dimensional characters are far more complex than their 2D counterparts, therefore we need to give them more detailed expressions if we are to "wow" the viewing audience.

For quite some time it's been said that 3D facial animation and expression is a complicated and exasperating task that can only be mastered by the seasoned professionals. Well, that simply isn't true. Anyone, and I mean anyone, can master the fine art of facial dialog in a matter of minutes by simply understanding a few simple rules, which we will cover in the coming chapters. We'll be shattering many myths surrounding facial animation, making it easier than ever before to perfectly synch your animation to an audio file. You'd be amazed at how simple facial animation really is.

In fact, what are we waiting for? Let's get started.

5 Speech/Lip Synch

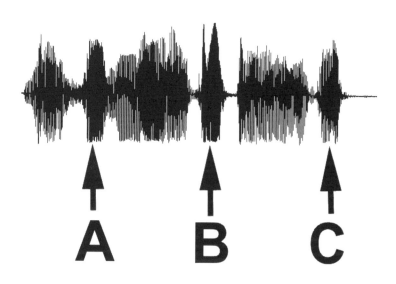

In this chapter we're going to concentrate on the process of matching a character's facial movement to recorded dialog. In principle this is a rather simple process. First, we build a library of character model variations, that include the basic mouth shapes necessary for speech (phonemes) and expressive variations such as the brows lifted, an angry scowl, or a grimace. This is usually done in the modeling portion of your program. The expressions and phonemes are typically saved as individual model files that can be reloaded and edited.

The next step is to break down the recorded dialog, which is the process of translating what is heard in the dialog track into a list of facial shapes that, when run in sequence, will create the illusion that the character is producing the recorded sounds. The exact facial shapes and the keyframes numbers they will occupy are entered into a timing chart.

Finally, the facial shapes that were built in the first step are arranged according to the sequence listed in the timing chart. This can be done by supplying the software with a list of files to be morphed, or by building the phonemes and expressions with weighted targets, as we'll be discussing in more detail in Chapter 6.

While it may appear to be a mechanical process, there is a great deal of creativity in deciding how the character's face will transform throughout the animation. Lip synch is a part of acting, so the personality of your character defines the message being delivered. The spoken word can have several meanings depending on the nuances you give your character, such as eye movement and facial expressions.

The first step in the lip synch process is to understand the foundation— *phonemes*. Phonemes are the most misunderstood aspect of facial animation. Nearly all of the information available to animators is incorrect, making it challenging to create really dynamic lip synch animation. In the coming segment we will dig deep into the world of phonemes and pull back the shroud that has been covering the real story behind phonemes.

Let's take a look at phonemes and the role they play in lip synch animation.

Getting to Know Phonemes

What is a phoneme? A phoneme is the smallest part of a grammatical system that distinguishes one utterance from another in a language or dialect. Basically, it's the sounds we hear in speech patterns. In phonetic speech, combining phonemes, rather than the actual letters in the word, creates words. For example, in the word "foot", the "oo" sound would be represented by the "UH" phoneme. The phonetic spelling of the word would be "F-UH-T." It does look a bit odd, but phonemes are the backbone of speech and therefore paramount to the success of lip synch.

When we create lip synch animation, we synch the facial movement of our character to the recorded dialog. When the phonemes are spoken, the mouth changes shape to form the sounds being spoken, not the words but the sounds. There are 40 phonemes in the American English language, which are listed in Table 5.1.

As you can see, the phonemes don't actually look like the printed word, but when you speak them they sound identical. What determines a phoneme? Well, a unit of speech is considered a phoneme if replacing it in a word results in a change of meaning. For example, "pin" becomes "bin" when we replace the "p" therefore the "p," is a phoneme. Other examples would include:

- "Bat" becomes "rat," making "b" a phoneme.
- "Cot" becomes "cut," making "o" a phoneme.
- "Chat" becomes "cat," making "ch" a phoneme.

Of course, the phonemes in Table 5.1 apply only to American English. When is comes to international phonemes things get very complicated. Because there is a lack of correspondence between letters and sounds, a symbolic system was created that better represents sounds. It's referred to as the *International Phonetic Alphabet (IPA)*. The IPA assigns a set of symbols to phonemes. Most of these symbols are not available on an ordinary typewriter setting, so I have converted the IPA to English letters. You can find the IAP phonemes in Table 5.2.

As you can see, the IPA basically the same as the English phonemes, with the exception of one phoneme that has been dropped—YU, as used in "be*au*ty."

Now that we know what a phoneme is and how phonemes are created, let's take a look at how they translate to visual phonetics.

VISUAL PHONEMES

Visual phonemes are the mouth positions that represent the sounds we hear in speech. These are the building blocks for lip synch animation. When you are creating 3D character lip synch, you start by modeling the phonemes. The important thing to identify is how many actual visual phonemes there really are. The common myth is that there are nine visual phonemes. While nine can be used to create adequate lip synch animation, there are actually sixteen visual phonemes, which are shown in Figure 5.1 and 5.2.

Under each visual phoneme you'll find the audible phonemes that are associated to that specific mouth position. Now I'm sure you've noticed that several of the visual phonemes look the same. Well, they do look very similar, but upon closer inspection we see that the tongue is in different positions. To see the tongue positions more clearly, you can jump to Appendix B in the back of

Table 5.1 American English Phonemes

Articulation	Phoneme	Example	Visual Phoneme	Articulation	Phoneme	Example	Visual Phoneme
Vowels (unitary)	IY	Beat	1	Nasals	M	Maim	9
	IH	Bit	2		N	None	10
	EY	Bay	2		AN	Bang	2
	EH	Bet	2	Fricatives	F	Fluff	11
	AE	Bat	2		V	Valve	11
	AA	Hot	3		TH	Thin	12
	AO	Bought	3		DH	THen	12
	OW	Boat	4		S	Sass	13
	UH	Foot	5		Z	Zoo	13
	UW	Boot	4		SH	SHoe	14
	AH	But	2		ZH	Measure	14
	ER	Bird	5		H	how	2
	AX	About	4	Plosive (Stops)	P	Pop	9
Diphthongs	AY	Buy	2		B	Bib	9
	OY	Boy	4		T	Top	7
	AW	How	2		D	Did	7
	YU	Beauty	4		K	Kick	15
Glides	Y	You	6		G	Gig	15
	W	Wow	4	Affricatives	CH	Church	14
Liquids	L	Lull	7		J	Judge	16
	R	Roar	8				

the book. This appendix features larger images of each phoneme and illustrates the actual tongue position for each.

The tongue may seem to be an insignificant element in lip synch, but it's not if you want to create truly realistic dialog. We can see the tongue movement of people when they speak. We may not focus on it but we definitely know it is happening. Now if the tongue movement is unnatural because too few visual phonemes were used, then the animation will look unrealistic. Of course, it you want to save time you can always opt for fewer phonemes, such as the ten listed in Figure 5.3.

In the short list, several of the visual phonemes with similar exterior appearances have been combined. Of course, the subtle tongue movement will not be accurate, but that isn't always important, particularly if the shot isn't a close-up. There are times when you'll want to shorten the phoneme list to expedite the

Table 5.2 International Phonetic Alphabet (IPA)

Articulation	IPA Code	Example	Articulation	IPA Code	Example
Vowels	EY	Gate	Fricatives	F	Fault
	EH	Get		V	Vault
	AE	Fat		TH	Ether
	AA	Father		DH	Either
	AO	Lawn		S	Sue
	OW	Loan		Z	Zoo
	UH	Full		SH	Leash
	UW	Fool		ZH	Leisure
	AH	But		HH	How
	ER	Murder		WH	WHere
	AX	About	Plosive (Stops)	P	Pack
Diphthongs	AY	Hide		B	Back
	OY	Toy		T	Time
	AW	How		D	Dime
Glides	Y	Young		K	Coat
	W	Wear		G	Goat
Liquids	L	Laugh	Affricatives	CH	Churn
	R	Rate		J	Jar
Nasals	M	Sum			
	N	Sun			
	NG	Sung			

editing process, though once you truly understand phonemes, you'll find it doesn't take any longer to use the long list.

Speaking of understanding phonemes, now would be a great time to explore the classifications of phonemes, which is invaluable knowledge when it comes to synching your animation to the dialog.

PHONEME CLASSIFICATION

The classification of a phoneme plays a vital role in lip synch animation. When you are trying to synch your animation to a dialog you need to fully understand the duration and inflection of the phonemes so you can make an informed decision as to which phoneme to use and when. The classifications of phonemes make this task very simple. Let's take a look at the different phoneme classifications and how they are applied to lip synch.

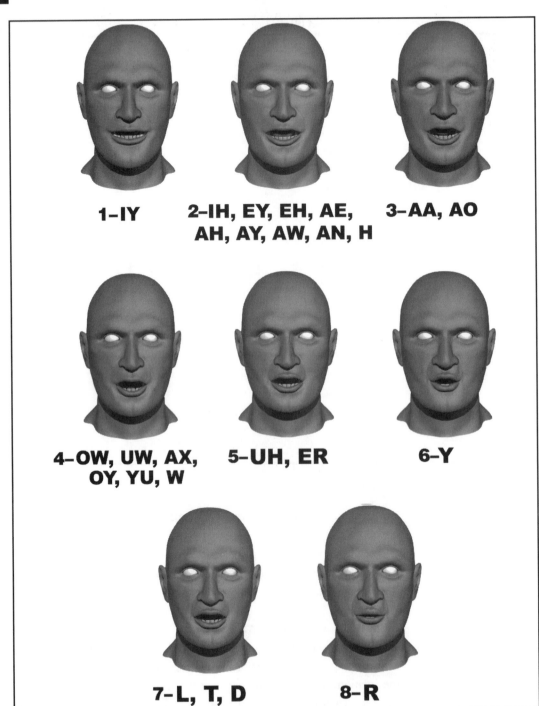

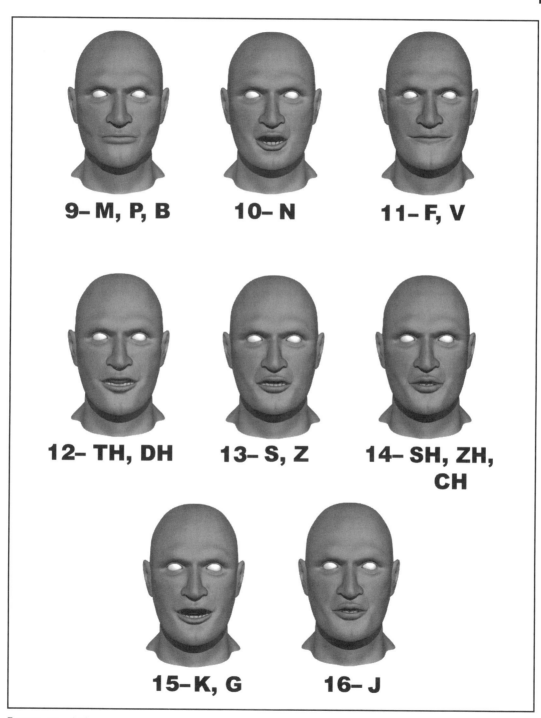

FIGURE   *Visual Phonemes.*
5.2

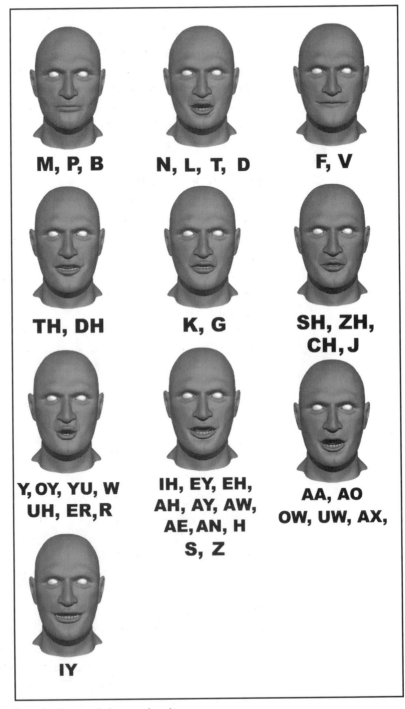

FIGURE *The visual phoneme short list.*

5.3

Once a phoneme is identified, it's then given a classification based on several characteristics. In Table 5.1 there is a column named *Articulation*. This is the classification of the phoneme. There are generally eight classifications of phonemes. These classifications break the phonemes down into logical groups, making them easier to understand and apply to facial animation. Once you have a solid handle on phonemes, you'll be able to rapidly synch even the most complicated dialog. Let's take a look at the phoneme characteristics. We'll start with the *point of articulation*.

Point of Articulation

The point of articulation is the point where the airstream is obstructed. In general, the point of articulation is simply that place on the palate where the tongue is placed to block the stream of air. After the air has left the larynx, it passes into the vocal tract. The constriction of airflow determines whether the phoneme is a vowel or consonant. If the air, once out of the glottis, is allowed to pass freely through the resonators, the sound is a vowel. If the air, once out of the glottis, is obstructed in one or more places, partially or totally, the sound is a consonant. There are a number of places where these obstructions can take place. These places are known as the *articulators,* several of which are indicated below.

- Lips (labial)
- Teeth (dental)
- Hard palate (palatal)
- Soft palate (velar)
- Back of throat (uvula/glottis)

The place of articulation is paramount when creating truly realistic dialog. Remember the long list of sixteen visual phonemes? Well, that list takes into consideration the many points of articulation. While the face may be the same on the exterior, the tongue on the interior is positioned differently to create a unique sound. When shooting close-ups of your characters, it's strongly recommended that you utilize the long list of visual phonemes.

Manner of Articulation

As well as indicating the place of articulation, it is also necessary to determine the nature and extent of the obstruction involved. The type of obstruction is known as the *manner of articulation.* An example of this can be found by looking at the following words: *nine, dine,* and *line.* They all begin with voiced consonants, yet they are all clearly different in both sound and meaning. The manner of articulation only relates to consonants since they are the sounds that are obstructed.

Vowels don't have a manner of articulation since the air passes freely. There are four kinds of consonant constriction that often occur in English. Let's take a moment the types of constriction and the role they play in lip synch.

- **Fricative:** A fricative is the type of consonant that is formed by forcing air through a narrow gap, creating a hissing sound. Typically, air is forced between the tongue and the point of articulation for the particular sound. Try it yourself. Say the "f" in *fun,* the "v" in *victor,* and the "z" in *zoo.* You should be able to feel the air turbulence created by the sounds. Unlike the plosive, it's possible to maintain a fricative sound for as long as you have air to blow. The fricatives include:
  - F
  - V
  - TH
  - DH
  - S
  - Z
  - SH
  - ZH
  - H

  Fricative consonants are held for a longer duration than any other consonant. For example, say the word "shoe." Notice how the "sh" sound last longer than the rest of the word. That's because it's a fricative phoneme. The same applies for the "h" in *help* and "z" in *zoo.* When you are marking the timing sheet for your lip synch animation, it usually a good idea to mark the fricative phonemes so you are prepared to give that phoneme a higher frame count in your animation.

- **Plosives (stop fricatives):** Plosives involve the same restriction of the speech canal as fricatives, but the speech organs are substantially less tense during the articulation of a spirant. Rather than friction, a resonant sound is produced at the point of articulation. Basically, friction and fricatives develop from tense articulations. When the articulation is loose, a spirant occurs. For example, try to slowly say "p" to yourself. You should be able to feel the build up of air that bursts into the "p" sound when you open your lips. Of course, you cannot prolong a spirant because it's fueled by a burst of air. The plosives in the English language are listed below:
  - P
  - B
  - T

- D
- K
- G

Plosives are commonly referred to as the "drop consonants" when it comes to lip synch. These sounds are uttered quickly and abruptly, meaning they are quite often passed over by the visual phonemes. They happen so rapidly that you are already into another visual phoneme before they had a chance to be visually expressed. This is an important item to consider when creating your lip synch animation. Not all consonants need to be reflected with visual phonemes, particularly if they are plosive.

- **Affricative:** An affricative is a plosive immediately followed by a fricative in the same place of articulation. That's a bit confusing, so let's look at an example. Take the word *jump*. The "J" is an affricative made by combining a plosive "D" immediately followed by a fricative "Z." The two affricatives in the English language are:

- CH
- J

Affricative phonemes are strong sounds, therefore you'll want to ensure that you use a visual phoneme for them. These are consonant phonemes that cannot be dropped in your lip synch since they are so prominent.

- **Nasal:** A nasal consonant is a consonant in which air escapes only through the nose. For this to happen, the soft palate is lowered to allow air to pass it. At the same time a closure is made in the oral cavity to stop air from escaping through the mouth. You can feel whether a sound is a nasal sound by placing your hand in front of your mouth and feeling if any air is escaping. You'll feel air if it's a nasal sound. There are three nasal sounds in the English language:

- M
- N
- AN

Voicing

Phonemes are either *voiced* or *voiceless*. A sound is described as voiceless when the vocal cords do not vibrate during its articulation. If the vocal cords do vibrate, the sound is called voiced. The vocal cords are folds of muscle located at the level of the glottis (in fact, the glottis is nothing other than the space between the vocal cords). The vocal cords vibrate when they are closed to obstruct the airflow through the glottis. They vibrate under the pressure of the air being forced through them by the lungs. Technically, only consonants are classified as voiced or voiceless, because when a vowel is spoken, the vocal tract is wide open and the vocal chords are vibrating.

The easiest example of a voiceless phoneme is to whisper. When you whisper, your glottis is wide open, meaning all the sounds produced are voiceless. However, if the vocal cords are very close together, the air will blow them apart as it forces its way through, making the cords vibrate, producing a voiced sound. To feel the distinction between voiced and voiceless, place your finger and thumb lightly on your throat. Then say "FFFFF" to yourself. Now say "ZZZZ." Notice how you can feel the vocal chord vibrating when you said "ZZZZ," but nothing moved when you said "FFFF."

It is also possible to hear the vibration. Instead of putting your fingers on your throat, put your index fingers in your ears and repeat the above sounds. You should hear a low buzzing sound when you articulate "ZZZZ" but almost nothing for the "SSSS."

The important thing to consider about voicing is that the voice phonemes are more likely to be represented visually. For example, vowels are always voiced phonemes, so they are accentuated with visual phonemes. You should always hit the vowels when you are doing lip synch animation. Speaking of vowels, let's take a look at the vowel phonemes.

PHONEME VOWELS

Vowels differ from consonants in that there is no noticeable obstruction in the vocal tract during their production. When a vowel is spoken, the vocal tract is wide open and the vocal chords are vibrating. If you try saying "AAAA," "EEEE," "IIII," "OOOO," or "UUUU" to yourself, you should be able to feel the vibrating. While your tongue moves around in your mouth, it never actually obstructs the airflow.

Vowels are determined by changes in position of the lips, tongue, and palate. These changes can be very slight and difficult to detect. In English, vowels can also glide into one another to form diphthongs. Speaking of diphthongs, let's took at the different types of vowel sounds.

- **Unitary:** A single-syllable sound with no change in articulator position. The unitary vowel phonemes include:
  - IY
  - EY
  - EH
  - AE
  - AA
  - AO

- OW
- UH
- UW
- AH
- ER
- AX

- **Diphthong:** A diphthong is a gliding, single syllable vowel sound that starts at or near one articulator position and moves to or toward the position of another. Diphthongs are often referred to as semivowels and are relatively slow transitions. Diphthongs are those sounds that consist of a movement or glide from one vowel to another. The first part of a diphthong is always longer and stronger than the second part; as the sound glides into the second part of the diphthong the loudness of the sound decreases. One of the most frequent errors made by people doing lip synch animation is to use unitary vowels instead of diphthongs, which tends to make the animation choppy, particularly since a diphthong is slower than a unitary vowel. You'll want to give the diphthong phonemes a higher frame count to prevent your animation from appearing choppy. The English language diphthong phonemes include:
  - AY
  - OY
  - AW
  - YU

- **Glide:** Glides are a subclass of diphthongs, but they are even slower. Therefore, you'll need to allow even more frames for a glide phoneme. The English language glides phonemes include:
  - Y
  - W

- **Liquids:** Liquids are another subclass of diphthongs and tend to be more like a rolling or thrill sound. The English language liquid phonemes include:
  - L
  - R

  A liquid phoneme is pronounced rather quickly so you'll want to shorten the frame count to compensate.

Well, that does it for the classification of vowel phonemes. As you can see, phonemes are a great deal more involved than a few simple facial expressions. Of course, they aren't nearly as complicated as they may seem. It's simply a matter of getting used to how they are used. We'll be taking a look at how we use phonemes in lip synch animation later in this chapter. Right now let's take a moment to get familiar with a few simple rules that will simplify the task of lip synch animation.

The Lip Synch Rules

Creating the illusion that your character is actually speaking the dialog is challenging but you can achieve great success by following a few simple rules. Let's take a look at the rules of lip synch animation.

RECORD THE DIALOG FIRST

There are two reasons to record the dialog before animating:

- It's far easier to match a character's facial expressions to the dialog than it is to find voice talent that can accurately dub an existing animation. That is, unless you enjoy Kung-Fu theater. But seriously, you don't want to find yourself spending hours in a recording studio trying to match words to a preexisting animation.
- The recorded dialog will help you determine where the keyframes go in your animation. Suitable sound editing software will even give you a visual representation of the dialog's shape, in effect a chart showing you where each sound goes in the time stream. In fact, we'll be covering such a program in Chapter 7 when we explore Magpie—a shareware utility for breaking down audio tracks for lip synch animation.

ANIMATE PHONEMES BASED ON THEIR ARTICULATION

The articulation of a phoneme determines the how much emphasis you will give the visual phoneme as well as the duration. When you are creating your lip synch timing charts, you should refer to Table 5.1 to see what the articulation is for each phoneme. In fact, while you are looking at the table, you'll also see that the actual morph targets for each phoneme have been indicated to make your job a great deal easier. The table is an invaluable tool that should stay by your side at all times when you are creating lip synched animation.

OK, let's take a look at each of the phoneme articulations and how they are expressed in lip synch animation.

Vowels

- **Unitary:** These are the strong vowel sounds and should be emphasized with your visual phonemes. Be sure to hit these phonemes in the dialog. You should never drop a vowel and always accentuate the unitary vowels. For example, the "EA" in *beat* is the strongest sound in the word. The same applies to the "O" in *hot.* Always emphasize the vowel phonemes by giving their visual phoneme the strongest strength in the morphing.

- **Diphthongs:** These are the lazy vowels, which tend to take longer to express. You should allow for plenty of frames when you encounter a diphthong. For example. In the word *beauty,* the "eau" is a "YU" diphthong. It actually takes up more audio time than the other sounds combined. The first part of a diphthong is always longer and stronger than the second part; as the sound glides into the second part of the diphthong, the loudness of the sound decreases. This means you'll want to hit the diphthong visual phoneme hard in the beginning of the sound, then taper the morph into the next phoneme. You won't want to drop any diphthongs because they form a substantial part of the words they inhabit. They are also a semivowel, which means they are voiced phonemes, and you can't drop a voiced phoneme. For example, dropping the "YU" in beauty would leave you with "bty," which would sound like *Betty.*

- **Glides:** Glides are slow diphthongs. Therefore, you'll need to allow even more frames for a glide phoneme. For example, the "Y" in *you* is a glide that lasts twice as long as the "ou"(UW). You always want to hit the glides since they form the bulk of any word they occupy.

- **Liquids:** Liquids are strong phonemes so you'll need to accentuate them. For example, take the word *lots.* If you dropped the "L," you'd be left with *ots,* which isn't much of a word. You'll always want to hit the liquids in your lip synch animation.

Consonants

- **Nasals:** The nasal phonemes are held for a longer period than most consonants, since they involve passing air through the sinuses. A nasal phoneme starts slow and ends on a high note. For example, in the word *mother* the "M" is started softly and slowly, then builds in tempo and volume until a sharp "M" sound is uttered. When animating nasal phonemes, you'll want to morph them gradually so you don't lead the sound.

- **Fricatives:** Fricatives are your middle-of-the-road consonants. They can be accentuated or passed over completely. For example, in the word *vice* the "V" is uttered quickly, so it can probably be dropped completely since it's followed by a strong vowel. On the other hand, in the word *voluptuous* the "V" is spoken slowly to make the word sexy. In this case you would need to accentuate the "V" and provide plenty of frames for it. Accentuating the "V" in voluptuous won't make the dialog choppy, because there is plenty of time to make the transition to the sharp vowels that follow.

- **Plosives:** Plosives are the stop consonants, so they are never emphasized in lip synch animation. In fact, more often than not they are completely dropped. For example, in the word *talk,* the "T" and "K" are both plosives, meaning they are abrupt. Since 'K' falls after the diphthong "AW," which tends to be slow and drawn out, it should be dropped to prevent the mouth from popping open and closing too rapidly. If it were left in the animation, the character would look like a cartoon, with the standard choppy Hanna-Barbera lip synch. Now why didn't we drop the "T"? Well, it's at the beginning of the word, so it can't be dropped without changing the visual appearance of the word. As a rule, you should drop plosives at the end of a word but never in the beginning.

- **Affricatives:** These are the consonants that you may never drop. They are the strong accent of the word and also feature two phonemes combined. Removing them will leave a large gap in your mouth movement. They are also long phonemes, so you'll need to provide them with an adequate number of frames to avoid chopping them.

If you take the time to identify the articulation of the phonemes in your dialog, you'll find it a great deal easier to synch the vocals. In fact, you'll be able to achieve a startling accuracy by merely editing the timing charts based on the phonemes alone, without even testing the actual animation synch.

NEVER ANIMATE BEHIND SYNCH

There are occasions when a lip synch will work better if it is actually one or two frames ahead of the dialog, but you should never try to synch behind the dialog. Think about it: You can form your mouth into an "o" shape and then say *oh,* but you can't say *oh* before you shape your mouth. It is best to start by animating exactly on synch. Then, if necessary, you can always move parts of the animation forward a frame and see if it works better.

DON'T EXAGGERATE

This is another important rule that is often overlooked. Study your own mouth while talking. The actual range of movement is fairly limited. Unless your subject is supposed to be a zany cartoon-type character, overly pronounced poses will look forced and unnatural. It is far better to underplay it than overdo it. Americans naturally talk in an almost abbreviated manner—you'd be surprised how many syllables we slur over or skip in normal daily speech. You'll find that the mouth doesn't open very much at all during speech, so you don't want your visual phonemes to be exaggerated.

KEEP A MIRROR ON YOUR DESK

When it comes to lip synching animation, this is not just a good idea—it's the law. There is no way to animate lip synch properly without having a model at hand, and you are best qualified to fill the position. Yes, your friends, family, and coworkers will laugh at you as you sit staring into a mirror for hours, endlessly repeating nonsense syllables and contorting your mouth into every imaginable shape. There is an easy solution, though. Simply make the people who are laughing serve as your models for an afternoon. You can be sure that after that they will stifle their snickers in the future and you can return to talking to your mirror in peace.

RULES WERE MADE TO BE BROKEN

Many consonants, and occasionally vowels, are actually pronounced in the transition between the preceding and following sounds. As a result, the full pose for that sound never occurs. Since consonants are often held for only one frame, there can be a major change in mouth position before and after the consonant. In these cases, it's best to drop the consonant pose or intermediate pose.

Also as mentioned above, Americans have a habit of abbreviating their speech. Depending on local dialect, syllables are often slurred or deleted entirely. Pay attention to your character's pronunciation and animate it, as the dialog dictates, not Webster's dictionary. For instance, in Kansas, where Darris Dobbs was raised, the phrase "That was a good rain we had the other night" would often be pronounced in casual conversation as something like "'ad'z uh gud rain wee'ad thuther nite."

And if you attend a rodeo in Western Kansas you will find that the natives have nearly eliminated consonants from the language altogether. Conversations go something like this:

"'ass a guh 'orse."
"Thanx, heez fum upparoun' Hays."
"Wha'ya giv foreem ?"
" roun'leben hunnerd."
"'ad us a guh deel."

You will find similarly abbreviated speech patterns in many other areas, particularly in the South and Southwest. In the New England area, speech is more clipped and precise, but vowels are often held even longer than usual. The important thing is to pay attention to the dialog. Try to hear it not as words but as sounds.

Your goal is to make the movements of the mouth appear natural and lifelike. Concentrate on smooth transitions between each pose. If you need to skip a consonant to maintain the tempo and avoid contorting the mouth, it will be far better to do so than forcing the mouth into unnatural poses or losing the rhythm of the dialog.

The rules laid out above are the basic guidelines to creating lifelike lip synch animation. As with everything in life, there are times when these rules must be broken, but in the vast majority of cases you will find that adhering to these principles will result in a very believable animation. Experience will make these rules second nature, but until it does, keep them close at hand as you animate dialog.

Now we are ready to get down to business and take a look at the actual process of lip synch animation.

The Lip Synch Process

The first step before animation can commence is to build variations on your original character model that correspond to the basic phonemes. This is where you put the knowledge you gained in the first part of this book to work. It's imperative that you properly model the phonemes, taking into consideration the muscle movements, or you'll end up with a very awkward animation, no matter how well you synch the dialog.

To make the process of developing the phoneme morph target easier, you'll find charts in Appendix B and Appendix D that illustrate the visual phonemes for both humans and cartoon characters. In addition to the visual reference of the appendices you'll also find image template of each phoneme in the Chapter5/Phoneme folder on the companion CD-ROM. You are provided with a front and side image of each phoneme to used as background template for creating your character's phonemes. While your heads will likely not match the ones in the images, they will be close enough to help you determine the shape of each visual phoneme expression.

Eventually the poses shown in the appendices will become as familiar to you as your own features. Until then, keep them nearby for reference, but never forget that they are only the starting place and must be modified to fit your character. Once the basic phonemes have been built, the process of lip synch can begin.

Lip-synching to dialog is really not all that difficult with the knowledge gained in the previous sections at hand. As a matter of fact, using the phoneme chart in Table 5.1 to translate what you hear in the dialog into their audible phonemes, then translating those phonemes into a predetermined set of visual phonemes makes it downright child's play. Well, it may not be all that simple, but you'd be surprised at how easy it can be one you get the hang of working with phonemes.

Typically, the first attempt at synching a character to a snippet of dialog will likely have some problems, but if we step through the process logically, they can be minimized. Let's take a look at the steps of lip synch animation.

THE STEPS OF ANIMATING LIP SYNCH

1. Break down the speech pattern.
2. Analyze the audible dialog and enter the phonemes into the timing chart.
3. Use the timing chart to set the keyframes in your animation.
4. Test the animation for synching and tweak the animation where necessary.

I know these steps seem oversimplified, but fortunately the phonemes make the process easier to manage.

For the purpose of this analysis we will be using a piece of dialog for the Living Toon character Knuckles, which was created for the Komodo Empire film, "Dwellers." Knuckles is a great choice because he tends to slur his speech, which gives us the opportunity to really see how the phonemes make a huge difference in lip synch animation. He also has greatly exaggerated features, which makes animating him more interesting than a standard human.

Let's take a look at the first step, analyzing the dialog and determining which phonemes make up the sounds we hear.

Step 1: Break down the Speech Pattern

The first step in lip synch is to determine the speech pattern of your dialog. Remember how we spoke about the slurred speech of the good old boys from Kansas, where the phrase "That was a good rain we had the other night" would often be pronounced in casual conversation as something like "'ad'z uh gud rain wee'ad thuther nite." Well, we couldn't properly assign the phonemes to this dialog if we didn't first convert it to a rough translation phonetically.

We're not talking actual phonemes here but rather a translation of how the dialog sounds using the normal alphabet. Let see how this is accomplished with a piece of dialog from Knuckles. In the Chapter5 folder on the companion CD-ROM you'll find an audio file named knuckles.wav. Take this opportunity to load the file and play it a few times.

Text:	**You shouldn't ought to talk to me like that.**						
Phonetic:	Ya	shudnada		tak	tuh	me	like	dat

FIGURE
5.4   *A phonetic translation of Knuckle's dialog.*

Notice how Knuckles tends to slur his speech, skipping a large majority of the consonants. What we need to do is convert the actual text of what he's trying to say into a rough phonetic translation as seen in Figure 5.4.

Notice how the phonetic translation doesn't closely resemble the actual written text. This is an important element, since we need to assign phonemes to the actual sounds we hear, not the text we see. You can see how Knuckles has slurred the words "shouldn't ought to" into a single word "shudnada." If we were to break down the words "shouldn't ought to" into phonemes it wouldn't match the actual dialog as you can see in Figure 5.5.

There certainly are some major differences. In fact, everything after "SH UH D N" is completely different. If we were to use the text phoneme translation, we would end up with something reminiscent of those classic Kung-Fu theater movies where the lip synch was completely off. It's always a necessity to phonetically translate the text before you actually start assigning the phonemes. Speaking of assigning phonemes, let's take a look at how that is accomplished.

Dialog:	**shouldn't**	**ought**	**to**
Phoneme:	SH UH D N T	AA T	T UW
Dialog:	**shudnada**		
Phoneme:	*SH UH D N AA D AH*		

FIGURE
5.5   *A comparison of the written and phonemic phonemes.*

Step 2: Analyze the Audible Dialog to Determine Phonemes

Now that we know Knuckles slurs his speech, we can break down the dialog into the proper phonemes. The first thing is to load his audio file into a sound-editing program; any will do as long as you can identify the actual times when sounds occur. There are a couple things to consider when selecting an audio-editing tool. You'll need a program that can relate the timing in frames, as well as actual time. While you can do the math to convert a real time to a specific frame number, it's much easier to use a program that does the work for you. Most lip synch animation is done at 30 frames per second so you would set the frame rate in the preferences of your audio-editing program to ensure it provides you with the proper frame numbers. If you had the wrong frame rate set, your animation would be out of synch.

The second thing to consider is whether the tool has a scrub tool. "Scrubbing" a sound is basically the same as running an audiotape back and forth over the play-head but only digitally. The scrub tool lets you drag the audio forward and backward so you can pinpoint the exact inflection of the phoneme. Without a scrub tool, you'll be spending a lot of time correcting guesswork. I like to use Adobe Premiere for my analyzing. While there are tools like Magpie that are specifically designed for lip synch analysis, I like the way Premiere handles the scrub tool.

Once you have your file loaded in your audio-editing program, listen to each sound in the knuckles.wav file and write down the corresponding phonemes, which are listed in you use the chart in Table 5.1. Figure 5.6 shows what you should end up with when the file has been broken down phonetically.

It can take a bit of time to get used to applying phonemes to dialog, but it's easy once you've done it a few times. Just sound out the phonetic translation of the dialog we did in Step 1 and apply the phonemes to the unique sounds you

Dialog:	Ya	shu	dn	ada		tak		tuh		me
Phoneme:	Y AH	SH UH	D N	AA D AH		T AA K		T AH		M IY

Dialog:	like		dat	
Phoneme:	L AY K		D AE T	

FIGURE 5.6 The phoneme breakdown.

hear. Be sure to focus on the sound and not the written dialog so you won't be confused.

Now, with the completed phoneme breakdown in hand, we can begin determining the exact location of each sound in the audio file. We do this by scrubbing the sound back and forth. By scrubbing in small segments we can determine exactly where a particular phoneme occurs in the time sequence. One bonus to doing our scrubbing digitally is that these programs provide a visual representation of the sound, which helps us to determine the point where phonemes are registered. Figure 5.7 shows the visual wave analysis of the Knuckles audio file.

As you listen repeatedly to small portions of sound, you will come to recognize them in the visual representation, which in turn will assist you in pinning down a phoneme's location. The high points in the file represent words and the low points the space between words. For example, the sound burst at "A" is the word *should,* at "B" the word *talk,* and at "C" the word *that.*

On closer inspection you'll see that distinct phonemes stand out in the wave file. For example, the high peaks indicated in Figure 5.8 are plosives, or stop consonants.

The first arrow points to the "t" in *talk,* the second to the "k" in *talk,* and the third to the "t" in *to.* Plosives always will be the highest peaks in your wave file, since they are a burst of air. This is an important distinction when selecting

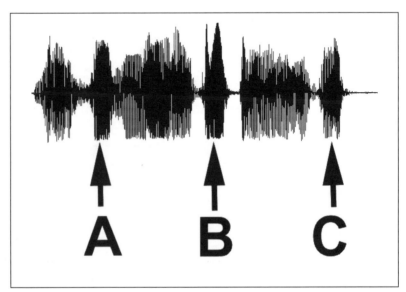

FIGURE *The Knuckles visual wave analysis.*
5.7

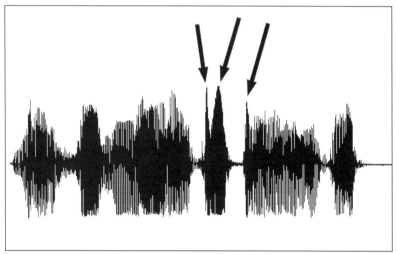

FIGURE   *Plosive peaks.*
5.8

your visual phonemes because you'll want to give priority to the strongest sounds in the dialog.

Other phonemes that will register as high peaks in your wave file will be vowels because they are voiced. The airflow isn't obscured by the articulation so they tend to be louder. Figure 5.9 shows some distinct vowels in the knuckles wave file.

A. This represents the "AH" in *Ya.*
B. The "UH" in *shu.*
C. And the "AA" in *ada.*

All three of these are single syllable unitary vowels, meaning they are hit hard in dialog; therefore, they need to be represented clearly with the visual phonemes. One distinction to make with Knuckles is that he slurs his vowels. In normal speech we hit the vowels hard and abruptly, unless they are diphthongs. This is another reason why we must start by analyzing the speech pattern of the dialog so we are prepared to compensate for accents and speech impediments.

The visual representation of phonemes in the wave file is very helpful since it gives us a visual means for identifying the location of phonemes. By scrubbing smaller intervals around the peaks we can extrapolate the precise location of each phoneme that goes into building up the phrase. Let's go ahead and an-

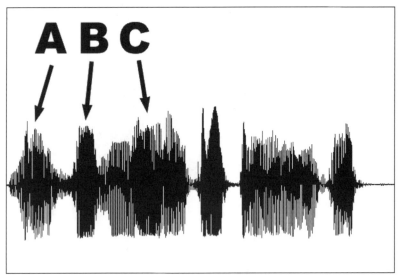

FIGURE *Vowel peaks.*
5.9

alyze the knuckles.wav file for lip synch animation to get a feel for how scrubbing works.

Scrubbing at the beginning of the file, we discover that the sound "Y" is located at frame 2. The phoneme "SH" of *should-a not-a* is at frame 10, and so on. Continue scrubbing through the file, picking out the sounds and their locations until you reach the end. Be sure to reference the visual waveform to help you locate the hard phonemes such as vowels and plosives.

Notice that we're hunting phonemes, not words. Shaping the sounds Knuckles speaks with your own mouth will help a great deal in deciding which phoneme is necessary for which sound. When scrubbing the phrase *You Should-a Nod-a Talked to me like dat,* you need to move your mouth to discover exactly what shapes it makes to form those words. Think in terms of sounds, not meaning.

Once the dialog track has been broken down into its component phonemes, they should to be entered into a chart along with the exact times at which they occurred. It's basically a table that shows the phonetic translation, the actual phoneme, and then the time when the phoneme occurs. Figure 5.10 shows the timing chart for Knuckles' dialog.

As you can see, in addition to the phoneme and the frame, the timing chart also has the visual phoneme target listed. Once you have identified a phoneme, you enter the designation for the visual phoneme target to be used. In Appen-

PHONEME	Target	Frame		PHONEME	Target	Frame
Y	7	2		L	2	53
AH	8	6		AY	8	57
				K	5	61
SH	6	10				
UH	7	15		D	2	62
D	2	19		AE	8	63
N	2	20		T	2	66
AA	9	25				
D	2	30				
AH	8	32				
T	2	37				
AA	9	38				
K	5	42				
T	2	45				
AH	8	46				
M	1	48				
IY	10	50				

FIGURE *The completed timing chart.*
5.10

dix B you will find a list of realistic human visual phonemes and Appendix D contains a list of ten visual phonemes built for human-like cartoon character. The cartoon visual phonemes were used for Knuckles' timing chart.

When you do the breakdown for the first time, you should be sure to enter the time for every phoneme. While it's likely you will be dropping plosives, you still want to add them in the initial pass in case they play a role in the visual lip synch. They are easy to delete later.

OK, with your completed timing chart in hand it's time to begin setting the keyframe poses.

Step 3: Use the Timing Chart to Set the Keyframes

Timing charts make setting keyframes for lip synch a trivial process. Once the sounds we heard have been translated into their visual phonemes and the frames identified for each, all we need to do is morph the visual phonemes from one to another at the appropriate frame in our animation.

In this particular example we're using straight morph animating. There are two types of morphing, straight and weighted. Straight morphing simply morphs the object in a linear progression from one object to another. The morphing can be any value from 0 to 100% and in many cases can even exceed 100%. The only issue is that you are limited to a single morph object so you can introduce subtleties into your animation like the occasional blinking eye without having to build hundreds of morph targets.

On the other hand, weighted morphing allows you to blend multiple objects in a single morph. This is very useful when adding facial expressions and emotions to your lip synch animation. You can not only add subtle eye blinks but also complete changes in the character's personality through facial expressions. Of course, this greatly complicates the animation process, but the end result is well worth the effort. We'll be taking a close look at animating facial expression with dialog in Chapter 6. For now we'll focus on straight morphing.

The Knuckles animation came out to be 70 frames in length at 30 frames per second. You can load the knuckles1.qtm movie file from the Chapter5 folder on the companion CD-ROM to see the resulting animation. In fact, why don't you do it now so we can discuss it in the next step.

Step 4: Tweak the Finished Animation

Don't be discouraged if your facial animations aren't perfect; lip-synching is not an exact science and it will almost always require a little tweaking. This may involve altering certain poses or tinkering with the timing. In some cases, the synch may appear more realistic if it's a frame or so ahead of the dialog, so that the mouth is moving as the viewer's brain is processing the sound rather than when their ear is receiving it. These are subtle things, but lip-synching is an exercise in subtlety. If you truly want the audience to suspend disbelief and accept your character as a living being, don't stop until it actually seems as if the character is speaking the dialog.

We can see by the animation that our timing is right on the money. You'll find that applying the articulation of phonemes to your lip synch will ensure that you hit the mark very close every time you do it. Of course, Knuckles' face seems to jitter too much in a few places, which is an issue of too many visual phonemes. This is where the tweaking begins. The first step is to go back to our timing sheet and add one more column. We then enter the articulation for each of the phonemes on the column as shown in Figure 5.11.

This is a vital step in lip synch because it allows us to identify the problems areas, eliminating the guesswork. Nothing wastes more time that blindly tweaking lip synch in hopes of resolving problems. Annotating the phoneme articulation takes out all of the guesswork. Why? It all comes down to the rules of lip synch we discussed earlier. There are times when you'll need to drop a

PHONEME	Target	Frame	Articulation		PHONEME	Target	Frame	Articulation
Y	7	2	Glide		L	2	53	Liquid
AH	8	6	Vowel		AY	8	57	Diphthong
					K	5	61	Plosive
SH	6	10	Fricative					
UH	7	15	Vowel		D	2	62	Plosive
D	2	19	Plosive		AE	8	63	Vowel
N	2	20	Nasal		T	2	66	Plosive
AA	9	25	Vowel					
D	2	30	Plosive					
AH	8	32	Vowel					
T	2	37	Plosive					
AA	9	38	Vowel					
K	5	42	Plosive					
T	2	45	Plosive					
AH	8	46	Vowel					
M	1	48	Nasal					
IY	10	50	Vowel					

FIGURE *Adding the articulation to the timing sheet.*
5.11

phoneme to make the animation flow smoothly. We don't always pronounce every letter when we speak, particularly if we have an accent. The consonants are the typical phonemes that fall prey to lazy and slurred speech, though there are times when you can and can't drop them in lip-synch. Let's take a look some guidelines for dropping phonemes.

PHONEME DROPPING GUIDELINES

1. **Never drop a phoneme in the beginning of a word.** You can drop consonants at the ends of words but never in the beginning. If you take them off the beginning, it will change the visual phonetic pronunciation for the word. The consonants at the ends of words can be dropped without having much impact on the word. In fact, it usually improves animation because most people end their words on a soft note rather than hitting a strong phoneme. The most common phonemes to drop are the plosives because they are very fast and therefore don't really register visually. If we look at the timing chart we just annotated with articulation, we'll see there are several plosives. Now we can't drop all of them. However, there

are several that are causing some stuttering problems. They are indicated in Figure 5.12.

You can see that we've selected the trailing plosives in the words *talk, like,* and *dat.* These are the visual phonemes that made the first animation test choppy. With them removed, the animation will flow smoothly from one word to another.

In addition to Plosives, there is another type of consonant that is often wise to drop - the Nasal phonemes. Let's take a look at the rule for dropping Nasal phonemes.

2. **Drop nasal visual phonemes to smooth transitions.** Nasals are the anti-visual phoneme. The majority of their sound comes through the nasal passage so they tend to be quick mouth movements, often nearly undetectable, yet the sound lingers well after the mouth has moved. This is a very important issue when animating. The most offensive of the nasal phonemes is the "M," since it requires a closed mouth. This can be a problem since in reality the mouth movement is nearly undetectable but in animation it stands out like a sore thumb. The problem is that

PHONEME	Target	Frame	Articulation		PHONEME	Target	Frame	Articulation
Y	7	2	Glide		L	2	53	Liquid
AH	8	6	Vowel		AY	8	57	Diphthong
					K		5	61	Plosive
SH	6	10	Fricative					
UH	7	15	Vowel		D	2	62	Plosive
D	2	19	Plosive		AE	8	63	Vowel
N	2	20	Nasal		T	2	66	Plosive
AA	9	25	Vowel					
D	2	30	Plosive					
AH	8	32	Vowel					
T	2	37	Plosive					
AA	9	38	Vowel					
K		5	42	Plosive					
T	2	45	Plosive					
AH	8	46	Vowel					
M	1	48	Nasal					
IY	10	50	Vowel					

FIGURE *Selecting consonants to drop.*
5.12

there is no way to tween the movements within a single frame in lip synch. This, of course, isn't a problem in reality because reality isn't 30 frames per second.

In the Knuckles animation we have several nasal phonemes but only one that is a problem. Play the Knuckles animation again and you'll see that his mouth jumps closed and open again when he says the letter "M." The movement looks unbelievably unnatural, yet it's synched perfectly to the sound. The problem is that the mouth has to cover a long range to reach closed from a vowel and then a long range back to get to a vowel that follows. This created the snapping movement of the jaw, which we need to remove. You'll typically want to drop a nasal when it lands between two vowels since the vowels are voiced, meaning they have the widest mouth gap to allow the free passage of air. Of course, if the nasal visual phoneme is the same as the preceding or following vowel, then it won't be necessary to delete it. Figure 5.13 shows the nasal "M" in the Knuckles' animation selected for deletion.

With this phoneme dropped, the mouth will flow smoothly from the AH to the IY visual phonemes so we won't see the sharp snap of his mouth.

As you can see, the rules for dropping consonants are fairly straightforward. In fact, they are an absolute blessing when it comes to lip synch problem solving. You merely need to go through your timing chart and identify the plosive and nasal phonemes, then delete them based on whether their location qualifies. It's really that simple. You actually don't even need to listen to the audio file. It will save you countless hours of tweaking, which is the standard by which most lip synch animation is done today. It's unfortunate, but most studios tend to do lip synch the old fashioned way, tweaking and tweaking until they are blue in the face with agony. Let them do that, while you take a few minutes to annotate the articulation of the phonemes so you can perform immediate and accurate tweaking of your lip synch animation.

Now that we have the problem visual phonemes deleted from our sequence, we can create another animation to see the results. You'll find the corrected Knuckles animation in the Chapter5 folder of the companion CD-ROM, entitled Knucklesfix.qtm. Take a minute to load the file and play it a few times. You'll see that it now flows very naturally and the missing "M" isn't even discernable.

By taking a deep exploration of phonemes we've managed to make a very difficult task rather trivial. Lip synching a cartoon character with an exaggerated face and slurred speech is one of the most challenging lip synch challenges

PHONEME	Target	Frame	Articulation		PHONEME	Target	Frame	Articulation
Y	7	2	Glide		L	2	53	Liquid
AH	8	6	Vowel		AY	8	57	Diphthong
					K			Plosive
SH	6	10	Fricative					
UH	7	15	Vowel		D	2	62	Plosive
D			Plosive		AE	8	63	Vowel
N	2	20	Nasal		T			Plosive
AA	9	25	Vowel					
D	2	30	Plosive					
AH	8	32	Vowel					
T	2	37	Plosive					
AA	9	38	Vowel					
K			Plosive					
T	2	45	Plosive					
AH	8	46	Vowel					
M	1	48	Nasal					
IY	10	50	Vowel					

FIGURE *Identifying the problem nasal phoneme.*
5.13

you will find, yet the proper application of phoneme principles has made it rather enjoyable and very quick to complete.

Be sure to read through this chapter a number of times until you feel confident that you have a handle on the process of lip synch animation using visual phonemes. You'll be happy you did the next time you tackle a big lip synch project.

Wrap Up

No one is ever going to claim that lip synching animation is easy. But few things are as rewarding as seeing audiences watching your character speak dialog and accepting that character as a real entity. By carefully following the rules and procedures laid out in this chapter you should be able to effectively synch your character's animation to its dialog. The more experience you get, the easier it will become.

Of course, simple lip synch is a long way from interesting. The real excitement comes from blending emotions with lip synch animation, which is what we'll be exploring in the next chapter. Flip the page and we'll take a look at how we bring characters to life with animated expressions.

CHAPTER

6 Weighted Morphing Animation

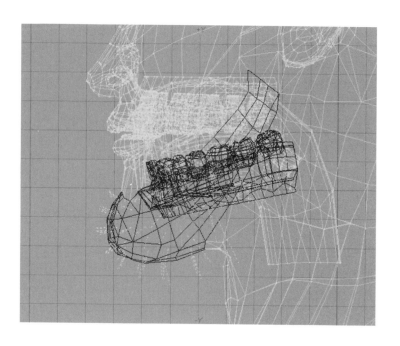

In this chapter we'll explore the techniques of animating the face using weighted morph-targets and segmented weighted morph-targets. What exactly does this mean? Well, have you ever played with one of those children's flip books that were segmented vertically into three groups of pages, one for the eyes and head, one for the nose, and one for the mouth? You were able to try different combinations of eyes, nose, and mouth just by turning the pages. The results were often incongruous and hilarious.

Well, we can perform a similar operation on our 3D characters through segmented morphing, with the added bonus that we can apply weighted morphs to each section, which means combining variations of the same section of the face to create a totally new expression. There are a few programs that utilize weighted morphing, including LightWave, which uses Morph Gizmo; and 3D Studio MAX, which has two plug-ins, Smirk and Morph Magic. You can also apply weighted morphing in Alias with Shape Shifter and Softimage with weighted shapes. There are also weighted morphing plug-ins being developed for trueSpace and RayDream Studio. It's safe to say that weighted morphing is becoming more of a standard with 3D programs.

In this chapter we'll be exploring how a short facial animation was made with Guido, a character from the Komodo Empire film "Dwellers." Guido's animation was created using segmented morphing, which we will cover later in this chapter. First let's take a closer look at weighted morphing.

Weighted Morphing

Weighted morphing is the ability to morph a base or anchor model into two target models simultaneously. This is a major advantage when you are creating lip synch animation that includes both dialog and facial expressions. Figure 6.1 illustrates this the process of weighted morphing.

The anchor object in column A was morphed 50% of the way toward the model at the top of column B and 50% of the way toward the model at the bottom of column B, effectively reaching a shape halfway between the two. The result is the model in column C.

If we chose to, we could have changed the weight of the morphs to 20/80, 60/40, or any other two percentages. The numbers don't have to add up to 100. In fact, in many programs you can exceed 100% to create very interesting results. Typically, a weighted morphing system will allow you to assign a slider to each target, as Figure 6.2 illustrates.

This is a common weighted morphing system interface. The targets are listed in the left-hand column and the sliders in the right-hand column control the percentage. For instance, we can see Figure 6.2 that the Mouth Crying tar-

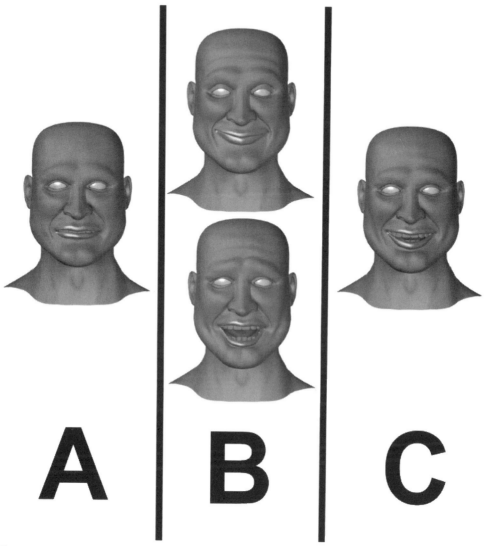

A   B   C

FIGURE   *Two morph targets combined.*
6.1

get is set to 20% and the Mouth Laughter target to 70%. To get a better idea of how weighted morphing works, load 2targetmorph.mov animation file found in the Chapter6 folder in the companion CD-ROM .

The anchor and two targets shown earlier in Figure 6.1 were the only models used, and keyframes were created by adjusting the sliders, keying them, and moving on to the next keyframe. Weighted morphing is an excellent tool because it allows us to derive a larger number of expressions from a given set of

Target Objects (Page 1 of 2)	Morph Percentage
Mouth_Closed.lwo	0
Mouth_crying.lwo	20
Mouth_cryopen.lwo	0
Mouth_Disgust.lwo	0
Mouth_Frightened.lwo	0
Mouth_Laughter.lwo	70
Mouth_purse.lwo	0
Mouth_repulsion.lwo	0

Page Up   Page Down

FIGURE **6.2** *A typical weighted morph slider interface.*

targets than can be achieved with straight morphing. Remember, with straight morphing the percentage of a morph can be set, but multiple targets cannot be morphed to simultaneously.

On the other hand, animating with weighted morphs is very similar to animating with straight morphs. In fact, the only difference is that you can combine two targets to create a totally new expression. Of course, there is a subset of weighted morphing that gives us the power to morph sections of the face independently of each other: segmented morphing. Let's take a look at how it works.

Segmented Morphing

Segmented morphing allows us to morph separate areas of the face individually. Working with segmented morphs is a little bit like playing with a Mr. Potato Head, mixing and matching expressions on different areas of the face. You might create separate targets for the eyebrows, eyes, and mouth. If you created only two targets for the brows, eyes, and mouth, you could create eight separate expressions, using combinations of them with 100% morph values.

Additionally, you can combine individual segment targets with weights, making for an astounding variety of expressions with these six simple targets.

The term *weight* refers to the percentage of the morph. By using percentages less than 100%, you can create literally thousands of variations from a simple few targets. You can even save combined morph objects as totally new objects that can be loaded into a modeler for tweaking, then loaded back into the weighted morphing system for creating even more combinations. The possibilities are truly limitless.

The real power of segmented morphing, however, is that we can keyframe each facial group individually. This means that we can hold the eyebrows in an arched position while the mouth goes about its business of forming visual phonemes, then we can lower the brows and use the same visual phoneme targets to continue the speech. With straight morphing we would have to build two sets of visual phoneme targets, one with the brows raised and one with the brows lowered. This may not sound so bad, but considering the variations of shape the brows can assume, it can become a very time-consuming task—not to mention taxing on your system resources having to load hundreds of morph targets.

Segmented morphing has two advantages over straight morphing: the ability to build a large number of expressions from a smaller set of targets and the ability to animate changing expressions while the character is talking. There is one more interesting use of segmented morphing we need to discuss: animating the jaw separately from the lips.

Animating the Jaw with Segmented Morphing

To illustrate for yourself why animating the jaw separately from the lips is a desirable technique, utter the phrase "I climbed the Washington Monument" in a natural speaking voice. Notice that while the lips changed shape at least 15 times while forming visual phonemes, the jaw pumped open and closed a mere 6 times. This means that, while jaw motion is definitely determined by the words being spoken, it operates independently from the lips.

So, how do we achieve this effect in animation? With segmented morphing. By creating separate morph targets for the lips and the jaw, each one will be given a separate set of sliders in your weighted morphing program and can be keyframed individually.

Figure 6.3 illustrates how the Guido model we discussed earlier is segmented in preparation for segmented morphing.

He looks a bit funny because the jaw has been lowered independently of the mouth, allowing us to select it and the lips with ease. Don't worry, it will be rotated to the proper position when he's animated. The anchor will never actually be keyframed without morphing it to another target.

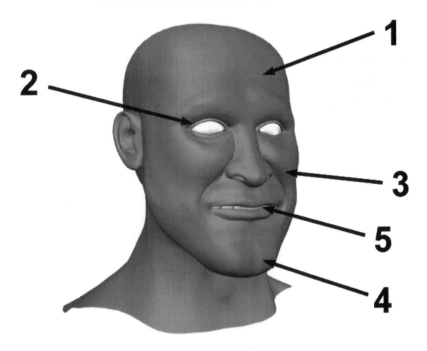

FIGURE *The segmented face.*
6.3

Guido's face is segmented into the following five groups:

1. **The forehead and brows.** This group gives Guido the ability to raise and lower the eyebrows independently of the rest of the face.
2. **The eyelids.** With this group one or both eyelids can be opened or closed, making blinking, squinting, and winking possible.
3. **The mouth, nose and cheeks.** The mouth is given a separate group so speech is possible in combination with a wide variety of eye and brow combinations.
4. **The jaw.** The jaw is given a separate group so it can operate independently from the mouth as discussed earlier in the chapter.
5. **The tongue.** By giving the tongue a separate group, actions such as licking the lips are possible, as well as more detailed representation of the visual phonemes, as we'll discuss later on in the chapter.

Once the segmentation of the character has been worked out, the next step is to build a library of morph-targets. Let's take a look at how that is accomplished.

Creating a Library of Segmented Morph-Targets

Three types of targets need to be created for Guido:

- Expression targets for creating expressive poses.
- The visual phonemes.
- Five tongue targets for the remaining visual phonemes that rely on the tongue.

Let's examine each of these target types.

CREATING AN EXPRESSION WITH SEGMENTED TARGETS

In Appendix E, Facial Expression Examples, you'll find a reference of expressions broken down by morph-weight percentages. These percentages point to the individual segment targets found in Appendix A, Typical Human Expression Weighted Morph Targets. Figure 6.4 shows the expression "Evil Laughter" that will be built in this section.

The first step to creating this expression is to build the component segmented morph-targets in your modeling program. We can see from Table 6.1 that we'll need to build five targets: two for the brows, two for the mouth and one for the jaw.

We'll start by taking a look at how the targets for the brows are created.

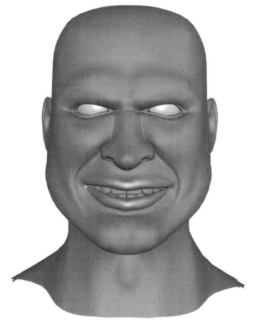
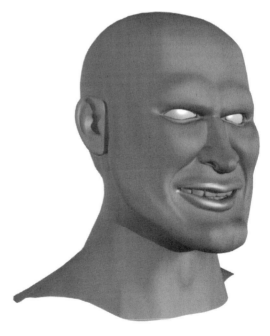

FIGURE *Guido's Evil Laughter.*
6.4

Table 6.1 Evil Laughter Morph Targets

Morph Target Group	Morph Target	Percentage
Brows	• Brows angry	70
	• Brows compressed	100
Eyes	• NONE	N/A
Mouth	• Laughter	60
	• Smile closed	70
Jaw	• Jaw closed	80

Creating the Brow Targets

Figure 6.5 shows the Brows Angry target, which can also be found in Appendix A.

To create the Brows Angry target, you would open the anchor object in your modeling program and pull the points on the inside portion of the brows down toward the eyes to form a bulge in the middle. Chapter 3 contains an excellent discussion of the movement of the brows. The important thing here is to affect only the points of the brow and forehead. Weighted morph systems work on

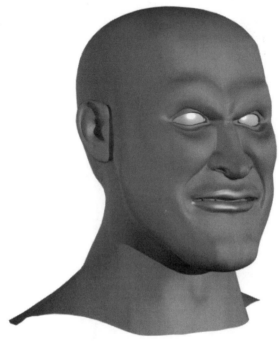

FIGURE *The Brows Angry target.*
6.5

the principle that only those points that deviate from the position of the points in the anchor model will move when morphed. If the location of points on the mouth were altered while building a brow target, those points would move toward their new position when the brows were morphed, deforming the mouth when we only wanted to affect the brow. If a separate target were applied to the mouth, it would be spoiled by the interference of the mouth points that were moved when building the brow target. When building segmented targets, be sure to alter only those points that belong to the target group.

Once the Brows Angry target has been created, it is saved as a new model with an appropriate name. The same procedure would be used to create the Brows Compressed target, shown in Figure 6.5.

In this target the whole brow is lowered, partially obscuring the eyes. Again it would be saved as a totally new object to be loaded into the morphing software later as a target.

Creating the Mouth Targets

The chart under the Evil Laughter expression specifies that the mouth requires two targets: Laughter and Smile Closed. These would be combined in the weighted morph program at the percentages specified in the table. Figure 6.6 shows the two morph targets.

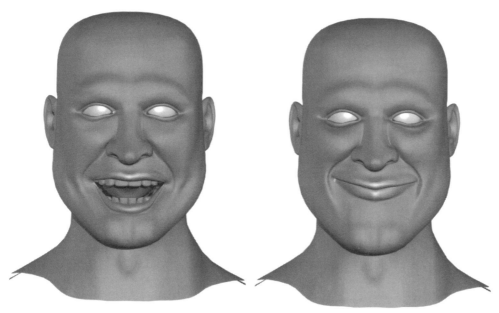

FIGURE *The two mouth targets.*
6.6

You'll notice that the mouth penetrates the chin in some of the Weighted Morph Targets in Appendix A. This is because the jaw remained stationary while the mouth was deformed. When these targets are loaded into the weighted morph program, the jaw would be adjusted to its correct position. Working with segmented, weighted morph targets may look odd at first, but once the objects are applied in the morphing program, you'll soon see the reasoning for the madness. Since we are creating individual morph targets for each segment, we can't afford to move the other segment so the model looks nice. If we did that we'd run into the problem of uncontrollable ancillary morphing like we discussed a minute ago.

Speaking of the jaw, let's take a look at creating the jaw targets. While the expression "Evil Laughter" only uses the Jaw Closed target, it couldn't hurt to take a look at building all five.

Creating the Jaw Targets

Before beginning, read the section on jaw rotation in Chapter 1 if you haven't already. It is important that the jaw is rotated at the proper axis point. Starting with the default anchor object, the points of the jaw and lower teeth are selected, but not those belonging to the mouth, as shown in Figure 6.7.

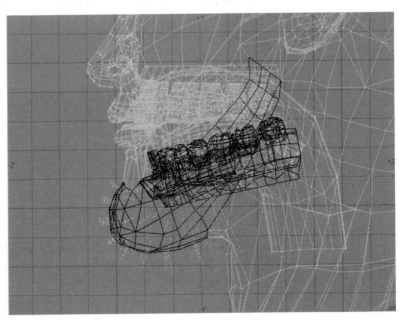

FIGURE *Select the points of the jaw and lower teeth.*

6.7

Since in the neutral pose for Guido the jaw is opened to about the halfway point, two jaw rotation targets would be built: Jaw Open and Jaw Closed.

The Jaw Open target is built by rotating the jaw from the correct axis at the base of the ear opening to its maximum position as shown in Figure 6.8.

Notice that some of the points at the base of the jaw penetrated the neck. These points are pulled out to create a little fold where the skin has bunched up. Also, when the jaw opens, the skin underneath the chin bulges out. Figure 6.9 shows the Jaw Open target with the points adjusted to recreate this effect.

As usual the target is saved as a new object. Let's move on to creating the Jaw Closed target.

The same points of the jaw and lower teeth that were grouped for the Jaw Open target are selected and rotated from the proper axis until the teeth are together in a natural position. Some points of the jaw may penetrate the mouth, but as we mentioned earlier, this would be corrected in the weighted morph program. Figure 6.10 shows the jaw rotated shut.

Some of the points of the jaw may have moved dangerously close to points on the cheek. When the jaw opens and closes, the skin of the face naturally stretches and contracts. Points would need to be adjusted on the side of the jaw to compensate for this. Figure 6.11 shows a more natural positioning of points.

Three more targets are necessary for natural jaw motion: first, a target in which the jaw is moved to the right side of the head with the gap between the two front lower teeth lining up with the right side of the upper right incisors; then a similar target with the jaw shifted to the left; and finally, a target with the jaw jutting forward.

These three jaw movement targets are created in the same way we created the jaw rotation targets, by selecting the points of the jaw and lower teeth, moving them left, right, or forward, and adjusting the points to simulate natural stretching and contraction of the skin.

Now that the Brows Angry and Brows Compressed targets, the Laughter and Smile Closed targets, and the jaw rotation and movement targets have been built. They're ready to be loaded into the weighted morphing program to create the Evil Laughter expression.

COMBINING THE SEGMENTED TARGETS

It took a bit of work and a lot of tweaking to create the targets, but now we get to put them together and watch Guido as he hatches an evil plan. First, the default head is loaded into the weighted morph program as the anchor. This is the base model that will morph to the targets that were created.

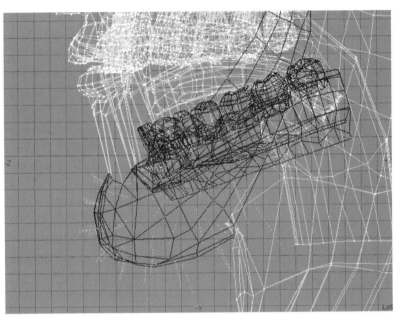

FIGURE *The Jaw Open target.*
6.8

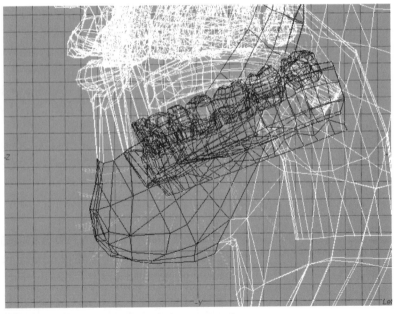

FIGURE *The Jaw Open target tweaked into proper shape.*
6.9

Next three groups of sliders are created: one for the brow targets, one for the mouth targets, and one for the jaw targets. Then the target models we created in the last section are loaded into the appropriate group where they will be assigned individual sliders.

That's all it takes to set up a segmented morph project. Later, when additional targets have been built, there will be a bank of sliders for each group that can be keyframed individually. For now, a single expression will be created with the targets at hand.

The Brows group is selected and the Brows Angry slider is moved to 100%. Guido's brows deform smoothly into the target shape while the rest of the face remains in the strange anchor pose.

Next the Mouth group is selected and the slider for the Smile Closed target to is moved 100%. The mouth deforms to its target while the brows remain unaffected in their angry position.

Now for the real power of segmented weighted morphing: The Laughter slider is moved to 100% and the two mouth targets are combined while, again, the brows hold their shape.

If the model's jaw is in an incorrect position in relation to the mouth pose, the jaw sliders are moved to open or close it into a more natural position. That's it, the Evil Smile pose has been created. If you've built your own model and tar-

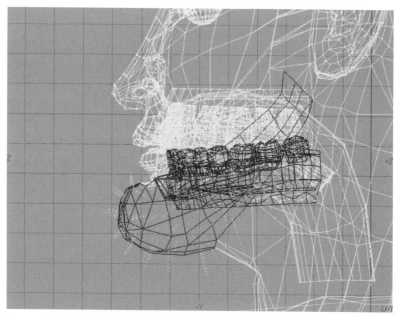

FIGURE   *The jaw rotated shut.*
6.10

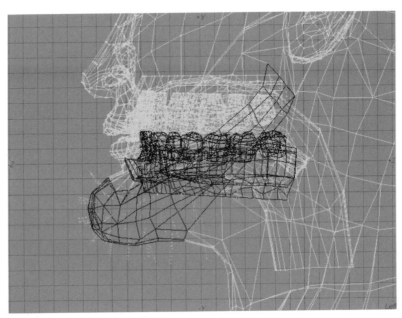

FIGURE   *The Jaw Closed target tweaked into proper position.*
6.11

gets, go ahead and play with the sliders a bit to get a feel for how the segmented targets interact with each other and how the targets in the same group can be mixed at various percentages. It's fun. And when all the weighted morph targets found in Appendix A have been created and loaded into the weighted morph program, the possibilities are endless.

Of course, before Guido can be animated speaking, we need to create the visual phoneme targets.

CREATING VISUAL PHONEMES FOR SEGMENTED MORPHING

The visual phonemes used for Guido's lip synch are the reduced set of ten human phonemes discussed in Chapter 5 and illustrated in Figure 5.2. The reduced set is used because they represent changes in the mouth only. The remaining six rely on tongue changes, and since the tongue has been assigned to a separate morph group, it can be keyframed separately from the mouth. If you weren't using weighted morphing with segments, you'd have to create all sixteen visual phoneme targets.

Building the ten visual phonemes shown in Figure 6.12 follows the same procedure followed for building the expression targets.

The differences between the shapes are subtle, but it is important these are accurately reproduced to create natural and flowing lip synch. Also, while creating visual phoneme shapes for your models, be sure to sound out the phonemes in a mirror as you work. Don't completely rely on a printed graphic—examine your own mouth or someone else's. You can never be too neurotic when it comes to perfecting the phonemes, or anything else in facial animation.

After the ten mouth shapes have been built, the five basic tongue positions are created.

THE FIVE BASIC TONGUE POSITIONS

To complete the sixteen visual phonemes, six tongue targets are needed. These affect the liquids, nasals, fricatives, spirants, and africatives, which are listed in Table 5.1 in the previous chapter.

Take a look at Figure 6.13, which shows the six basic tongue positions needed to complete the sixteen visual phonemes.

These tongue targets are:

1. Floating in the center of the mouth cavity
2. The tip pressed against the hard palate just above the upper teeth
3. The tip pressed against the lower teeth
4. The tongue curled upward
5. Between the teeth
6. At the base of the mouth

Creating these targets is no more difficult than creating the mouth or eyebrow targets. The tongue is simply isolated and rotated section by section until the shapes in Figure 6.13 are reproduced.

To use these, refer to Appendix B, Typical Human Phoneme Morph Targets. There you will find each of the sixteen phonemes with their associated tongue position. Simply combine the appropriate mouth shape with the tongue shape shown to create the new visual phoneme.

Let's move on now to creating a brief animation with Guido using segmented weighted morphing.

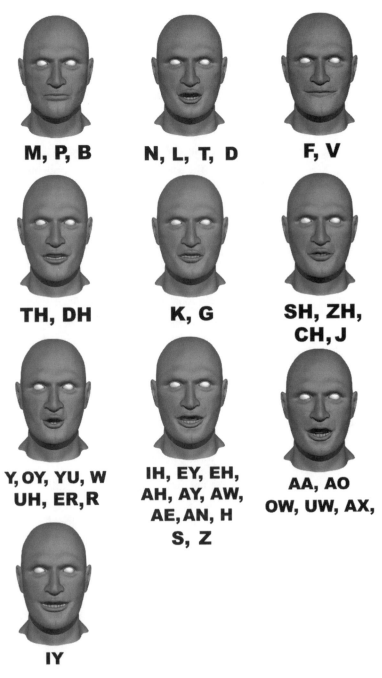

M, P, B **N, L, T, D** **F, V**

TH, DH **K, G** **SH, ZH, CH, J**

Y, OY, YU, W UH, ER, R **IH, EY, EH, AH, AY, AW, AE, AN, H S, Z** **AA, AO OW, UW, AX,**

IY

FIGURE *The reduced set of ten visual phonemes.*
6.12

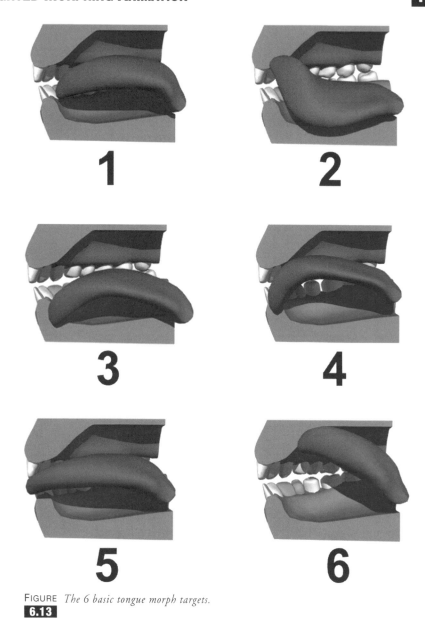

FIGURE   *The 6 basic tongue morph targets.*
6.13

Creating a Facial Animation with Segmented Morphing

In this section Guido's face will be animated to the recorded dialog *"Ya want some? Ya want a piece of me? Huh? Do ya?"* The audio file can be found in the Chapter6 folder of the companion CD-ROM. The file is entitled youwant.wav. The targets needed for the walkthrough are as follows:

- Brows
  - Brows Angry
  - Brows Arched
- Eyes
  - Left Lid Closed
  - Right Lid Closed
- Mouth
  - All visual phonemes listed in Appendix B, affecting only the mouth, cheeks, and nose
  - Smile
  - The five basic tongue positions
- Jaw
  - Jaw Open
  - Jaw Closed

These are loaded into your weighted morph program as described in the last section, and keyframes are set on the sliders to create animation.

Since Chapter 5 discussed a great method for breaking dialog into phonemes and translating these into a timing chart with notations for keyframes and visual phoneme targets, we'll skip over this process and jump to animating the face. But first, let's discuss an additional unique element of a timing chart: the jaw movement breakdown.

THE JAW MOVEMENT BREAKDOWN

Earlier in this chapter we mouthed the phrase "I climbed the Washington monument" and noted that while the mouth formed fifteen visual phonemes, the jaw pumped open and closed only six times. Since the reason for creating individual jaw targets is so that the jaw can be moved independently from the lips, when and how far the jaw opens and closes needs to be notated on the chart.

Jaw rotation is notated with numbers ranging from 1 to 10, where 1 signifies the jaw at its closed position and 10 signifies the jaw opened to its fullest extent.

Figure 6.14 shows the timing chart for the recorded dialog.

The rotation timing for the jaw is notated in the Jaw column. The rotation

Jaw	PHONEME	Target	Frame	Jaw	PHONEME	Target	Frame
2	YU	4	7	4	(Silence)		75-90
	W	4	10				
3	AA	3		6	AH	2	95-106
1	S	13	14				
	AH	2		2	(Silence)		110-125
4	M	9	20				
				2	D	7	127
	(Silence)		35-50		UW	4	
4				2	Y	6	131
3	YU	4	54	5	AA	3	133-140
	W	4	56				
5	AA	3					
5	N	10	59				
6	AA	3					
6	P	9	61				
	IY	1					
1	S	13	65				
4	AH	2					
3	M	9	69				
4	IY	1	70-74				

FIGURE 6.14 *The timing chart for Guido's facial animation.*

values were extracted from the dialog by repeating the voice actor's performance and noting where the jaw opened and closed, how wide it opened, and where it held its position.

Now that we've learned how to create a jaw movement breakdown, it's time to set the keyframes.

KEYFRAMING THE SEGMENTED MORPH ANIMATION

With the timing chart completed, setting keyframes for the dialog is a simple matter of moving the sliders for the visual phoneme targets listed in the chart at the specified times and setting keyframes.

It's important that the lips are animated before the jaw rotation because jaw motion is directly related to the mouth shapes. While the jaw rotation levels have been specified in the timing chart, some of them may turn out to be too extreme to look natural with the mouth target. It is only when the mouth targets have been set that we can tell how far to open or close the jaw.

First, the keyframes for the mouth are set as specified in the timing chart, then the jaw rotation is keyframed. Next, keyframes are set for the tongue on the visual phonemes that require it. It's important to render a test animation and check it against the dialog so the speech can be nailed down before mixing in the brow motion and the smile expression targets. A test render of the animation at this stage can be found on the companion CD-ROM in the Chapter 6 folder in the file Ptest1.mov.

Once the timing for speech has been tweaked, and possibly phonemes dropped as discussed in Chapter 5, animated expressions may be added to the face. Let's take a look at how this is done.

ADDING ANIMATED EXPRESSIONS

Expressiveness is an important element of realistic facial animation. Consider the phrase lip synched in the previous section, *"Ya want some? Ya want a piece of me? Huh? Do ya?"* You would need to act this out in a mirror and take note of when the character's brows might be raised or lowered, and when he might smile deviously.

For instance, the brows might be lowered for the first sentence *"Ya want some?"*, raised slightly for the sentence *"You wanna piece of me?"*, raised even higher for the *"Huh?"*, and still more for the final *"Do ya?"*. Since timings have already been determined for these phrases, it's easy to see where the brows should be keyframes. They'll be set as follows:

- Brows Angry 20% at frame 1
- Brows Angry 20% at frame 40
- Brows neutral at frame 20
- Brows neutral at frame 85
- Brows Arched at frame 90
- Brows Arched 30% at frame 110
- Brows Arched 60% at frame 120

The sliders are simply keyframed at those percentages at the designated frames. Most of the work of lip synch is done before keyframes are set.

Now for the smile. When the voice actor spoke the dialog, he smiled between the words *some* and *you wanna* and between the words *me* and *huh*. He also smiled somewhat as he spoke the whole phrase, so the mouth smile slider can be set to about 20% for the whole animation and cranked to 60% or 70% for the pauses.

The voice actor who spoke these lines didn't blink once while acting out the lines. If he had, the delivery of the lines wouldn't have been as poignant. The lack of blinking adds a taunting quality to the animation. If he did blink, it would be as easy as keying the Eye Lid Closed sliders to 100% on one frame and back to 0% on the next.

To see what the final animation looks like load the Guidofinal.mov animation file found in the in the Chapter6 folder the companion CD-ROM. You can see how Guido has come to life with the addition of the expressive targets mixed in. He's no longer mouthing the words like a puppet, but thinking and egging us on with his words. Of course, we could easily change his attitude by making the smiling targets anger or even fear. This is the beauty of segmented morph target animation. We have a tremendous level of flexibility to change things on the fly until we find something that suits us.

Wrap Up

Both segmented and weighted morphing are extremely powerful techniques, as we've seen in this chapter. Weighted morphing adds the ability to mix morph targets to create large numbers of expressions, and segmented morphing adds the ability to morph separate areas of the face individually, allowing us to create an even larger variety of expressions. We've also seen that segmented morphing allows us to animate the features of the face, namely the jaw and mouth, in an independent manner that makes for more realistic facial animation. These tools are invaluable when it comes to animating your character's face. They allow you to add an unprecedented amount of detail without investing a lot of time. If you don't already have a tool for weighted morphing I suggest you get one—you'll be glad you did.

Well, that does it for our discussion of animating facial features and expressions. Facial animation really isn't too difficult if you take the time to study the process. I know there is plenty of information in this book but really most of it is all common sense. It's really all a matter of attention to detail. All you need is a little patience.

By the way, if you want to learn more about Magpie, a shareware lip synch breakdown tool, be sure to read Chapter 7, which was written by Mike Comet—a great guy and a whiz at Magpie.

CHAPTER

7 Lip Synch with Magpie

Add mouth

Mouth Name: Closed

Picture: Browse...

Hotkey:

Value 1:

Value 2:

Value 3:

Ok   Cancel

Before you jump right in and start animating your character's face, you need to know not only what your character is saying, but also the timing and pacing of the speech. The art of listening to a pre-recorded track of dialogue and figuring out the timing is known as *Track Analysis* or *Breakdown*. Traditionally, the audio would be played on a mechanical device with a counter. The person analyzing it would listen over and over, and write down the best estimate of when each sound or phoneme occurred. For cartoons this information was (and is) recorded on what is called an exposure sheet, or X-sheet for short. An X-Sheet is really nothing more than a glorified table, as shown in Figure 7.1.

As you can see, it has a column with numbers that represent the frames and then other areas where you can pencil in dialogue notes, camera instructions, expression indications, and so on.

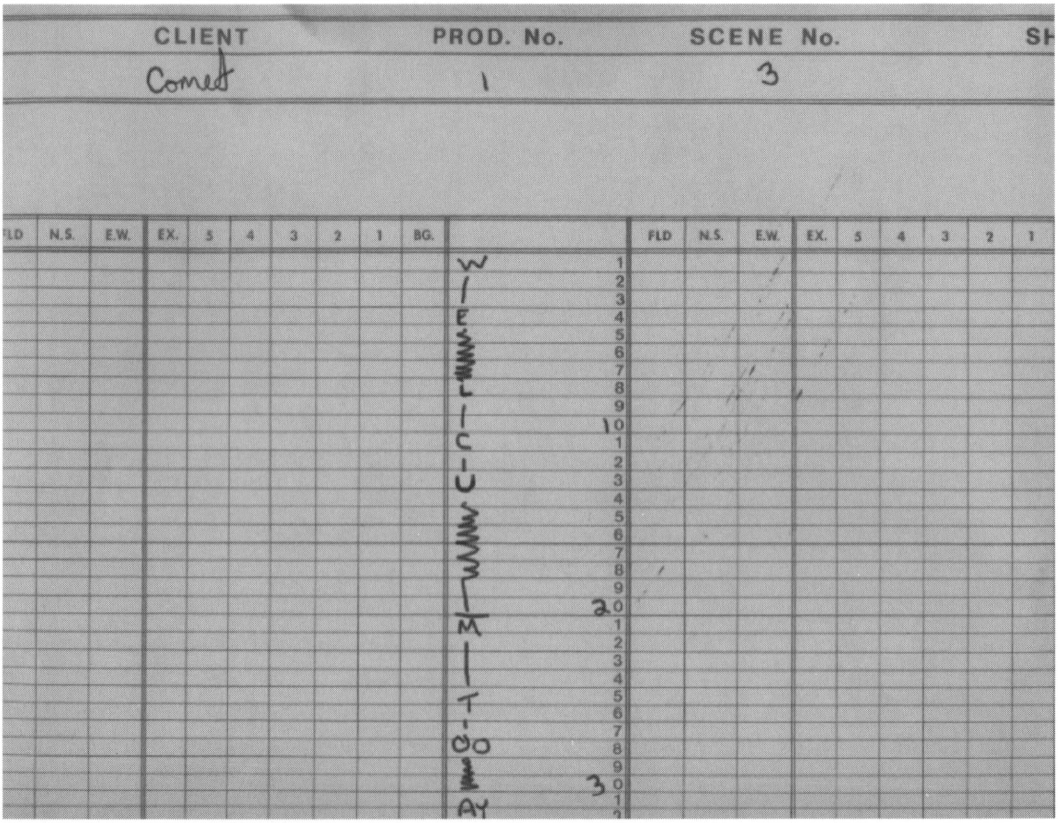

FIGURE *An exposure sheet.*
7.1

With the advent of computer animation, the process of track analysis has been greatly simplified. We are now able to visually examine the timing of a particular audio file and be supplied with the exact times at which the sound is uttered. There are a number of tools available for track analysis. In this chapter we will be looking at a shareware application called "Magpie" by Miguel Grinberg, which runs on Windows 95 and Windows NT. This is a popular application that provides you with a digital exposure sheet and a way to easily listen to, preview, and adjust the breakdown for an audio file. Before we get into how Magpie works, you should download the trial version at the Magpie homepage: http://thirdwish.simplenet.com/Magpie.html. The program is shareware, so after 30 days you must register it if you wish to continue using it. The cost is nominal compared to the time saved by working with Magpie. Registration information is included with the utility, as well as on the web page.

Now that we have Magpie installed, let's take a look at how it is used to break down a sound track.

Using Magpie for Track Analysis

The following exercise illustrates how to use Magpie for a lip synch breakdown. The first step in beginning a project with Magpie is to load an audio file.

LOADING AN AUDIO FILE

1. Double-click on the Magpie program icon to start the application.
2. Click on the Magpie copyright screen to enter the program.
3. Now load the Sweet.WAV from the Magpie folder on the companion DR-ROM. This is a standard windows WAV format audio file. You should now have a view of the waveform as shown in Figure 7.2.

At the top of the screen is the menu and toolbar. The toolbar has buttons for the most commonly used functions in Magpie. Along the left side is a tall vertical frame with sample mouth images and phoneme letters. This is the mouth frame. Along the top, just below the toolbar, is the waveform frame with the audio file represented in the color blue. The waveform frame is subdivided by dashed lines, with each division representing one frame of animation. To the right of waveform is what currently looks like a blank, white square area. This is the preview frame, which is used to show how the lip synch looks in real time. Below the waveform and preview frame is the largest section housing the exposure sheet. The exposure sheet mimics a traditional X-sheet and displays the frame number, time, and phonemes for the breakdown.

Let's take a look at how we work with audio in the program.

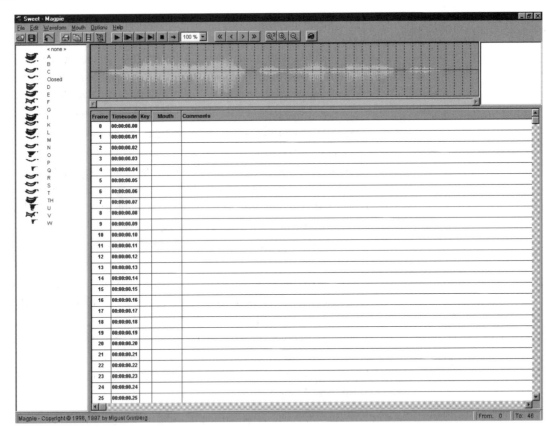

FIGURE *Magpie with the audio file loaded.*
7.2

WORKING WITH AUDIO

1. First, click on the Play button on the toolbar. This is the button with a black triangle that is similar to the play button on audio devices. The waveform frame shows a vertical black bar as the sound plays back. You should hear a voice saying "All right Sweethearts" as this occurs.

2. Using the left mouse button, click on the fourth segment in the waveform frame. That frame is now shown in red. Still holding down the left mouse button, drag the mouse to the right to select frames 3 through 7. Notice how those frames are highlighted in the exposure sheet window. This is how we select a range of frames.

3. Now click on the Play Selected button to the right of the Play button on the toolbar. This is the button with the black play triangle and red lines on the left and right of it. Notice how only the highlighted selection

plays back. Using this method, you can selectively listen to just a portion of the audio file.

4. To expand or contract the selection of frames, hold down the shift button and at the same time left-click on a segment in the waveform frame.

5. Another way to select frames is by clicking on the exposure sheet. Click the left mouse button on the exposure sheet. Now click in the Frame, Timecode, or Mouth column. As you click, that frame will be selected and highlighted in red.

6. To select a range of frames, hold down the shift button and at the same time click on another frame in the exposure sheet frame. For example, you can left click the number 3 in the exposure sheet frame, then, holding down the shift key, left-click again on number 7, and frames 3 to 7 will be selected. The waveform frame matches the selection you make in the exposure sheet.

7. To zoom in to see the waveform in more detail press the Zoom-In button on the toolbar. The button has a magnifying glass with a plus symbol inside. The waveform frame now shows a zoomed in section of these frames. This is useful when dealing with longer WAV files. It also allows you to use the Play button to play only that section of audio.

8. Now press the Zoom-Out button to the right of the toolbar to zoom back out and return to the entire waveform.

You should now be familiar with selecting frames and playing portions of audio within Magpie. This is the basis of analyzing the timing for lip synch. The next step is to actually start marking the phrases on the digital exposure sheet. Let's take a look at how this is done.

Track Analysis— When Is a Fish Not a Fish?

When analyzing the voice for lip synch, each sound is broken up into a small discrete unit called a *phoneme*. For example, in the word *Track,* the "A" would use the phoneme for "AAA." The word *Animation* could be described phonetically as "a-nee-may-shun" or more like a breakdown as "a-n-ee-m-ay-sh-u-n."

For basic breakdown purposes, the fewest number of phonemes most people use is nine, which are listed below.

1. A, I
2. O
3. E (as in sweet)
4. U

5. C, K, G, J, R, S, TH, Y, Z
6. D, L, N, T
7. W, Q
8. M, B, P
9. F, V

The more phonemes you use, the more detailed you can get in your break-down. If you are aiming for realistic animation, you should use the categories listed in Chapter 5. This allows the exposure sheet to have more detail, making the final result more realistic. The fewer phonemes you use, the more animated the speech will appear. As an example, Hanna-Barbera used three phonemes in all of their cartoons, which looked very choppy, but was acceptable for the type of animation they were creating. On the other hand, if you are trying to create realistic human animation, you'll need to use at least nine phonemes.

One thing to keep in mind when doing track analysis is that not every phoneme sounds or looks like the letters in the alphabet that spell the word. It's very important to actually listen to the sound to figure out which phoneme to use. This is especially true when dealing with accents. One classic example is that "ghoti" spells the word "fish." Granted, it looks like it would sound like "goat-tea," but phonetically it can just as easily sound like the aquatic animal. Here's how: Take the "gh" from the word *enough,* the "o" from the word *women,* and finally, "ti" from the word *nation.* As you can see, all of these words have sections that are spelled one way but sound another. Keep this in mind and listen carefully to the sound of each phrase as you do the breakdown.

If you look at the Magpie screen, you'll see the basic phonemes in the mouth frame. The mouth frame has images of how the mouth looks for that phoneme and the letter next to it. Click once on a phoneme with the left mouse button and the image of that phoneme will appear in the preview win-dow to the right.

Now let's start analyzing the dialogue. Looking at the waveform you can al-most "see" the audio and how it is timed. The areas that are quiet are flatter and closer to the center. The vowels that are louder and longer tend to be repre-sented by a balloon-type shape in the waveform frame. For our analysis we'll start with the words "All right" in the audio file. I'll be providing you with se-quences of frames to edit, which were derived by playing the audio track and marking where the sounds changed. This process takes a bit of tweaking, so for the purpose of our tutorial we'll jump right to the actual sequences.

ANALYZING THE WORDS "ALL RIGHT"

1. The first three frames of the audio track are silent, so we need to assign them a "Closed Mouth" image. Start by selecting frames 0-1. You can do this by left-clicking on the "frame 0" text in the exposure window and then holding down shift and left-clicking on the "frame 1" square.

2. Now press the Play Selected audio button. This is the black triangle with the red lines on the left and right. There is a slight click but not really any sound. We'll mark these frames as being a closed mouth.

3. With frames 0 and 1 still selected, click the left mouse button on the phoneme marked "Closed" in the mouth frame. The image of the closed mouth is shown in the preview window.

4. Now double-click the "Closed" phoneme. The exposure sheet shows the phonemes "Closed" for frames 1 and 2. Now we need to Keyframe this sequence.

5. In the exposure sheet, under the "Key" column click the left mouse button once under Key for frame 0. A blue checkmark appears. This marks the frame as Keyframe. If you are exporting the lip synch data to another package, this tells the software to use the frame with the selected phoneme. Any frames not marked with the checkbox will be tweened in the final software you export to. Magpie exports lip synch data to such programs as LightWave and Animation Master.

6. Now we are ready to break down the actual dialog. Select frames 2-12 by left-clicking on frame 2, then hold down shift and click on frame 12. Then press the Play Selected button. You should hear an "Alr" sound. This actually covers a few phonemes, the "AAA," "L," and "R" sounds. What we need to do is divided this into more detail. We'll start with the "AAA" sound.

7. To do so, we first select frames 2-6, and press Play Selected. This is just the "AAA" sound, so we will assign the "A" phoneme. With frames 2-6 still selected, double-click the "A" phoneme in the mouth frame. Frames 2-6 are now marked with the phoneme A. To mark frame 2 as a keyframe, click the square in the Key column.

   It's also a good idea to mark the actual words in the comment field of the exposure sheet. That way you can easily find a section at a later time. To do so, double-click in the comment field for frame 2 of the exposure sheet. In the comment dialog box type the words "All right" and press Enter. The text is placed in the comment field.

At this point we have just started to breakdown the words "All right". Your Magpie screen should look similar to that in Figure 7.3.

Now let's finish the words "All right" analysis:

1. Select the "LL" frames 7-10 and choose Play Selected. This is the "L" sound. Now double-click on the "L" phoneme for these frames and mark the start of this phoneme as a key frame by clicking the key box for frame 7.

2. Now let's complete the rest of the phonemes. Select frames 11-12, double-click the "R" phoneme in the mouth frame, and assign Frame 11 as a keyframe.

3. Then select frames 13-17, which are the "IGH" sound in the syllable *right*. Now double-click the "I" phoneme. Mark frame 13 as a keyframe.

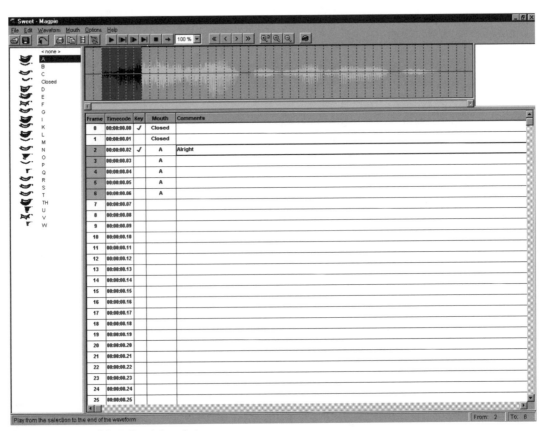

FIGURE   *The start of the "All right" analysis.*

7.3

4. Next, select frames 18-19, which represent the "T" in *right*. Double-click the "T" phoneme in the mouth frame and mark frame 18 as a keyframe.

5. Now the words "all right" have been completely analyzed. To see the phonemes in action, press the Play button, which plays the entire waveform plays, showing an animation of the phonemes in the preview window.

6. Now let's save our work. You can use the file menus or press the blue disk/save icon from the toolbar. The default name for a Magpie breakdown file is the name of the WAV file you are editing with the MPS extension. In this case, it should default to Sweet.MPS. Select a directory to save it in and press the Save button. Your Magpie screen should now match Figure 7.4.

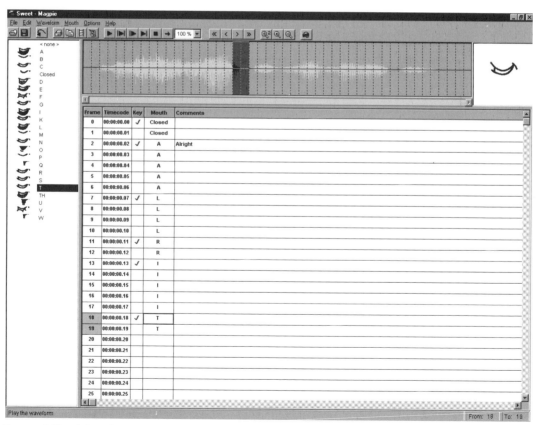

FIGURE *"All right" analyzed.*

7.4

Now we will finish the breakdown by analyzing the word "sweethearts." This gets a bit redundant, but that's what analysis is all about. Let's get started.

1. Select frame 20-22 and Press Play Selected. This is the "S" sound. It is very typical of "S" type sounds to be smaller thinner balloon shapes like this in the waveform.

2. Double-click on the "S" phoneme to assign it to frame 20-22, then mark frame 20 as a keyframe. Also, place the word "sweethearts" in the Comments field for frame 20 by double-clicking in the comment column for frame 20, typing the word "sweethearts," and pressing Enter.

3. Now select frames 23-25, assign the "W" phoneme to them and mark frame 23 as a keyframe. Then assign the "E" phoneme to frames 26-28 and mark 26 as a keyframe.

4. Now mark frames 29-30 with the "T" phoneme and make frame 29 the keyframe.

5. Next, make frame 31 a keyframe, and assign the "A" phoneme to frames 31-35.

6. Frames 36-37 are the end of the "R" sound, so assign the "R" phoneme to them and mark 36 as the keyframe.

7. Frames 38-42 are another "S" phoneme, so set frame 38 as a key and assign the "S" phoneme to that range.

8. Finally, frames 43-46 are silent. Select them, and assign the "Closed" phoneme to that range, then set frame 43 as a key.

9. OK, now save your progress so far by clicking on the blue disk Save icon from the toolbar.

Well, that was a bit of work. To see your lip synch, choose Play. During playback the preview window should be synched fairly well to the dialogue. Now let's take a moment to examine a few segments of the dialogue.

Examine the words "all right" that we synched earlier. Notice that in frames 36-38 the T in the syllable "right" is dropped. It's common to drop phonemes in speech, especially when the dialog is spoken quickly. In general, if you hit the M/B/P phonemes and S and W/OO phonemes, your animation will usually look correct.

Generally, you should leave at least one in-between frame for each phoneme. The exception is the M/B/P phonemes followed by a vowel. These are quick transitions so you usually don't want any tweening. But generally, if you have too many phonemes too close together, the lip synch will look off because the mouth will be moving too fast. One of the key points in doing breakdown is learning what to drop and where. You don't want the animation to appear unnatural. We may speak quickly as a rule but there is still some transition between phonemes.

Now that we've analyzed and synched the phonemes, let's take a look at the most important aspect of lip synch—timing.

Timing Is Everything

Ensuring that your timing is accurate is essential. To do this you should make an AVI of the lip synch, or export it to the software package you use. This will allow you accurately preview the animation to ensure it is correct, since real-time playback may differ a little from system to system. Let's take a look at how we create the test AVI from within Magpie.

CREATING THE TEST AVI

1. First, load the Magpie Sweet.MPS file we've been working with.
2. Then click on the File menu and select Export. A submenu appears with four options. Select Video for Windows. Alternatively, you can click on the Export Video for Windows button on the toolbar, which appears like a filmstrip.
3. By default Magpie will make an AVI in the same directory as the .MPS file. In this case it defaults to the filename Sweet.MPS. Feel free to change the filename or directory. Then press Save.
4. After a few moments, an AVI file should appear. Click on the play button on the AVI player.

Well, it appears the timing is off a bit. The lip motion is delayed too much so it doesn't synch with the audio. It is very common to have the mouth lead the sound. That is, you'll want to shift your mouth poses to actually appear 2 to 4 frames before it actually occurs in the WAV file. This method makes the lip synch look more correct. It's not uncommon to anticipate poses 12 to 16 frames ahead of when they occur when creating film quality animation. In addition, it is very common to lead the M/B/P and sometimes F/V sounds even more since they are rapid.

There are two ways to handle pose leading. First, you can break down your track 100% accurate to the waveform. Look at the pattern, listen to the sound and place the correct phoneme. Then simply slip your audio to start a little later. The other option is to actually compensate in the breakdown itself. This is the best method because it will give more precise control over the animation, since you can tweak the timing of the poses within Magpie without any farther modification.

In Magpie, you can use the offset option to slip the track for the real-time preview. Unfortunately, this doesn't affect the output to the AVI or other exporting. However, it can be useful for quickly deciding if the audio or video needs to be delayed. Let's take a look at how this is accomplished.

OFFSETTING THE REAL-TIME PLAYBACK

1. With the Sweet.MPS file opened, choose Play from the toolbar. The real-time preview shows the playback, which is fairly close, but the video is trailing the audio. We need to shift the video forward. To do so, choose "Audio/Video Sync" from the "Options" menu.

2. The dialog box allows you to enter a value in frames to offset the audio. The default is 0. Negative frames will make the audio start earlier, while positive frames will make the audio start later. We want the audio to be delayed a little bit so the video appears first, therefore we need to enter a value of 3. This will delay the audio 3 frames. It can take a bit of tweaking to find the exact number of frames to shift the audio.

3. Now press OK and choose Play from the toolbar. The real-time appears more accurate now but the timing should be closer since the video precedes the audio a little. You can try playing with different values in the offset dialog to get a feel for how it works. Note that there is no way to offset only selected portions. The entire audio is offset at once. If you make an AVI, or export to another package this information isn't accounted for.

You can see how this isn't a very precise solution, since the changes won't appear if you export the data to your rendering program. Your program won't know the audio file was slipped. The best method is to change the timing in the exposure sheet. Let's take a look at how this is accomplished.

OFFSETTING THE BREAKDOWN IN THE EXPOSURE SHEET

1. Reload up the Magpie Sweet.MPS file you have been working on. We don't want to use the one we just edited because the audio track has been edited. Another option would have been to reset the offset to 0 with the Audio/Video Sync dialog box, though it's safer to reload the file.

2. We'll start by deleting the first three frames of the breakdown to bring the audio and video closer to synching. Select frames 0-2 by left clicking on frame 0, then hold down shift and click on frame 2. From the Edit menu, choose Delete Frames. The first three frames are removed from the breakdown, and all the later frames slide up to fill the gap.

3. Now make frame 0 a key frame by clicking on Key column in the exposure sheet for frame 0. You should also enter the words "All right" in the Comments field so you have a visual reference.

4. Now let's test the animation. Press the Play button. Notice how it looks better than the original file. The video is now preceding the audio track correctly. Next, save the animation as an AVI. Use the name Sweet-FIX.AVI so you can distinguish it from the original. Then press the Play button on the AVI window. The audio and video now look correct.

5. Now is a good time to save this edited breakdown with a different name, such as SweetFIX.MPS.

As you can see, Magpie makes it easy to offset keys by simply deleting or adding frames. The changes will also remain in the exported data since we actually changed the frames.

Now I'm sure you've noticed that the preceding examples were done with a simple cartoon mouth, which makes it rather easy to edit. Now let's take a look at a more complicated model.

Changing Mouth Sets

The preceding samples have used the default cartoon mouth drawings. This is fine for a basic breakdown, but it's more useful to check your work with other images. Magpie allows different phonemes and mouth sets to be used. The following example lets you view the previous breakdown, with the three sample mouth sets that come with Magpie.

1. Load the SweetFIX.MPS and press the play button. The preview frame shows the default cartoon mouth with the dialogue.

2. From the toolbar click the last button with the open mouth icon. This opens the Change Mouth Set dialogue, which allows you to switch mouth sets. It also allows the creation and editing of custom mouth sets and phonemes. There should be three sets available with the basic version of Magpie. Default which is what has been used so far, and also Billy and Cartoon. Select the cartoon set in the list and press OK.

3. After a moment the mouth set is loaded. The phoneme list and images on the mouth frame update. Press the Play button and you'll see lip synch with the new head.

4. Now open Change Mouth Set dialogue again and select Billy. Another mouth set is loaded that replaces the cartoon phonemes. Press play and you'll see Billy talking.

As you can see different phoneme images can yield different looking results even with the same track analysis. Magpie even allows you to load in your own custom phonemes, which allows you to preview and create your breakdown with images of the actual head you will use when animating. Let's take a look at how we build custom mouth sets.

CREATING CUSTOM MOUTH SETS AND PHONEMES

In order to get a better feel for how an animation will look, it's a good idea to create a mouth set with images of the actual model you are using. The first step in making a custom mouth set is to take your 3D model in whichever program you use and generate one image for each phoneme. In Chapter 5 we discussed the different phonemes and in Chapter 3 we covered the process of modeling a head. You should refer to these chapters when creating your phonemes.

The images you import into Magpie must be 128 × 128 sized Windows Bitmap files. Typically, it's easier to create an animation file with each frame being a different phoneme. Then, you can just render the animation out to sequenced BMP files. Generally the images for mouth sets are stored under the \MAGPIE\MOUTHS directory. For this section, you can use the sample images under the AnimeF folder of the CDROM. This has several BMP files used for an Anime-style female head.

Before starting this tutorial you need to copy the BMP files in the AnimeF folder to a local directory. Creating a \MAGPIE\MOUTHS\AnimeF\ directory is probably the best idea. Now let's build our custom mouth set for the Anime character.

1. With the SweetFIX.MPS file loaded, click the Change Mouth Set button and select the "Edit Set >>>" button. The dialog box expands and should looks like Figure 7.5.

2. To add a set click on the Add Set... button. This creates a new Mouth Set with no phonemes in it. Name this set AnimeF. The set is now added and selected on the left side of the dialogue. The list on the right is blank, showing that no phonemes/mouths exist for this set. Now we'll add the first mouth.

3. Click the Add Mouth... button to the right of the dialog box. This dialog is used to add a phoneme to the mouth set. It shows the name of the phoneme, a sample image once a file has been selected, and other optional settings such as a hotkey.

4. Click on the Browse... button and select the "Closed.bmp" from the directory you created earlier. Then press Open. The file dialog closes and brings you back to the Add Mouth dialog box. The image of the Closed

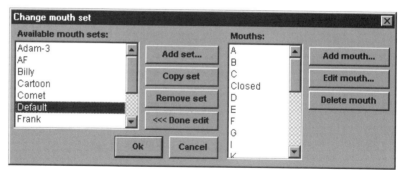

FIGURE *The Change Mouth Set dialogue expanded.*
7.5

phoneme is shown in the window. Under mouth name type the word Closed without quotes. Make sure the first letter is uppercase because Magpie will not recognize the file with a lowercase letter. The dialog box should now look like Figure 7.6.

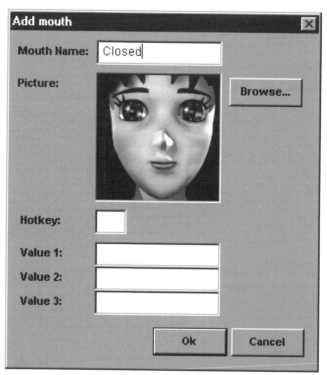

FIGURE *The Add Mouth dialog with the Closed phoneme.*
7.6

5. Now press the OK button to accept this new mouth shape. The list in the Change Mouth Set dialog now shows the Closed phoneme. Next we'll add the A phoneme. Once again, click on the Add Mouth... button. Then click on Browse... and select the A.BMP file. Then choose Open.

6. Under Mouth Name type in the letter A in UPPERCASE, then press OK to add the mouth. Repeat this procedure for each of the remaining mouth shapes listed below:

Phoneme/Mouth Name	BMP File to Select
C	CGJKY.BMP
G	CGJKY.BMP
J	CGJKY.BMP
K	CGJKY.BMP
Y	CGJKY.BMP
E	E.BMP
F	F.BMP
V	V.BMP
I	I.BMP
L	L.BMP
M	MBP.BMP
B	MBP.BMP
P	MBP.BMP
N	NDT.BMP
D	NDT.BMP
T	NDT.BMP
O	O.BMP
R	R.BMP
S	SZSH.BMP
Z	SZSH.BMP
SH	SZSH.BMP
TH	TH.BMP
U	U.BMP
W	W.BMP
Q	W.BMP
OO	W.BMP

7. At this point the Change Mouth Set dialog should now show all the mouths added to the AnimeF mouth set as shown in Figure 7.7.

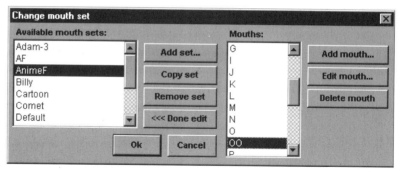

FIGURE   *The AnimeF phonemes added.*
7.7

8. Click the OK button to accept this new mouth set. After a moment, the new mouth set is loaded and shown to the left. Press Play to view the animation with the new set. It looks a little odd because some of the mouth shapes don't look quite right. This is because the mouth shapes for this character are slightly different than the shapes used on the 2D default mouth set. Here is an example where it is important to listen to the sounds and to choose what looks correct, rather than strictly following how a word is spelled or pronounced phonetically.

9. Let's fix the breakdown by changing some of the phonemes in the exposure sheet to better match this character. Select frames 4-7, which are currently marked with an "L" phoneme. In the mouth frame double-click on the "T" phoneme. The T and L phonemes are similar, but the T phoneme is slightly more closed and looks a little better. Frames 4-7 now use the T mouth.

10. Now select frames 8-9, which are currently an "R" phoneme. Double-click on the "S" phoneme in the mouth frame. The mouth closes down more, looking more natural.

11. OK, one last change. Select frames 20-22, which are the "O" phoneme. Double-click on the "W" phoneme in the mouth frame. The W phoneme is more contracted, which looks better. Now press Play to review the changes. Notice how it now looks more natural. While the phonemes aren't accurate for the spoken word, they are visually accurate. Facial animation is all about tweaking, and plenty of it.

12. Now let's save the file under a new name, such as "SweetANM.MPS."

As you can see, changing mouth sets sometimes necessitates tweaking of the track analysis. However, doing so means the preview shown in Magpie will closely match your final animation when it is exported, which, after all is the goal.

Exporting Exposure Data

Once you're done with the track analysis, you're ready to animate. You can either print out the exposure sheet from Magpie to animate by hand, or use some of Magpie's built-in exporting features to copy the keyframe information into your 3D animation package.

Magpie 1.1 supports exporting to Animation Master and LightWave. For Hash Animation Master, Magpie will export the frames with the checkmarks as keyframes, letting Animation Master use the normal tweening for the other frames. If you haven't marked any keyframes, then every frame will be exported as a key, likely making your animation look very rough.

For LightWave Magpie can export in the ObjList format, or if you own a registered copy of Magpie, also for the Morph Gizmo plug-in format. The ObjList format uses the replacement method for animation. That is, on specified keyframes LightWave will actually do a full mesh replacement for the head, which doesn't allow for any real tweaking within LightWave. It also requires a lot of overhead and is not very extensible. The newer Morph Gizmo method is usually preferred, since it's far less taxing on resources and has greater control.

For Morph Gizmo, the Magpie export lets you match a phoneme name to a Lightwave object file. After all the phonemes have a corresponding object file, it will export to Morph Gizmo. This allows you to go in later to add tweaks or other movement into the face like eye blinking or even the occasional nervous twitch.

3D Studio MAX can also import a Magpie breakdown if you animate your character's face with bones. There is a freeware plug-in available on the Magpie web page (http://thirdwish.simplenet.com/Magpie.html) called MagImp.dlu by Andrew Reid. It allows you to make bone poses on negative frames in MAX. Then each phoneme is matched to one of these frames. The bone position, rotation, and scale information is then automatically copied from these phoneme setup frames to the actual animation frames via the importer and the Magpie breakdown file.

Magpie can also print directly to a printer, or export to a user-defined format. The default user-defined format outputs a standard ASCII text file with the breakdown information. The SweetFIX.txt file in the Magpie folder on the CD-ROM shows a sample text output. You can customize how the text format is exported so Magpie can be used with other applications in addition to those listed above.

Even with all this automated exporting, there is still something to be said for simply taking the text exposure sheet and animating it by hand in your 3D package. Generally, using a mirror, looking at yourself, and keyframing it by hand yields results that look better and seem to have more life. The problem with using a predefined export is that the motion can look canned, all the A's will look the same, and so on. However, for a tight deadline, auto exporting with some hand tweaking of the animation can be a good thing.

The Future of Magpie

That's about all there is to track analysis with Magpie. It's actually rather simple. You should now be able to create breakdown any audio file for facial animation. Like anything in animation, lip synch takes time. The best way to improve is to practice and keep on practicing. The more you practice, the better the facial animation will appear.

Also, keep your eye out for the new releases of Magpie. A new version has already been in the works, and the next release, "Magpie Pro," is already in beta-testing. You can download a trial version on the Magpie web page. The new version supports multiple channels in the X-sheet and preview window. This allows the breakdown and animation of individual sections of the image or facial features. So besides mouth motion, eyebrow, eyes, and other areas can be analyzed as well.

Magpie Pro will also allow a video window to played with the breakdown so there will be video reference right there as you work. Finally, Magpie Pro also has a feature to automatically analyze and break down a dialogue track for you. For more information and a more complete feature list, be sure to check out the web page at: http://thirdwish.simplenet.com/Magpie.html.

Wrap Up

Well, there you have it, facial expression and animation with 3D characters. As you can see there is much to consider. You can never be too detailed. The important thing to remember is it all starts with a good model. You need to build a solid foundation before you can expect to create dazzling facial animation.

Also, it's a good idea to keep a mirror handy. While we've covered 50 expressions in this book there are literally thousands of variations. It wouldn't hurt to spend some time making faces in the mirror. Another good idea is to render some movies and spend a few days with the pause button under your thumb, capturing the expressions of actors. Just a few minutes with Robin Williams or Jim Carrey should do the trick. Even a B horror film is great for getting those expressions of terror.

The facial expression of your character is more important that any other element in your scene or animation, so be sure to invest enough time to ensure you have created a compelling expression or animation.

Well, that's all for now. I hope you've enjoyed reading this book as much as I did writing it. I'll see you in the next book.

Typical Human Expression Weighted Morph Targets

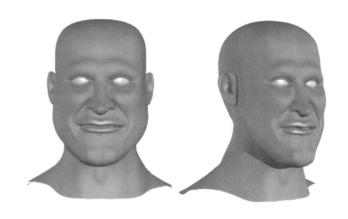

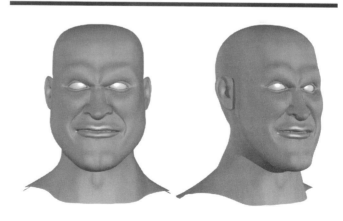

BROWS ANGRY

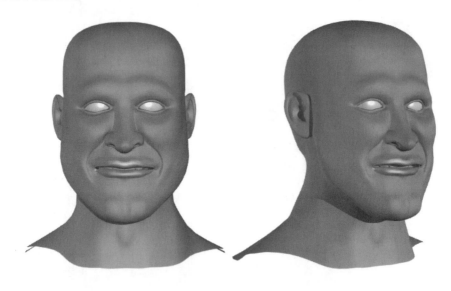

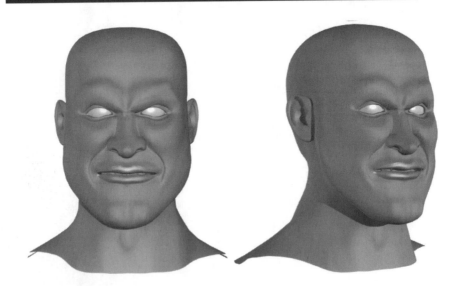

Distinguishing Features

The brows are pulled down and together at the inside corners. This target is used primarily for expressions of pain or effort.

BROWS ARCHED

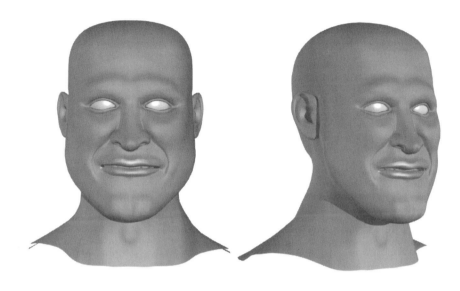

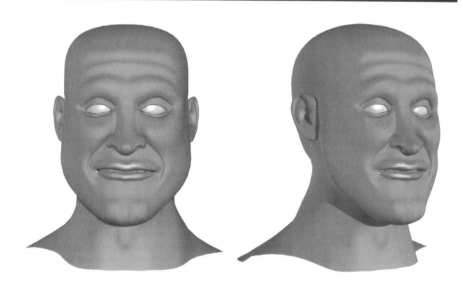

Distinguishing Features

The brows are raised straight up, creating deep furrows in the forehead. This target is used for expressions such as surprise, terror, and shock.

BROWS COMPRESSED

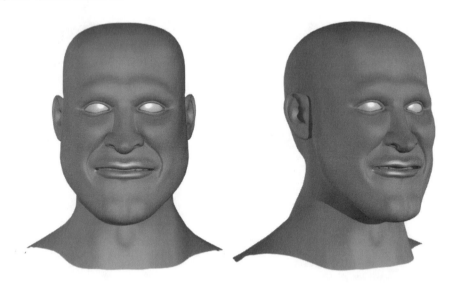

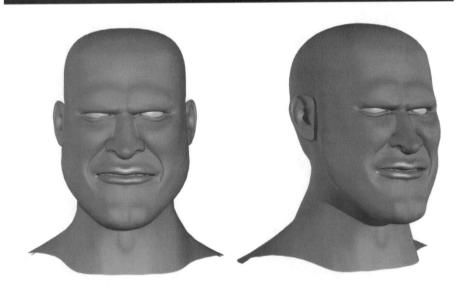

Distinguishing Features

The brows are drawn straight down, partially obscuring the eyes. This is used for expressions such as concentration, crying and anger, and to soften the raised and angry brow targets.

BROWS MIDDLE UP

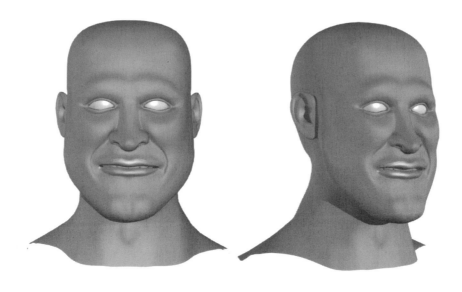

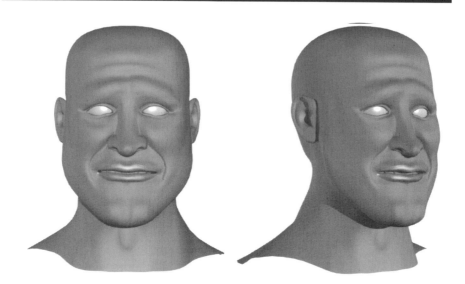

Distinguishing Features

The brows are drawn up in the middle. This target is used for many expressions of sadness.

EYES LEFT DOWN

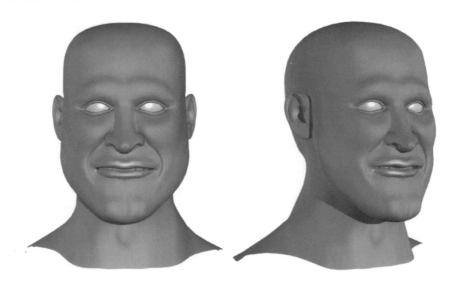

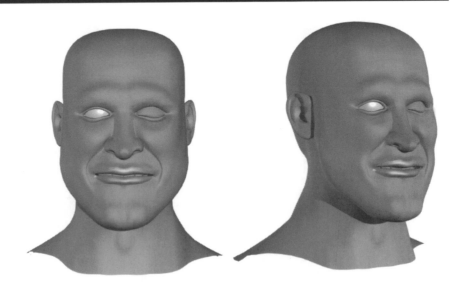

Distinguishing Features

The left eye is closed. By creating separate closing targets for the left and right, winking and asymmetrical squinting are possible.

EYES RIGHT DOWN

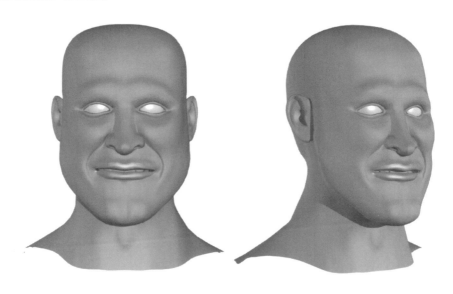

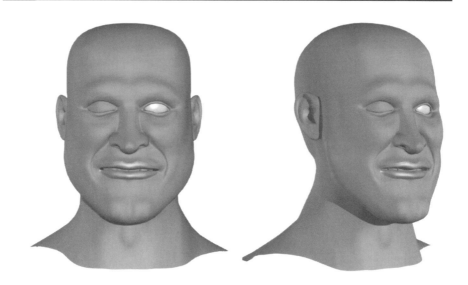

Distinguishing Features

The right eye is closed. By creating separate closing targets for the left and right, winking and asymmetrical squinting are possible.

EYES WIDE

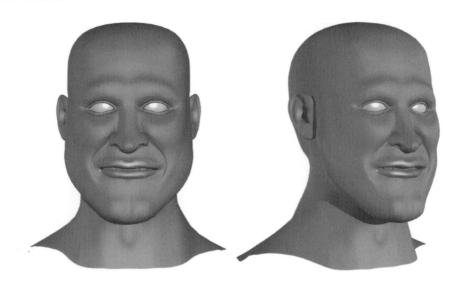

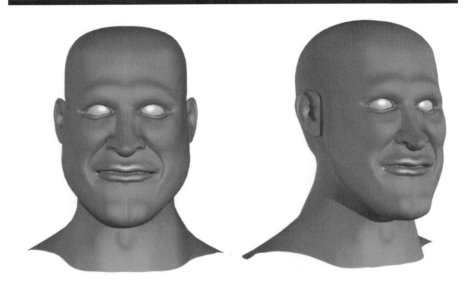

Distinguishing Features

The eyelids are drawn farther up than normal, making it useful for such poses as terror, fear, and eagerness.

MOUTH CLOSED

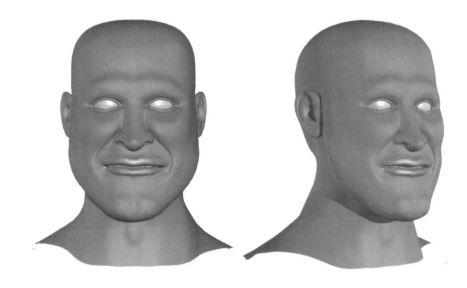

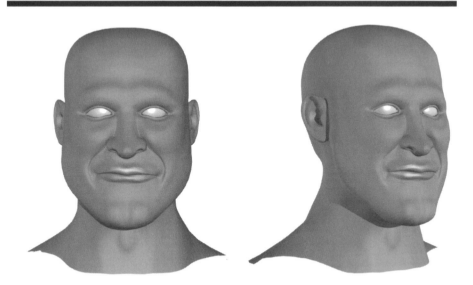

Distinguishing Features

The mouth is closed in a relaxed, somewhat neutral pose. This is useful for calm expressions, as well as toning down other open and closed mouth targets.

MOUTH CRYING

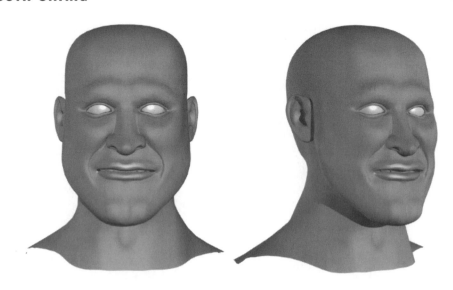

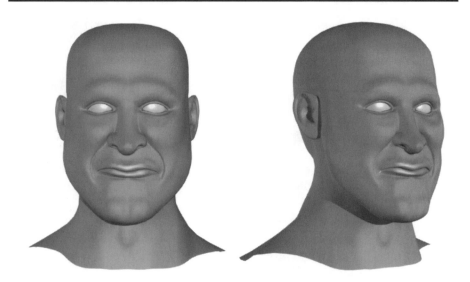

Distinguishing Features

This is a crying target with the mouth closed, making it useful for subdued crying expressions.

MOUTH CRY OPEN

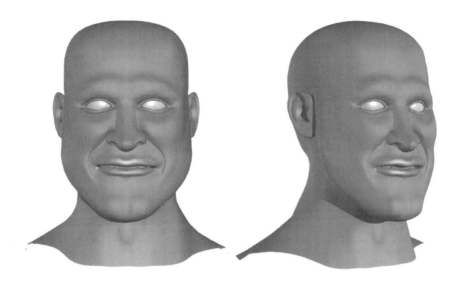

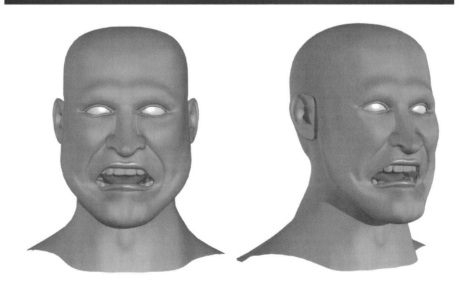

Distinguishing Features

This is an extreme crying mouth target. The mouth is open and the corners drawn down and back, causing the cheeks to bulge under the zygomatic bone.

MOUTH DISGUST

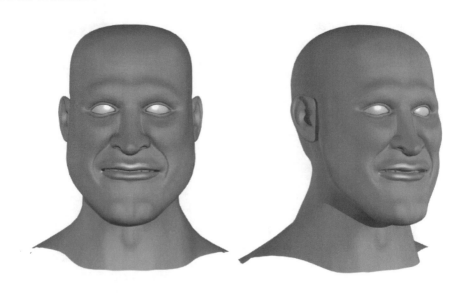

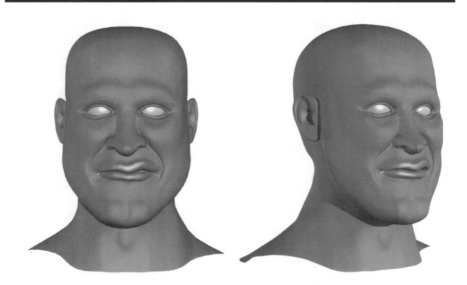

Distinguishing Features

One side of the upper lip is drawn upward, creating a bulge in the cheek and a crease around the nose on that side of the face. This is a useful target for expressions of distaste, or possibly a snarl.

MOUTH FRIGHTENED

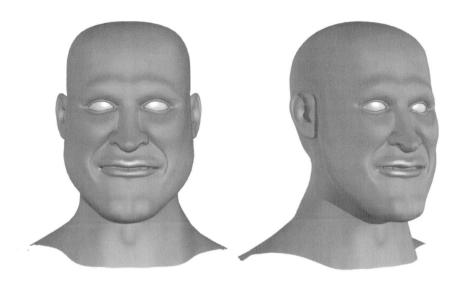

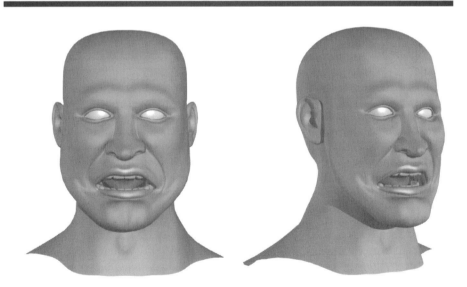

Distinguishing Features

The corners of the mouth are drawn back with the lower lip almost straight across. It's useful for expressions of fear. It can also be used to create effort, at less than 100% weight with the teeth together.

MOUTH LAUGHTER

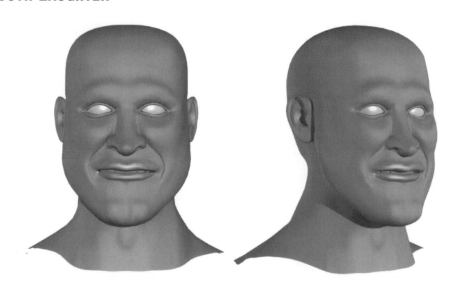

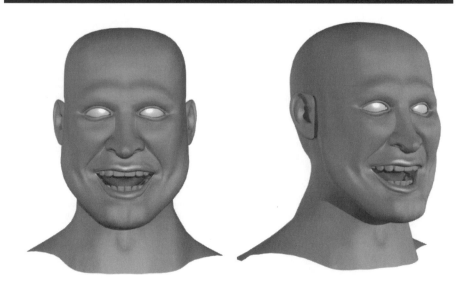

Distinguishing Features

The mouth is opened and the corners drawn up and back toward the ears, tightening the lips against the teeth. The cheeks bulge under the zygomatic bone.

MOUTH PURSE

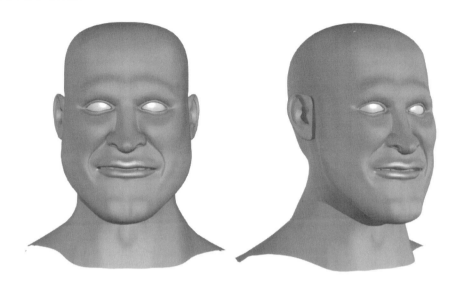

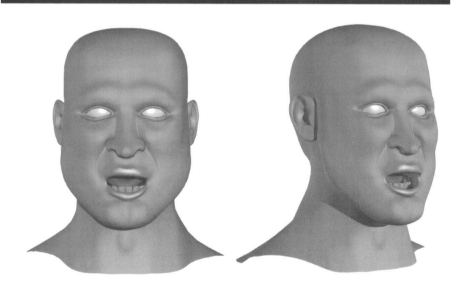

Distinguishing Features

The lips are compressed horizontally and drawn away from the teeth. This is useful for modifying expressions that need the lips drawn out somewhat, such as a false smile or a smirk.

MOUTH REPULSION

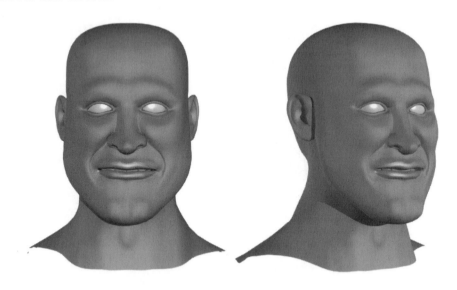

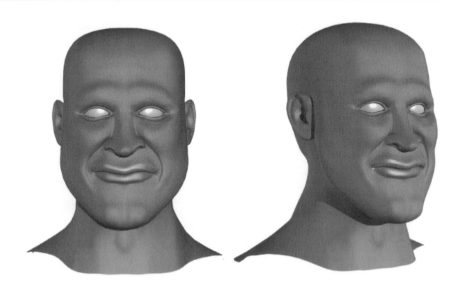

Distinguishing Features

The upper lip is curled into a sneer. Similar to disgust, but the lip is drawn up on both sides, which causes bulging in the cheeks.

MOUTH SMILE CLOSED

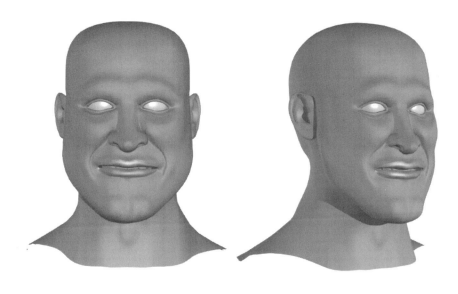

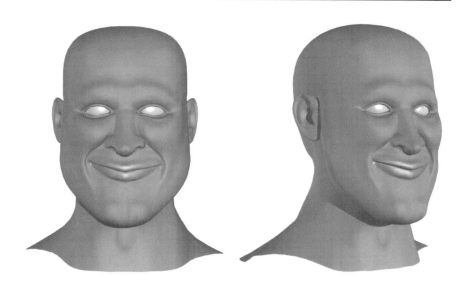

Distinguishing Features

The mouth is closed and the corners drawn up and back toward the ear. The cheeks bulge under the zygomatic bone and dimples may appear, depending on how chubby your character is.

MOUTH SUPPRESSED SADNESS

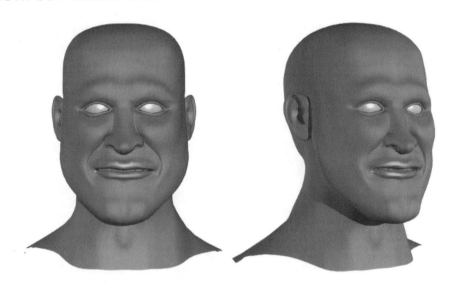

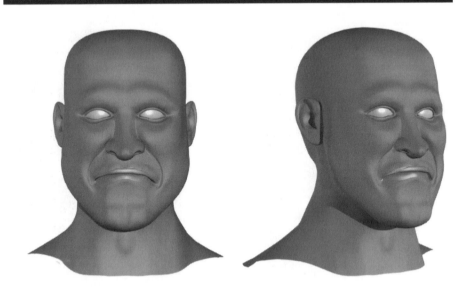

Distinguishing Features

The mouth is closed and the corners are dramatically curled downward. It's useful for expressions such as crying, sadness, and facial shrugs.

MOUTH SURPRISE

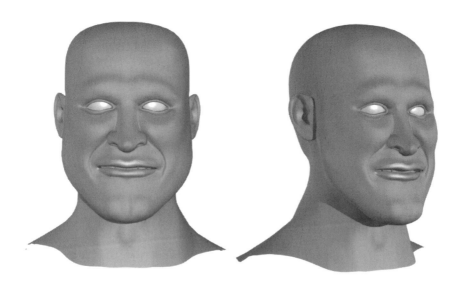

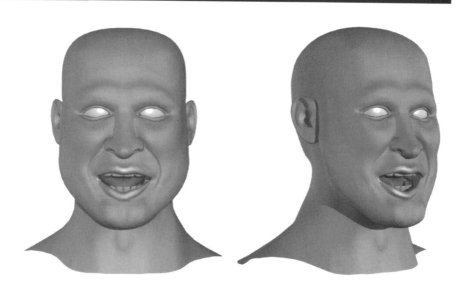

Distinguishing Features

The mouth is opened and somewhat relaxed, with the tips of the upper and lower teeth revealed.

MOUTH TERROR

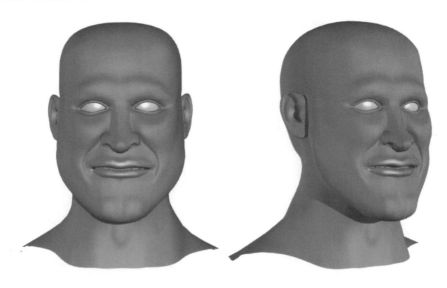

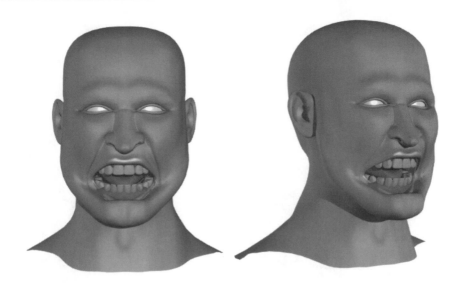

Distinguishing Features

The mouth is opened as wide as possible with the corners drawn down and back toward the ears. This is a necessary target for extreme forms of terror and yawning.

MOUTH YAWN

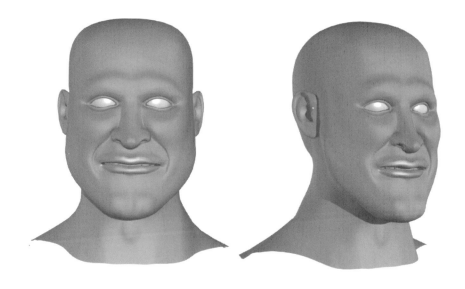

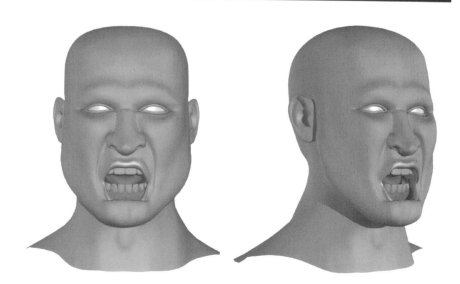

Distinguishing Features

The mouth is opened very wide, but the corners are drawn neither up nor down. This target is useful for modifying other targets that need a wide-open mouth, such as yawns.

JAW CLOSED

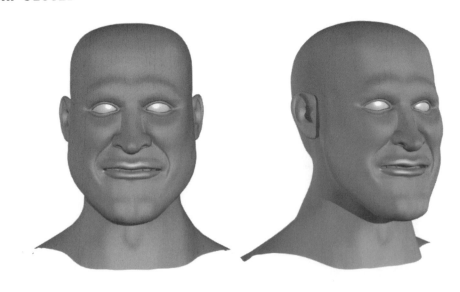

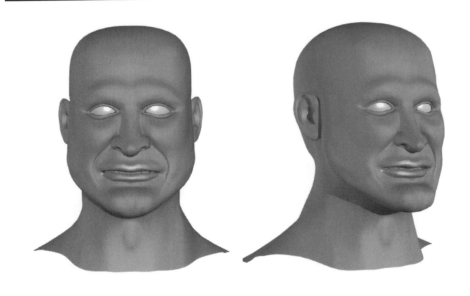

JAW OPEN

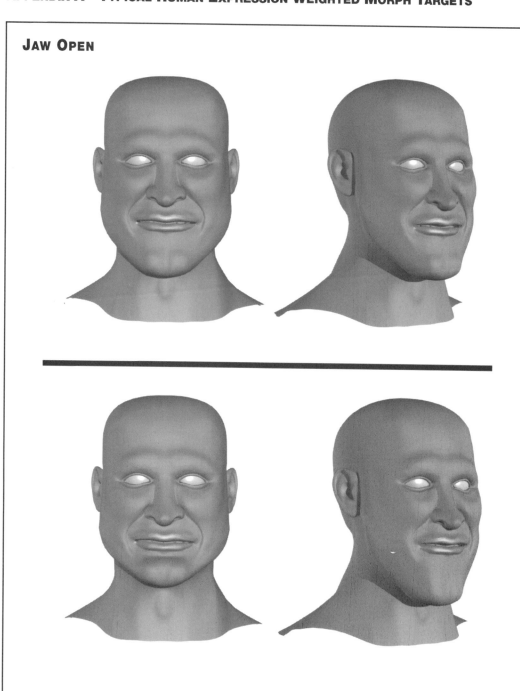

JAW FORWARD

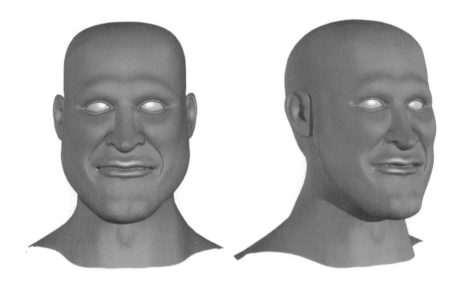

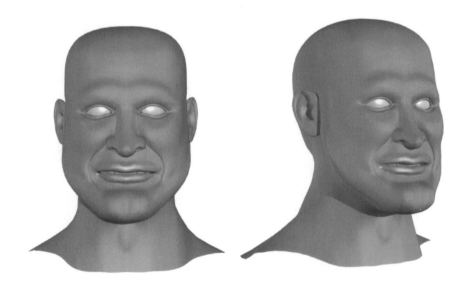

JAW LEFT

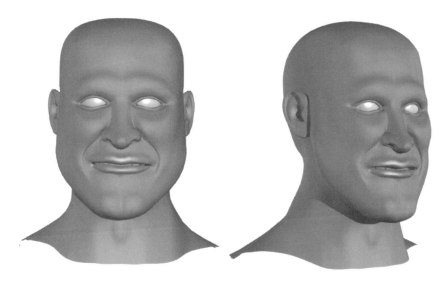

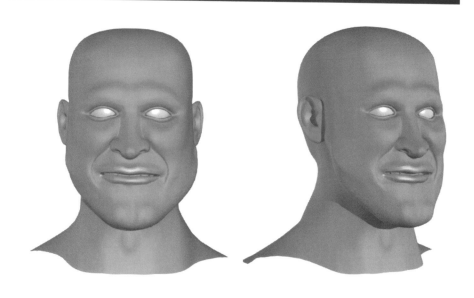

JAW RIGHT

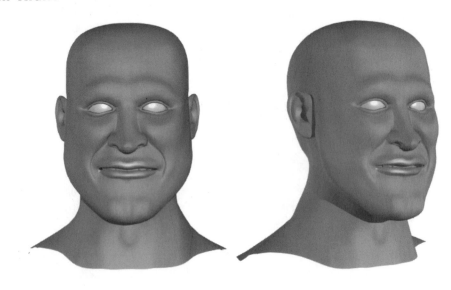

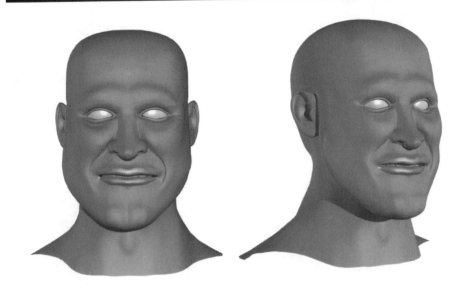

B Typical Human Visual Phonemes

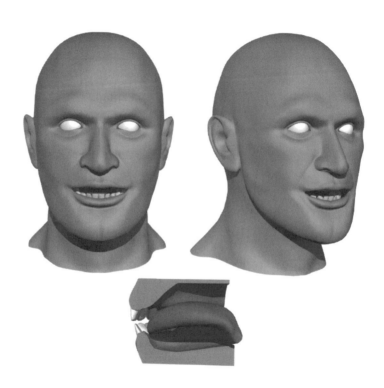

TARGET #1 PHONEME: IY

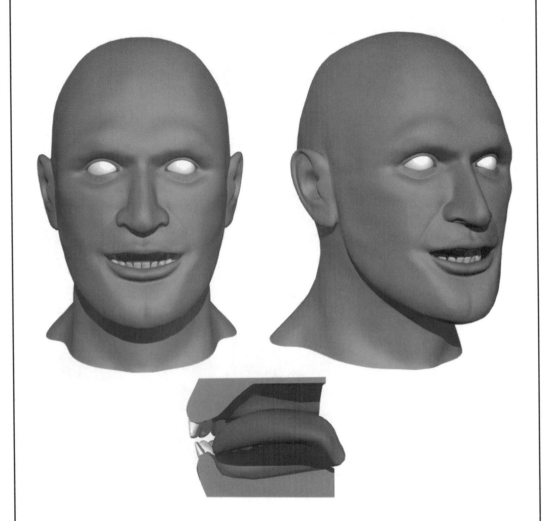

Distinguishing Features

The corners of mouth are pulled sideways and back over the teeth, partially revealing the upper and lower teeth. The tongue floats in the middle of the mouth cavity.

TARGET #2 PHONEMES: IH/ EY/ EH/ AE/ AH/ AY/ AW/ AN/ H

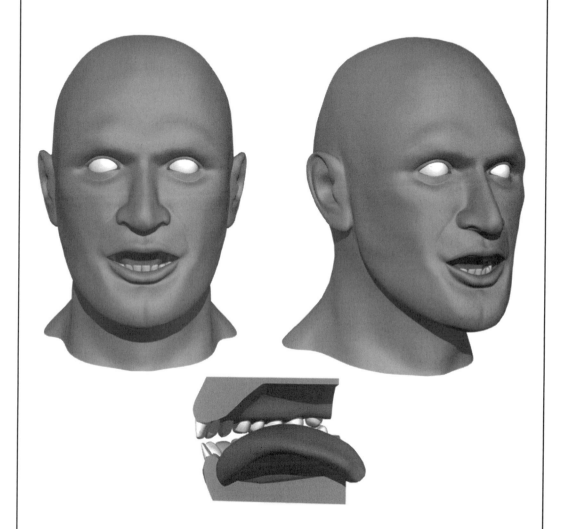

Distinguishing Features

The mouth is opened with the corners relaxed, revealing only the lower teeth. The back of tongue hovers and the tip is placed against the lower teeth.

TARGET #3 PHONEMES: AA/ AO

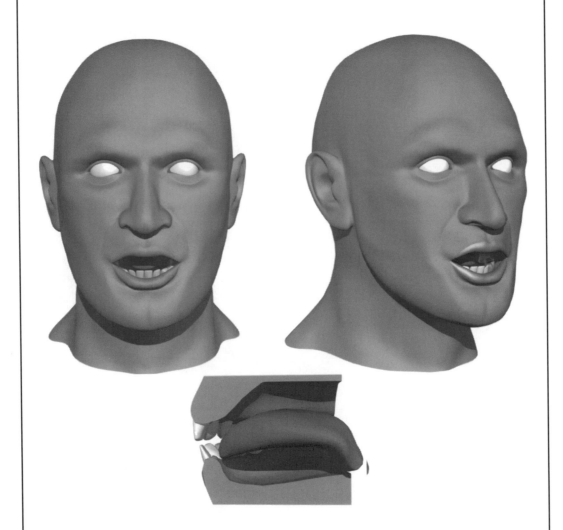

Distinguishing Features

The mouth gapes open, showing only the bottom teeth. The tongue floats in the center of the mouth cavity.

TARGET #4 PHONEMES: OW/ UW/ AX/ OY/ YU/

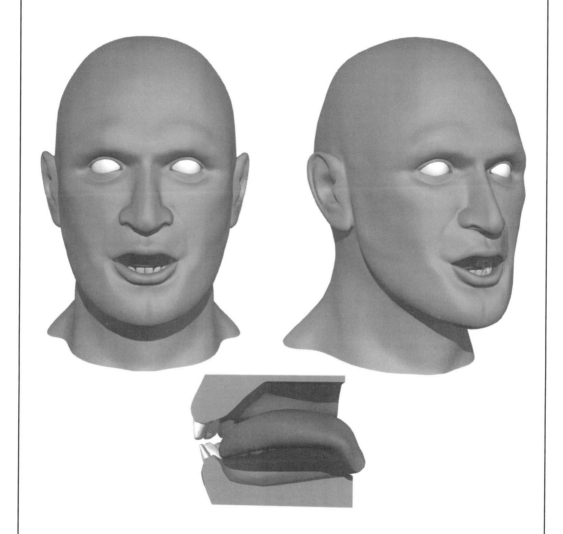

Distinguishing Features

The mouth is rounded with no teeth showing. The tongue floats in the middle of the mouth cavity.

TARGET #5 PHONEMES: UH/ ER

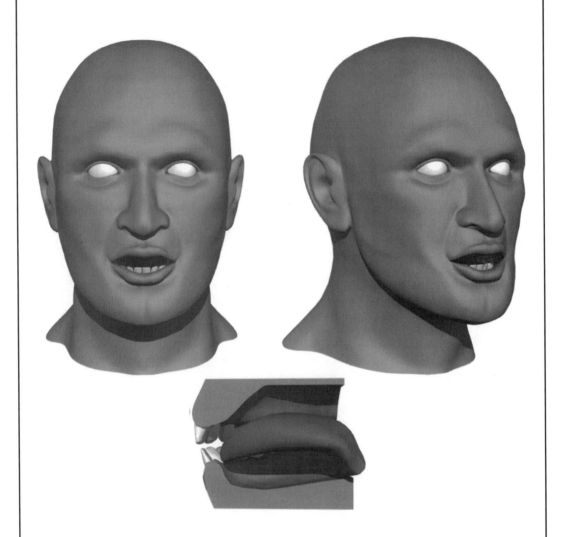

Distinguishing Features

The mouth is rounded and drawn away from the teeth, which are hidden. The tongue floats in the middle of the mouth cavity.

TARGET #6 PHONEME: Y

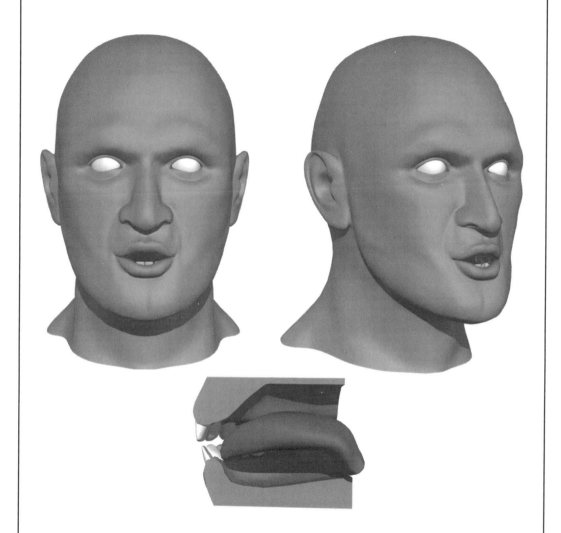

Distinguishing Features

The mouth is rounded with no teeth showing. The base of the tongue is pressed against the hard palate.

TARGET #7 PHONEMES: L/ T/ D

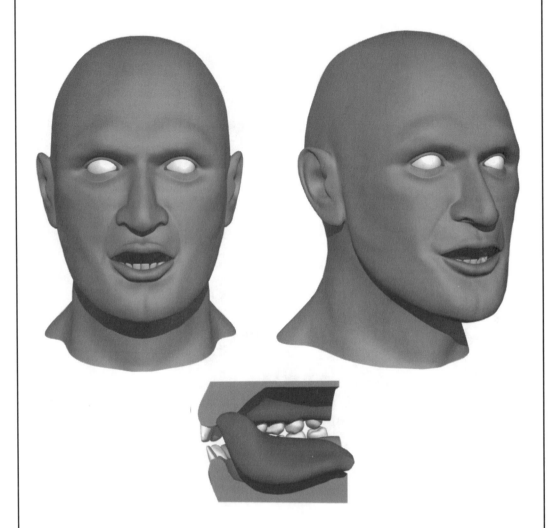

Distinguishing Features

The mouth is open slightly, revealing the tips of the upper and lower teeth. The tip of the tongue is pressed against the hard palate.

TARGET #8 PHONEME: R

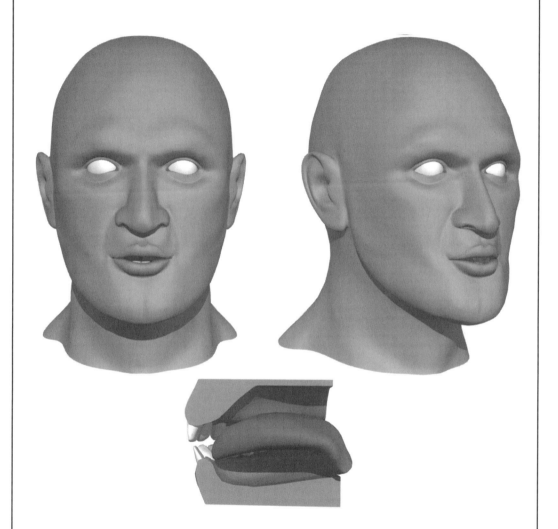

Distinguishing Features

The mouth is opened with the lips slightly pursed, hiding the teeth. The tongue floats in the middle of the mouth cavity.

TARGET #9 PHONEMES: M/ P/ B

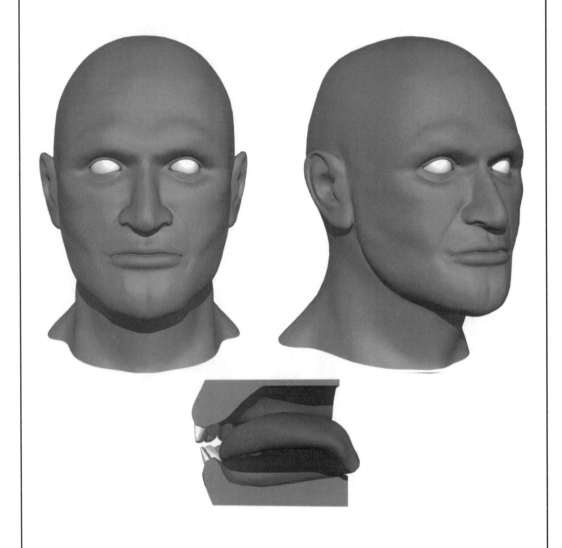

Distinguishing Features

The mouth is closed in a straight line.

TARGET #10 PHONEME: N

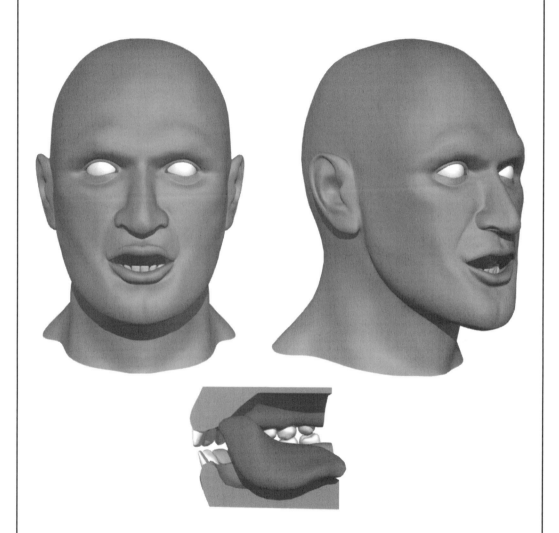

Distinguishing Features

The mouth is opened slightly, revealing the tips of the upper and lower teeth. The front portion of the tongue is pressed against the hard palate.

TARGET #11 PHONEMES: F/ V

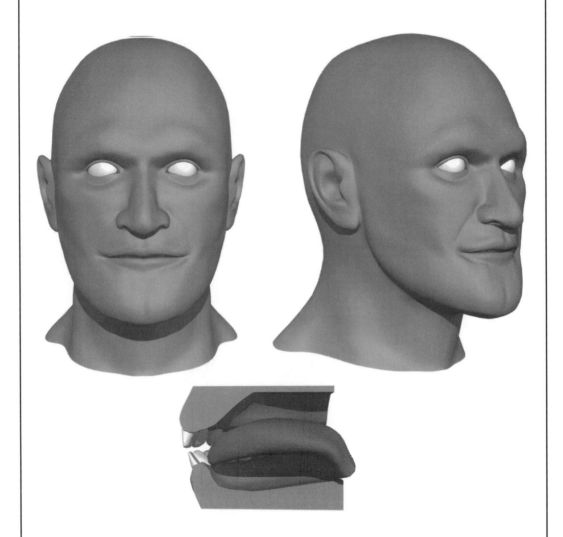

Distinguishing Features

The mouth is opened slightly, with the lower lip curled and pressed against the upper teeth. The tongue floats in the center of the mouth cavity.

TARGET #12 PHONEMES: TH/ DH

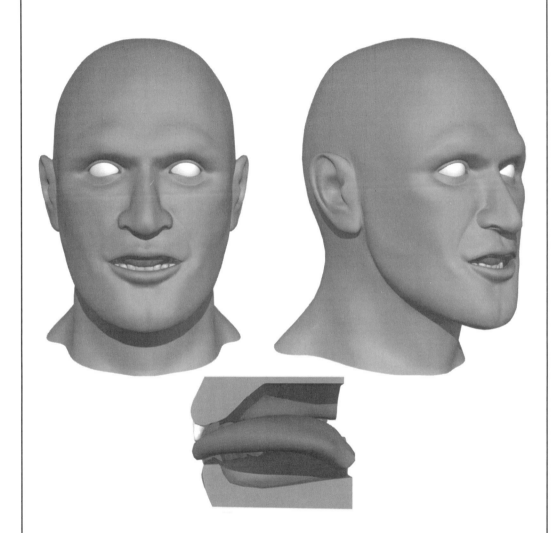

Distinguishing Features

The mouth is slightly opened and the tip of the tongue is placed between the upper and lower teeth.

TARGET #13 PHONEMES: S/ Z

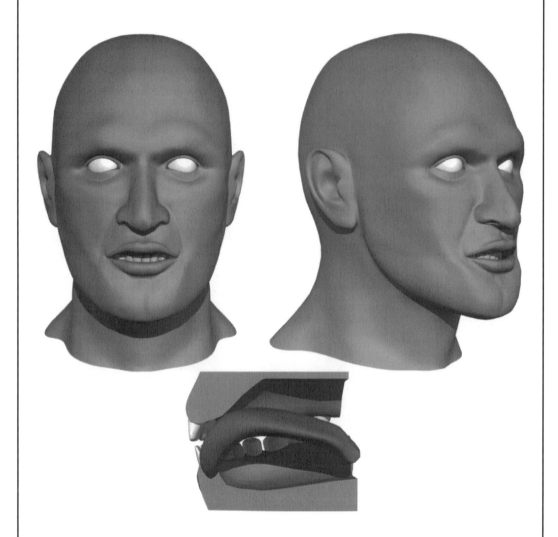

Distinguishing Features

The lips are parted, baring clenched teeth. The tip of the tongue is pressed against the lower teeth.

TARGET #14 PHONEMES: SH/ ZH/ CH

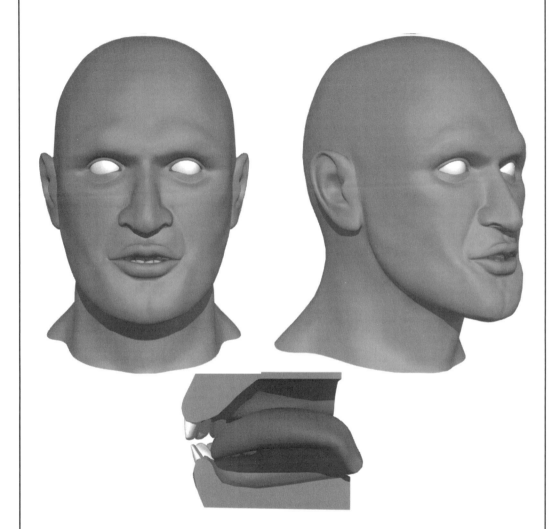

Distinguishing Features

The lips are parted, revealing clenched teeth. The tip of the tongue floats in the center of the mouth cavity.

TARGET #15 PHONEME: G

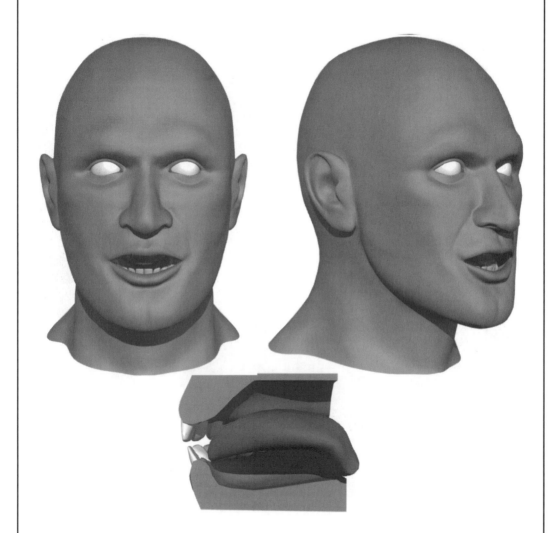

Distinguishing Features

The mouth is opened, revealing the tips of the upper and lower teeth. The back of tongue presses against the soft palate.

TARGET #16 PHONEME: J

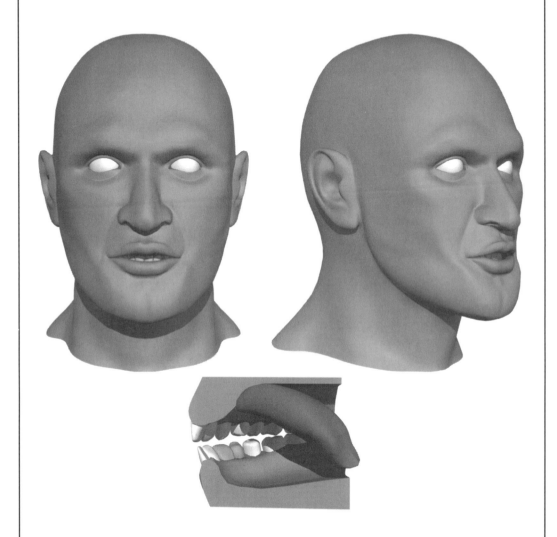

Distinguishing Features

The lips are parted, revealing clenched teeth. The tongue is pressed against the hard palate.

C Typical Cartoon Expression Weighted Morph Targets

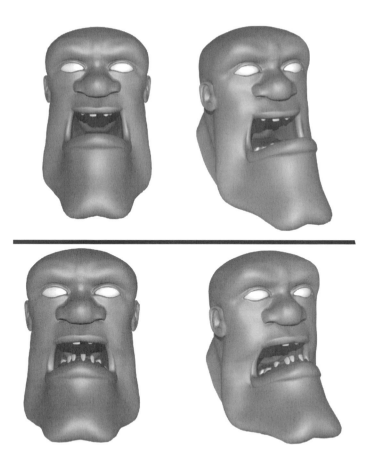

BROWS ANGER

Distinguishing Features

The brows are pulled down and together at the inside corners. This target is used primarily for expressions of anger, pain, or effort.

BROWS LEFT RAISED

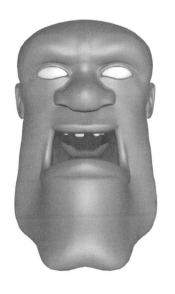 

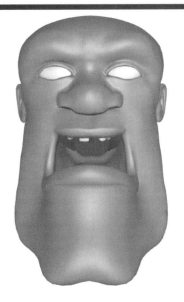 

Distinguishing Features

The left brow is arched. By giving separate morph targets to the right and left eyebrows, you can raise one or both, making possible such expressions as inquisitiveness.

BROWS RIGHT RAISED

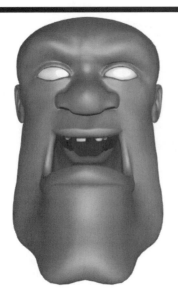 

Distinguishing Features

The right brow is arched. By giving separate morph targets to the right and left eyebrows, you can raise one or both, making possible such expressions as inquisitiveness.

BROWS LOWERED

Distinguishing Features

The brows are drawn straight down, partially obscuring the eyes. This is useful for expressions such as effort and concentration, and for modifying other brow targets.

BROWS MIDDLE RAISED

Distinguishing Features

The brows are drawn together and the inner portion is pulled upward. This is used for expressions such as sadness, questioning smiles, and facial shrugs.

BROWS AFRAID

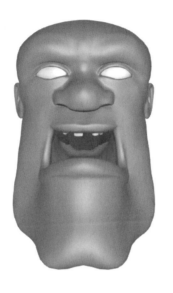

Distinguishing Features

The brows are drawn together in the center and create creases that are more pronounced than the Brows Middle Raised target. This is used primarily for expressions of fear.

EYES LEFT DOWN

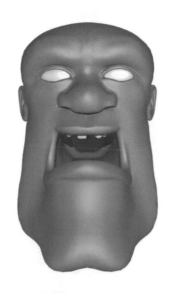

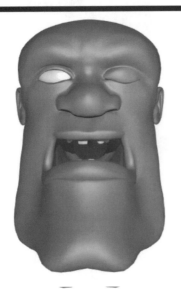

Distinguishing Features

The left eye is closed. Giving separate morph targets to the left and right eyelids allows us to pose the eyes asymmetrically.

EYES RIGHT DOWN

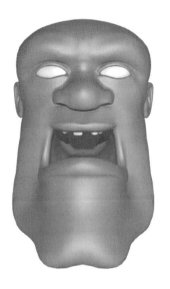 

Distinguishing Features

The right eye is closed. Giving separate morph targets to the left and right eyelids allows us to pose the eyes asymmetrically.

MOUTH CLOSED

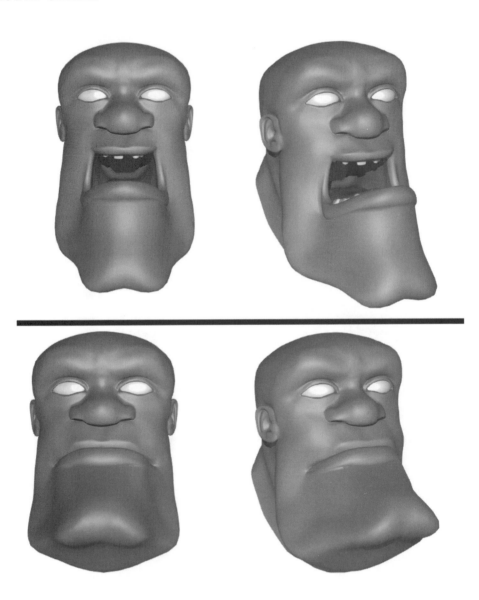

Distinguishing Features

The mouth is closed and relaxed. This can be used as the resting pose for a character, though in the case of our cartoon, the natural pose is with the mouth hanging open.

MOUTH CRY CLOSED

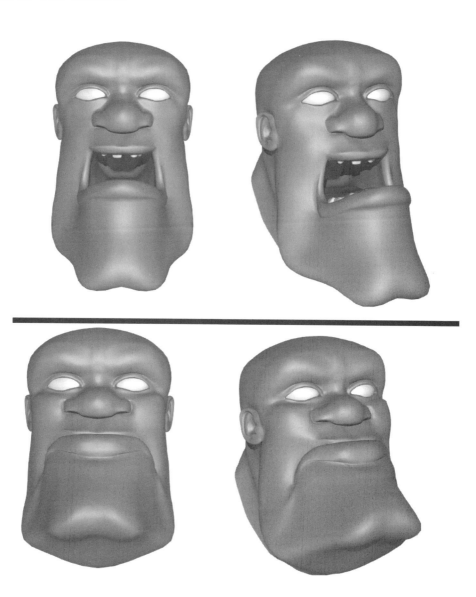

Distinguishing Features

The mouth is closed and the corners of the mouth turn down dramatically. The lower lip sticks out in a pout and the cheeks bulge under the zygomatic bone.

MOUTH CRY OPEN

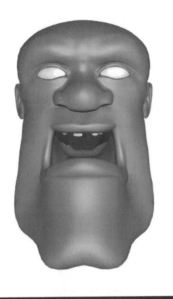 

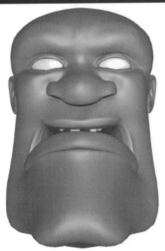 

Distinguishing Features

The mouth is open and the lower corners are pulled back and down. The cheeks bulge under the zygomatic bone.

MOUTH DISGUST

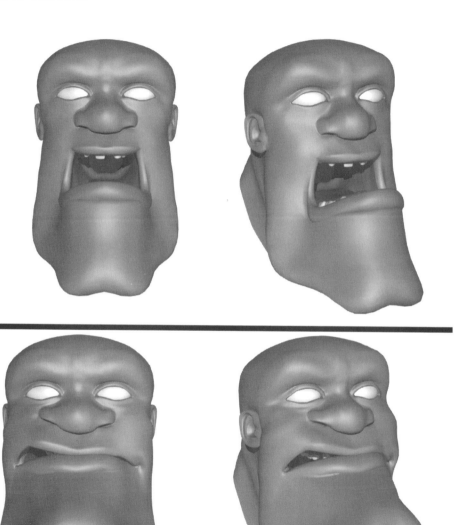

Distinguishing Features

The mouth is closed and one side of the upper lip is drawn upward in a sneer. This is useful for expressions such as disdain or hatred.

MOUTH FRIGHTENED

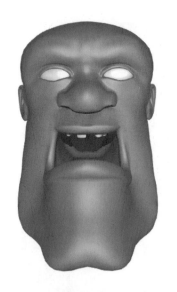

Distinguishing Features

The mouth is open and the lower corner of the mouth is pulled back. The cheeks don't bulge under the zygomatic bone.

MOUTH FROWN

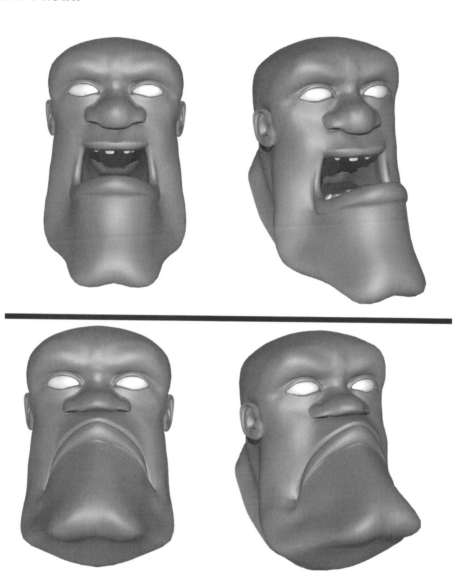

Distinguishing Features

The corners of the mouth are pulled down and the middle drawn up toward the nose. This is useful for all sorts of unhappy expressions, though it is not as dramatic as the crying or suppressed sadness targets. One reason for this is that the cheeks do not bulge under the zygomatic, arch so the character appears more upset than sad.

MOUTH LAUGHTER

Distinguishing Features

The jaw is dropped open and the mouth is open very wide, with the corners pulled up high. By creating a very extreme pose, you allow yourself the flexibility of generating a wide range of laughter from subdued to crazed.

MOUTH REPULSION

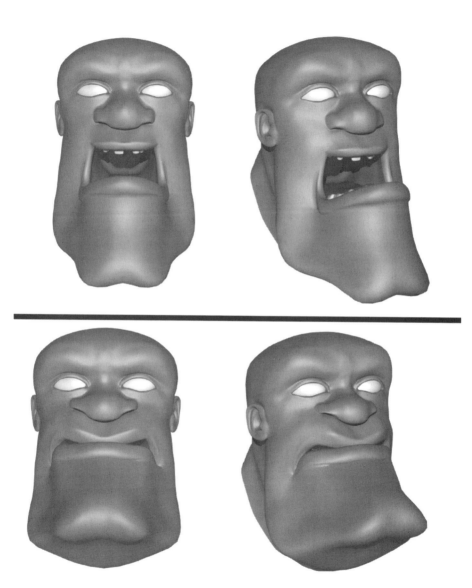

Distinguishing Features

The mouth is closed and both sides of the upper lip are drawn upward in a sneer. This target is useful for expressions such as disdain or physical repulsion. In a cartoony character such as Knuckles, the sneer may be so extreme that the upper teeth and gums appear.

MOUTH SMILE

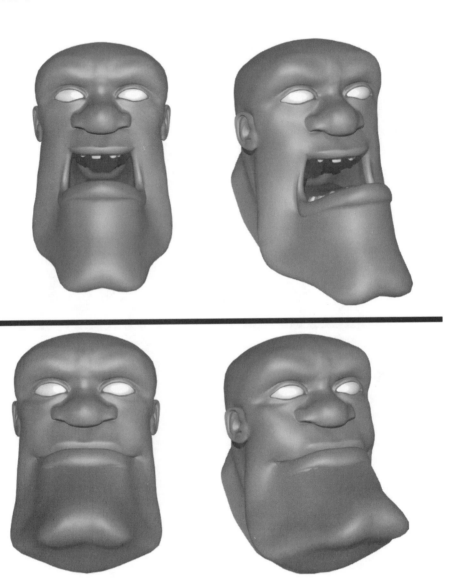

Distinguishing Features

The mouth is closed, stretched horizontally and back toward the ears, and the corners of the mouth are curled into a smile. The cheeks bulge somewhat under the zygomatic bone.

MOUTH SMILE OPEN

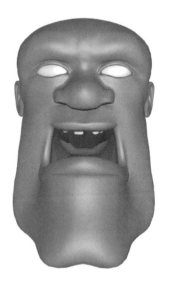 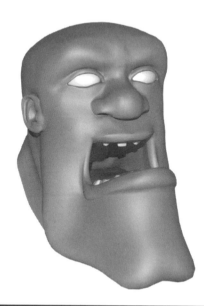

Distinguishing Features

The mouth is open with the corners pulled up and back toward the ears.

MOUTH SUPPRESSED SADNESS

Distinguishing Features

The mouth is closed and the corners are pulled into a frown. The lower lip is curled inward, blending into the chin as it bulges out at the base. This target is useful for building expressions such as facial shrugs and poses where the character is close to bursting into tears.

MOUTH SURPRISE

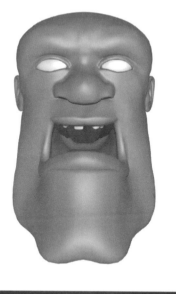 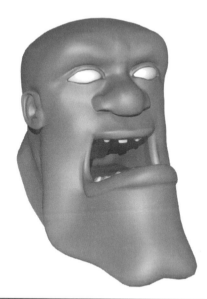

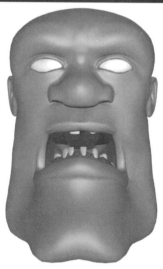 

Distinguishing Features

The jaw is dropped and the mouth is opened and pulled back. The lower lip is pulled down, revealing the lower teeth and possibly the gums.

MOUTH YAWN

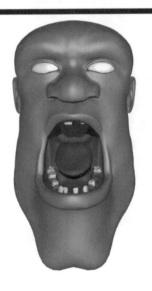 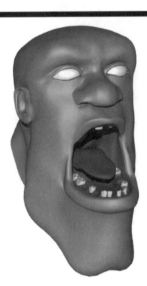

Distinguishing Features

The mouth is opened to its fullest extent. Unlike fear or laughter, the corners of the mouth are neither drawn up or down.

MOUTH MISERABLE

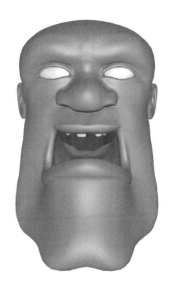 

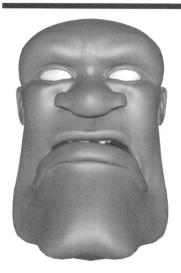 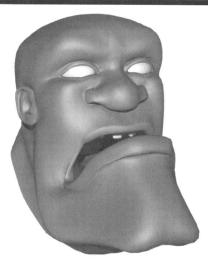

Distinguishing Features

The mouth is open and the lower corners are drawn back and rippled.

MOUTH CLOSED RAGE

Distinguishing Features

The mouth is closed and drawn into a frown. The nostrils are lifted and flare, and the cheeks bulge under the zygomatic bone.

APPENDIX

D

Typical Cartoon Visual Phonemes

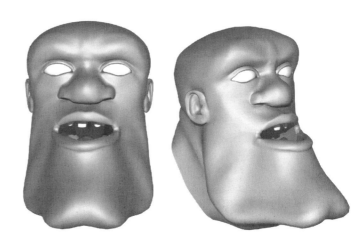

TARGET #1 PHONEMES: M/ B/ P

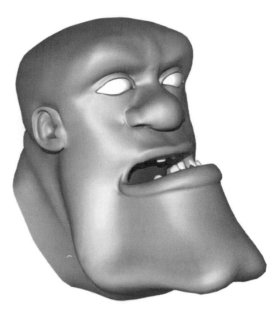

TARGET #2 PHONEMES: N/ L/ D T

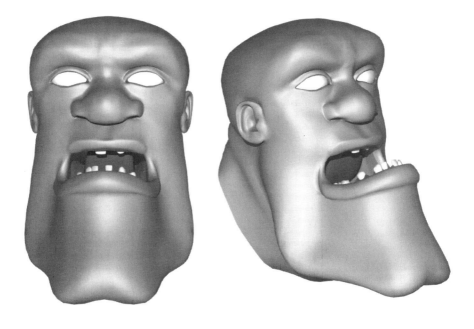

TARGET #3 PHONEMES: F/ V

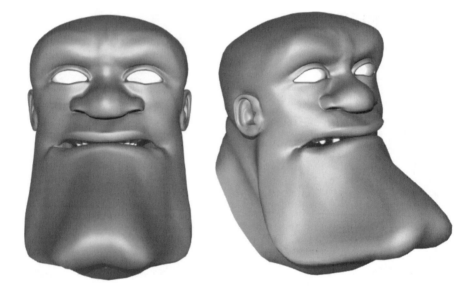

TARGET #4 PHONEMES: TH/ DH

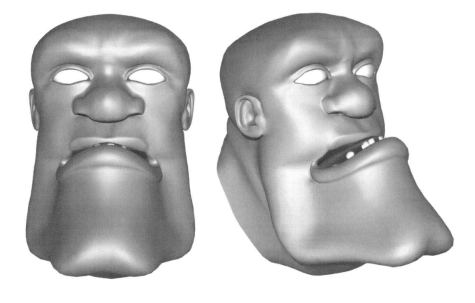

TARGET #5 PHONEMES: K, G

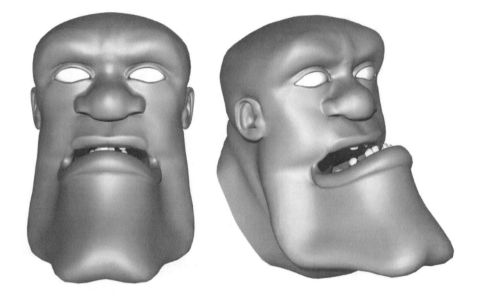

TARGET #6 PHONEMES: SH/ ZH/ CH/ J

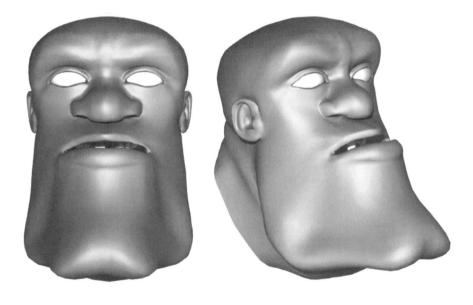

TARGET #7 PHONEMES: Y/ OY/ YU/ W/ UH/ ER

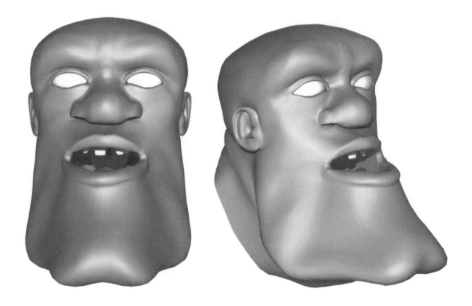

TARGET #8 PHONEMES: IH/ EY/ EH/ AH/ AY/ AW/ AE/ AN/ H/ S/ Z/ R

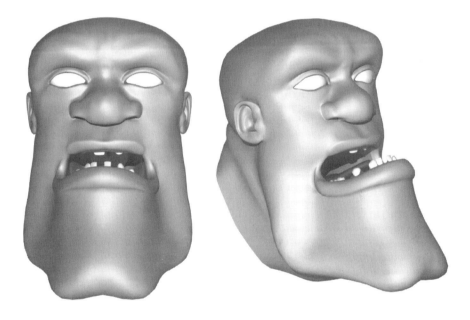

TARGET #9 PHONEMES: AA/ AO/ OW/ UW/ AX

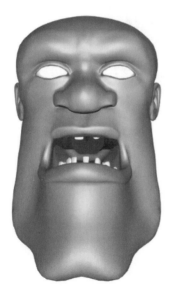
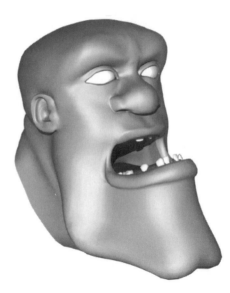

TARGET #10 PHONEMES: IY

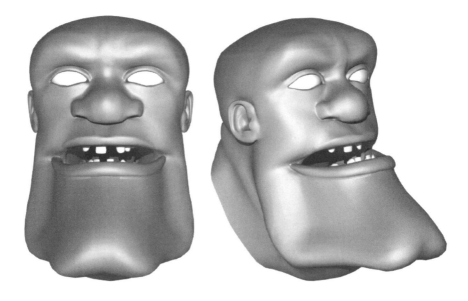

E

Facial
Expression
Examples

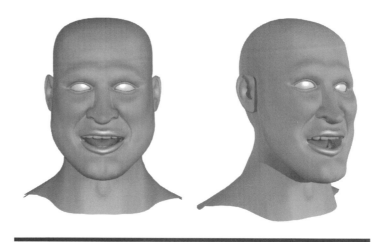

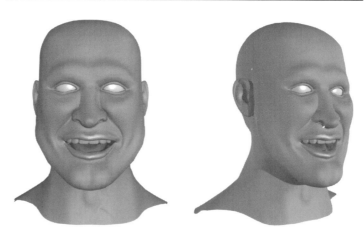

This appendix contains a large variety of facial expressions using a realistic human character and a Living Toon cartoon character as examples. While the expressions and their meanings will be clear from the images and headings alone, you can use the two tables under each heading as an aid in setting up your own characters' expressions. The upper table contains a verbal description of the expression broken down into four sections:

- **Brows:** Includes the forehead and eyebrows
- **Eyes:** The eyelids
- **Mouth:** The cheeks, nose, and mouth
- **Jaw:** The rotation and translation of the jaw

The lower table is a listing of the weighted morph targets listed in Appendices A and C that were used to construct the expression. An explanation of how expressions are built using multiple weighted morph targets is given in Chapter 6.

Modeling templates for creating human facial expressions are included in the AppendixE folder on the companion CD-ROM. The templates include a front and side render of the head, which can be used as background templates in your modeling program. While your head may be different from this particular human head, you'll find the proportions should be similar. The templates are meant to give you an approximate idea of how the face changes with each expression.

HUMAN SMILE WITH OPEN MOUTH

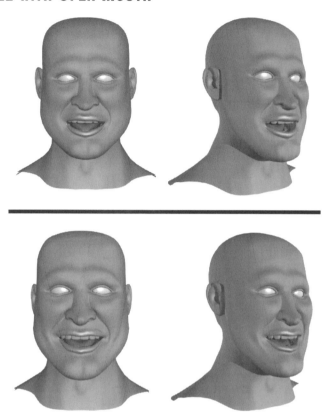

Distinguishing Features

Brows: The brow is relaxed.

Eyes: The eyelids are relaxed, though they may be slightly lowered. The eyeballs are alert, focusing steadily on whatever is making the character smile.

Mouth: The mouth is widened in front and pulled back towards the ears. Dimples may appear and the cheek creases running from the nose to the mouth deepen. In addition, the upper cheek bulges out slightly.

Jaw: The teeth are slightly parted, showing the upper teeth.

Morph Target Group	Morph Target	Percentage
Brows	• NONE	N/A
Eyes	• Left Eyelid Down	5
	• Right Eyelid Down	5
Mouth	• Laughter	
	• Smile Closed	70
Jaw	• NONE	N/A

CARTOON SMILE WITH OPEN MOUTH

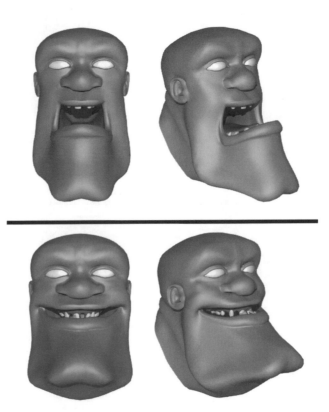

Distinguishing Features

Brows: The brow is relaxed.

Eyes: The eyelids are relaxed, though they may be slightly lowered. The eyeballs are alert, focusing steadily on whatever is making the character smile.

Mouth: The mouth is widened in front and pulled back towards the ears. Dimples may appear and the cheek creases running from the nose to the mouth deepen. In addition, the upper cheek bulges out slightly.

Jaw: The teeth are slightly parted, showing the upper teeth.

Morph Target Group	Morph Target	Percentage
Brows	• NONE	N/A
Eyes	• Left Eyelid Down	10
	• Right Eyelid Down	10
Mouth	• Smile	15
	• Smile Open	100

HUMAN SMILE WITH MOUTH CLOSED

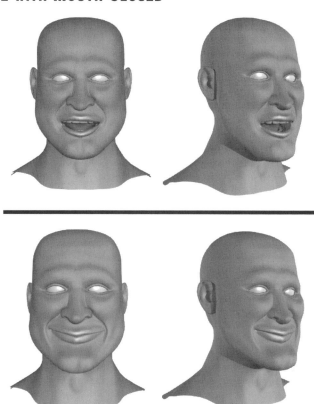

Distinguishing Features

Brows: The brow is relaxed

Eyes: The eyelid relaxed or lowered slightly.

Mouth: The mouth is widened and the corners pulled back toward the ears, tightening the mouth against the teeth. Dimples may show, though less pronounced than on the Smile with Open Mouth.

Jaw: The jaw is closed.

Morph Target Group	Morph Target	Percentage
Brows	• NONE	N/A
Eyes	• Left Eyelid Down	5
	• Right Eyelid Down	5
Mouth	• Smile Closed	70
	• Suppressed Sadness	60
Jaw	• Jaw Closed	75

CARTOON SMILE WITH MOUTH CLOSED

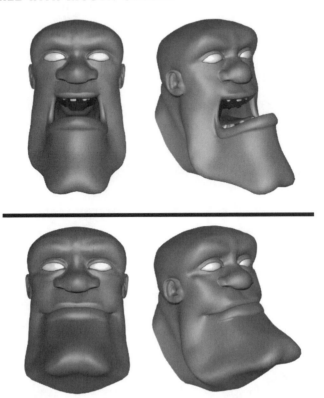

Distinguishing Features

Brows: The brow is relaxed.

Eyes: The lids are opened or lowered slightly.

Mouth: The mouth is widened and the corners pulled back toward the ears, tightening the mouth against the teeth. Dimples may show, though less pronounced than on the Smile with Open Mouth.

Jaw: The jaw is closed.

Morph Target Group	Morph Target	Percentage
Brows	• NONE	N/A
Eyes	• Left Eyelid Down	10
	• Right Eyelid Down	10
Mouth	• Smile	100

HUMAN SAD SMILE

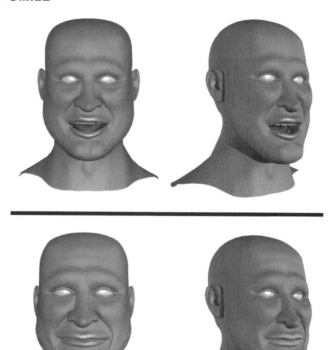

Distinguishing Features

Brows: The inner portion of the brows is lifted slightly.

Eyes: The lids might be slightly lowered.

Mouth: The mouth is widened and pulled back toward the ears, tightening it against the teeth. The appearance is virtually the same as the Smile with Mouth Closed. The cheeks may or may not bunch up under the eyes, depending upon how much effort the character is putting into the appearance of happiness.

Jaw: The jaw is closed.

Morph Target Group	Morph Target	Percentage
Brows	• Brows Middle Up	35
Eyes	• Eye Left Down	20
	• Eye Right Down	20
Mouth	• Smile Closed	40
	• Suppressed Sadness	30
Jaw	• Jaw Closed	100

CARTOON SAD SMILE

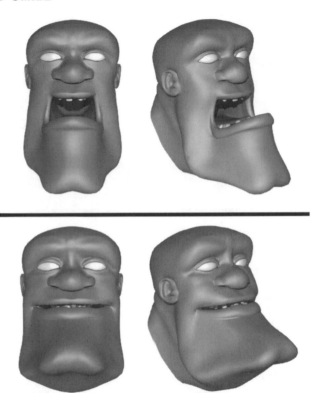

Distinguishing Features

Brows: The inner portion of the brows is lifted slightly.

Eyes: The lids might be slightly lowered.

Mouth: The mouth is widened and pulled back toward the ears, tightening it against the teeth. The cheeks may or may not bunch up under the eyes, depending upon how much effort the character is putting into the appearance of happiness. The character's intention is to betray its sadness. The weakness of the smile and the eyebrows give it away.

Jaw: The jaw closed or slightly opened.

Morph Target Group	Morph Target	Percentage
Brows	• Brows Middle Raised	70
Eyes	• Left Eyelid Down	10
	• Right Eyelid Down	10
Mouth	• Smile	70
	• Smile Open	90

HUMAN ENTHUSIASTIC SMILE

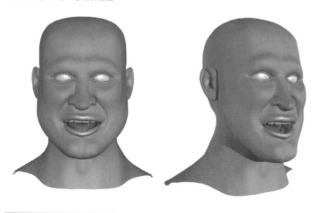

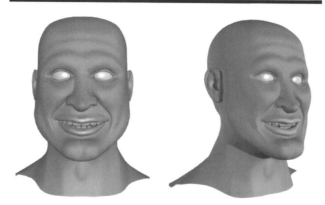

Distinguishing Features

Brows: The brows are lifted straight up, causing wrinkles on the forehead.

Eyes: The upper lid is opened wide. It's even possible that some white will show above the iris.

Mouth: The mouth is widened and pulled back toward the ears, pulling it tight against the teeth. The cheeks bunch up under the eyes.

Jaw: The jaw can be closed or slightly open.

Morph Target Group	Morph Target	Percentage
Brows	• Brows Arched	50
Eyes	• Eyes Wide	100
Mouth	• Mouth Laughter	80
	• Smile Closed	100
Jaw	• Jaw Closed	70

CARTOON ENTHUSIASTIC SMILE

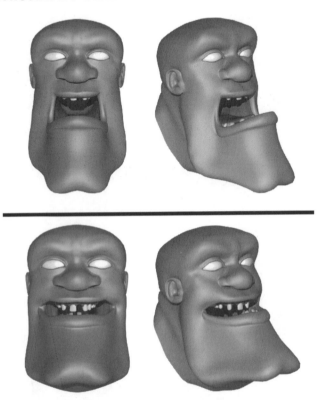

Distinguishing Features

Brows: The brows are arched, as if saying "I'm open to anything!"

Eyes: The eyes are open fully. If possible they can open even wider than normal, possibly even showing some white above the iris.

Mouth: The mouth is widened and pulled back toward the ears, pulling it tight against the teeth. The cheeks bunched up under the eyes.

Jaw: The jaw can be closed or slightly open.

Morph Target Group	Morph Target	Percentage
Brows	• Left Raised	20
	• Right Raised	20
Eyes	• NONE	N/A
Mouth	• Smile Open	75
	• Laughter	10

HUMAN CHARMING SMILE

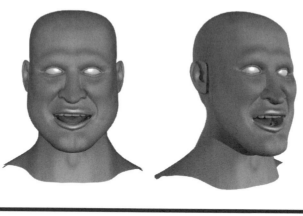

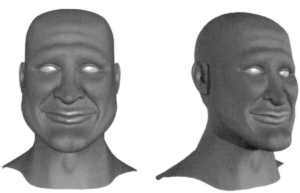

Distinguishing Features

Brows: The brows are lifted in the center in a manner similar to most sad and crying expressions. Deep furrows appear on the forehead.

Eyes: The eyes may fully open, or the lids may be lowered slightly.

Mouth: The mouth is widened and pulled back toward the ears, tightening it against the teeth. The cheeks bulge under the eyes.

Jaw: The jaw is closed.

Morph Target Group	Morph Target	Percentage
Brows	• Brows Middle Up	80
Eyes	• Eye Left Down	10
	• Eye Right Down	10
Mouth	• Smile Closed	75
Jaw	• Jaw Closed	85

CARTOON CHARMING SMILE

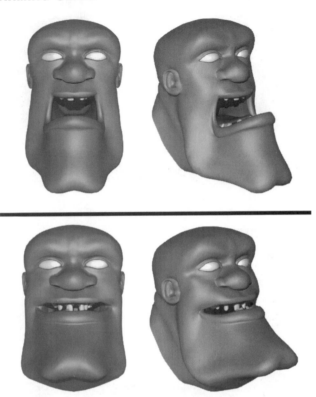

Distinguishing Features

Brows: The brows are lifted in the center, in effect posing the question "Do you like?" or "Is it okay?"

Eyes: The eye is fully open. The upper eyelid may be lowered slightly.

Mouth: The mouth is widened and pulled back toward the ears, tightening it against the teeth. The cheeks bunch up under the eyes.

Jaw: The jaw is closed.

Morph Target Group	Morph Target	Percentage
Brows	• Middle Raised	40
Eyes	• Eye Left Down	10
	• Eye Right Down	10
Mouth	• Smile	100

HUMAN DEVIOUS SMILE

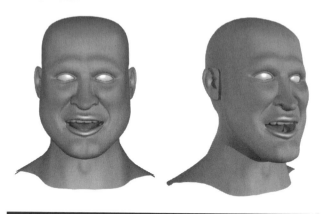

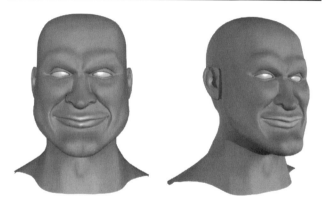

Distinguishing Features

Brows: The eyebrows are pulled down over the eye, almost as if in anger.

Eyes: The eyes are narrowed.

Mouth: The mouth is widened and pulled back toward the ears, pulling it tight against the teeth.

Jaw: The jaw is closed.

Morph Target Group	Morph Target	Percentage
Brows	• Brow Angry	90
Eyes	• Eye Left Down	25
	• Eye Right Down	25
Mouth	• Smile Closed	75
Jaw	• Jaw Closed	75

CARTOON DEVIOUS SMILE

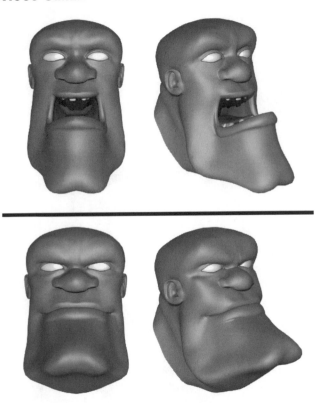

Distinguishing Features

Brows: The eyebrows are pulled down over the eye, almost as if in anger.

Eyes: The eyes are narrowed.

Mouth: The mouth is widened and pulled back toward the ears, pulling it tight against the teeth.

Jaw: The jaw is closed.

Morph Target Group	Morph Target	Percentage
Brows	• Brows Anger	100
Eyes	• Eye Left Down	10
	• Eye Right Down	10
Mouth	• Smile	100

HUMAN DRUNK SMILE

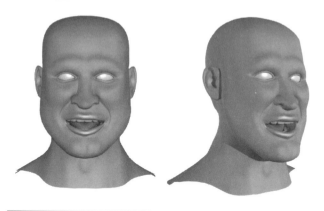

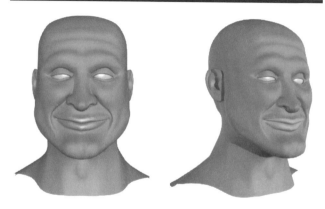

Distinguishing Features

Brows: The brows are lifted in a fruitless attempt to lift the eyelids.

Eyes: The upper lid is lowered almost to the halfway point in an attempt to focus the eye.

Mouth: The lips are widened, pulled back toward the ears and tightened against the teeth.

Jaw: The jaw is closed.

Morph Target Group	Morph Target	Percentage
Brows	• Brows Arched	70
Eyes	• Eye Left Down	30
	• Eye Right Down	30
Mouth	• Smile Closed	100
Jaw	• Jaw Closed	85

CARTOON DRUNK SMILE

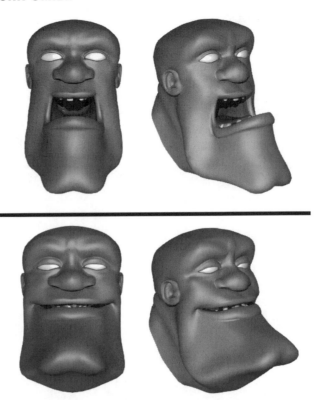

Distinguishing Features

Brows: The brows are lifted in a fruitless attempt to lift the eyelids.

Eyes: The upper lid is lowered almost to the halfway point in an attempt to focus the eye.

Mouth: The lips are widened, pulled back toward the ears, and tightened against the teeth.

Jaw: The jaw is closed.

Morph Target Group	Morph Target	Percentage
Brows	• Middle Raised	60
	• Right Raised	70
	• Left Raised	70
Eyes	• Eye Left Down	40
	• Eye Right Down	40
Mouth	• Smile	100
	• Smile open	100

HUMAN LAUGHTER

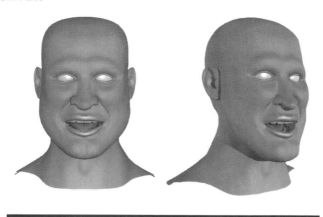

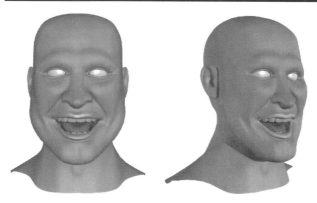

Distinguishing Features

Brows: The brows are relaxed.

Eyes: The lids are lowered slightly.

Mouth: The mouth is opened, widened, and pulled back toward the ears. The top lip is straightened out, revealing the upper teeth.

Jaw: The jaw is opened.

Morph Target Group	Morph Target	Percentage
Brows	• NONE	N/A
Eyes	• Eye Left Down	15
	• Eye Right Down	15
Mouth	• Laughter	100
Jaw	• Jaw Open	45

CARTOON LAUGHTER

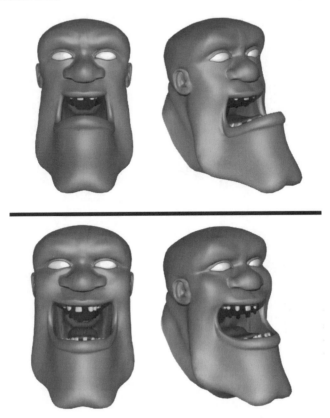

Distinguishing Features

Brows: The brows are relaxed.

Eyes: The upper eyelids are pushed down slightly by the pressure of the upper lid.

Mouth: The mouth is opened, widened, and pulled back toward the ears. The top lip is straightened out, revealing the upper teeth

Jaw: The jaw is opened.

Morph Target Group	Morph Target	Percentage
Brows	• Brows Lowered	50
Eyes	• Eye Left Down	10
	• Eye Right Down	10
Mouth	• Laughter	80
	• Smile Open	70

HUMAN LOUD LAUGHTER

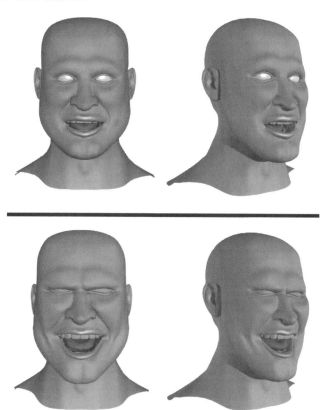

Distinguishing Features

Brows: The brows are lowered. In very extreme laughter they may be raised to their full extent.

Eyes: The lids are clamped shut. In extreme laughter they might be opened very wide as if in terror.

Mouth: The mouth is opened, widened, and pulled back toward the ears. The top lip is straightened out, revealing the upper teeth. The cheeks bulge under the eyes. In the very extreme positions mentioned under Brows and Eyes, the mouth is the only element that keeps the expression from fully appearing as terror.

Jaw: The jaw is opened.

Morph Target Group	Morph Target	Percentage
Brows	• Brows Compressed	100
Eyes	• Eye Left Down	100
	• Eye Right Down	100
Mouth	• Laughter	120
Jaw	• Jaw Open	100

CARTOON LOUD LAUGHTER

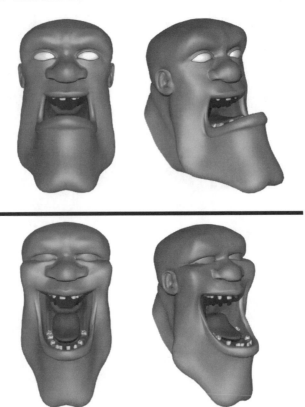

Distinguishing Features

Brows: The brows are relaxed

Eyes: The eyes are closed tight.

Mouth: The mouth is opened wide with raised corners, revealing the upper teeth.

Jaw: The jaw is opened wide.

Morph Target Group	Morph Target	Percentage
Brows	• Brows Lowered	100
Eyes	• Eye Left Down	100
	• Eye Right Down	100
Mouth	• Laughter	100

HUMAN PHONY SMILE

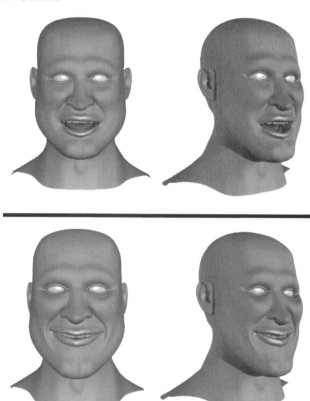

Distinguishing Features

Brows: The eyebrows are relaxed or slightly raised. If the character is attempting to appear endearing, the brows may be drawn up in the center.

Eyes: Eyes are open fully or narrowed very slightly.

Mouth: The mouth is opened slightly, widened, pulled back toward the ears, and tightened against the teeth. The cheeks don't bulge under the eyes as much as they do in a sincere smile.

Jaw: The jaw is slightly opened.

Morph Target Group	Morph Target	Percentage
Brows	• NONE	N/A
Eyes	• Eye Left Down	15
	• Eye Right Down	15
Mouth	• Laughter	60
	• Smile Closed	75
Jaw	• Jaw Open	10

CARTOON PHONY SMILE

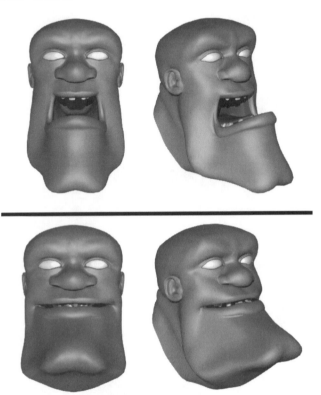

Distinguishing Features

Brows: The eyebrows are relaxed or slightly raised.

Eyes: Eyes are narrowed very slightly.

Mouth: The mouth is opened, widened, pulled back toward the ears, and tightened against the teeth. The cheeks don't bulge under the eyes as much as they do in a sincere smile.

Jaw: The jaw is slightly opened.

Morph Target Group	Morph Target	Percentage
Brows	• Brows Lowered	25
Eyes	• NONE	N/A
Mouth	• Smile Open	100
	• Closed	100

HUMAN PHONY LAUGHTER

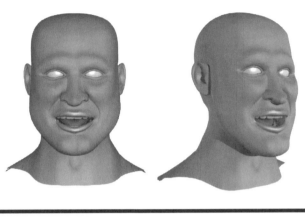

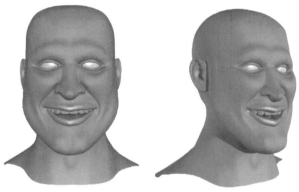

Distinguishing Features

Brows: The eyebrows are relaxed or slightly raised.

Eyes: Eyes are narrowed slightly.

Mouth: The mouth is opened, widened, pulled back toward the ears, and tightened against the teeth. The cheeks are bulged out only slightly and dimples appear.

Jaw: The jaw is opened about halfway.

Morph Target Group	Morph Target	Percentage
Brows	• NONE	N/A
Eyes	• Eye Left Down	15
	• Eye Right Down	15
Mouth	• Laughter	100
	• Smile Closed	100
Jaw	• Jaw Open	10

CARTOON PHONY LAUGHTER

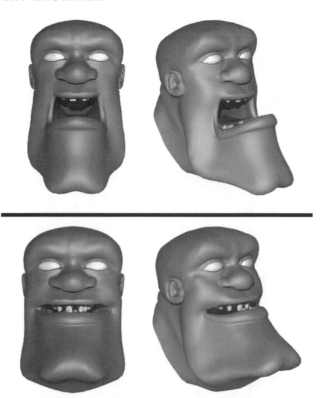

Distinguishing Features

Brows: The eyebrows are relaxed or slightly raised.

Eyes: Eyes are narrowed slightly.

Mouth: The mouth is opened, widened, pulled back toward the ears, and tightened against the teeth. The cheeks are bulged out only slightly and dimples appear.

Jaw: The jaw is opened about half way.

Morph Target Group	Morph Target	Percentage
Brows	• NONE	N/A
Eyes	• NONE	N/A
Mouth	• Smile	70
	• Smile Open	90

HUMAN CRYING WITH A CLOSED MOUTH

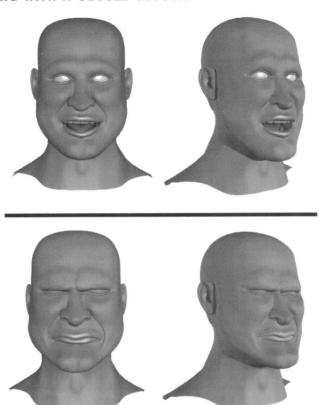

Distinguishing Features

Brows: The eyebrows are lowered, almost as if in anger.

Eyes: The eyes are clenched shut. If they do open, it's done with considerable effort.

Mouth: The mouth is clenched shut and in animation may tremble. The cheeks bunch up and dimples may appear on the chin.

Jaw: The jaw can be shut tight or open slightly. It might also quiver.

Morph Target Group	Morph Target	Percentage
Brows	• Brows Compressed	120
Eyes	• Eye Left Down	100
	• Eye Right Down	100
Mouth	• Crying	100
Jaw	• Jaw Closed	100

CARTOON CRYING WITH A CLOSED MOUTH

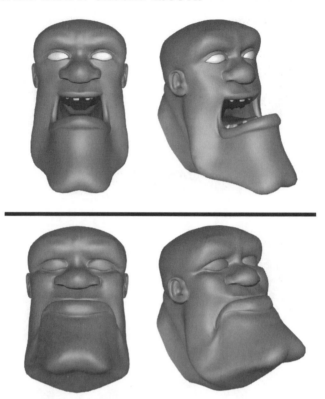

Distinguishing Features

Brows: The eyebrows are lowered, almost as if in anger.

Eyes: The eyes are clenched shut. If they do open, it's done with considerable effort.

Mouth: The mouth is clenched shut and in animation may tremble. The cheeks bunch up and dimples may appear on the chin.

Jaw: The jaw can be shut tight or open slightly. It might also quiver.

Morph Target Group	Morph Target	Percentage
Brows	• Brows Lowered	100
	• Brows Middle Raised	100
Eyes	• Eye Left Down	100
	• Eye Right Down	100
Mouth	• Cry Closed	100

HUMAN CRYING WITH MOUTH OPEN

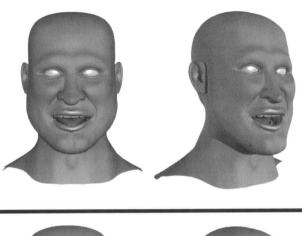

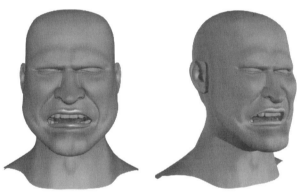

Distinguishing Features

Brows: The eyebrows are lowered.

Eyes: The eyes are clenched shut. If they do open, it's done with considerable effort.

Mouth: The mouth opened, and the lower corners pulled back. The cheeks bunch up under the eyes.

Jaw: The jaw is held stiffly open.

Morph Target Group	Morph Target	Percentage
Brows	• Brow Compressed	100
Eyes	• Eye Left Down	100
	• Eye Right Down	100
Mouth	• Cry Open	65
Jaw	• Jaw Closed	35

CARTOON CRYING WITH MOUTH OPEN

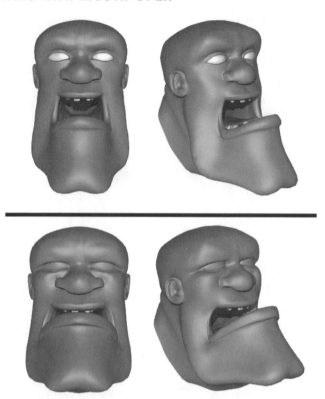

Distinguishing Features

Brows: The eyebrows are lowered.

Eyes: The eyes are clenched shut. If they do open, it's done with considerable effort.

Mouth: The mouth is open with the lower corners pulled back. The cheeks bunch up under the eyes.

Jaw: The jaw is open.

Morph Target Group	Morph Target	Percentage
Brows	• Brows Lowered	100
Eyes	• Eye Left Down	100
	• Eye Right Down	100
Mouth	• Cry Open	100

HUMAN NEARLY CRYING

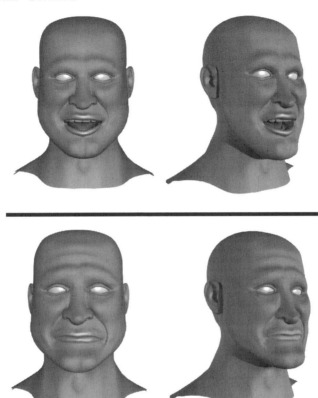

Distinguishing Features

Brows: The eyebrows are lowered, almost as if in anger.

Eyes: The eyes are clenched shut.

Mouth: The mouth is clenched shut and in animation may tremble. The cheeks bunch up and dimples may appear on the chin.

Jaw: The jaw can be shut tight or open slightly. It might also quiver.

Morph Target Group	Morph Target	Percentage
Brows	• Brows Arched	35
	• Brows Middle Up	100
Eyes	• Eye Left Down	15
	• Eye Right Down	15
Mouth	• Crying	80
	• Suppressed Sadness	80
Jaw	• Jaw Closed	90

CARTOON NEARLY CRYING

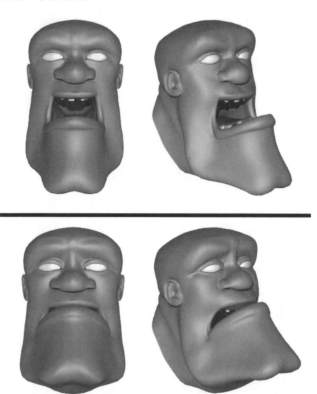

Distinguishing Features

Brows: The eyebrows are lowered, almost as if in anger.

Eyes: The eyes are clenched shut. If they do open, it's done with considerable effort.

Mouth: The mouth is clenched shut and in animation may tremble. The cheeks bunch up and dimples may appear on the chin.

Jaw: The jaw can be shut tight or open slightly. It might also quiver.

Morph Target Group	Morph Target	Percentage
Brows	• Brows Middle Raised	80
Eyes	• Eye Left Down	15
	• Eye Right Down	15
Mouth	• Cry Closed	70
	• Cry Open	100
	• Suppressed Sadness	100

HUMAN MISERABLE

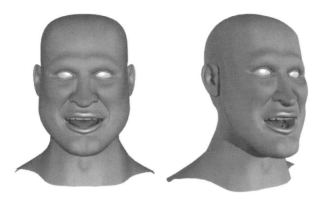

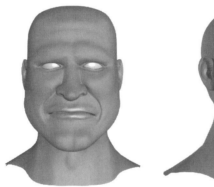

Distinguishing Features

Brows: The inner brows are bent upward and pinched together.

Eyes: The eyelids are lowered slightly.

Mouth: The mouth is slightly pouted, and the corners may be drawn down.

Jaw: The jaw is shut.

Morph Target Group	Morph Target	Percentage
Brows	• Brows Middle Up	90
	• Brows Compressed	100
Eyes	• Eye Left Down	100
	• Eye Right Down	100
Mouth	• Suppressed Sadness	40
Jaw	• Jaw Closed	90

CARTOON MISERABLE

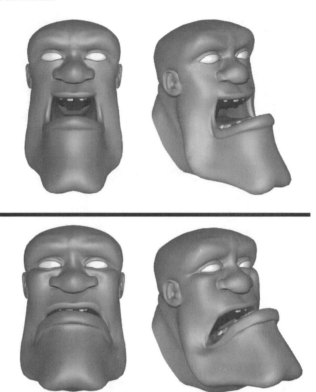

Distinguishing Features

Brows: The inner brows are bent upward and pinched together.

Eyes: The lids are relaxed or lowered and tightened slightly.

Mouth: The mouth is open and the corners of the mouth are drawn back and rippled. The lower lip might curl out

Jaw: The jaw hangs open.

Morph Target Group	Morph Target	Percentage
Brows	• Brows Lowered	50
	• Brows Middle Raised	100
Eyes	• Eye Left Down	15
	• Eye Right Down	15
Mouth	• Miserable	50

HUMAN WORRIED

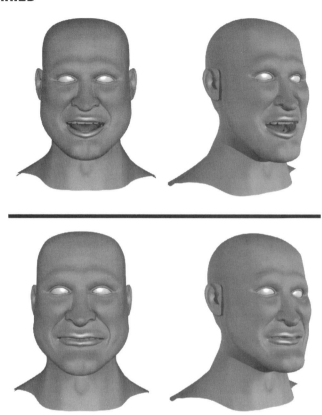

Distinguishing Features

Brows: The eyebrows may be relaxed or drawn up slightly as if sad.

Eyes: The eyes are open with a worried pose. Most action is taking place in the mind so the eyes are focused on nothing in particular.

Mouth: The mouth may be relaxed or squeezed together somewhat depending on the severity of the pose.

Jaw: The jaw is closed.

Morph Target Group	Morph Target	Percentage
Brows	• Brows Middle Up	75
Eyes	• NONE	N/A
Mouth	• Suppressed Sadness	50
Jaw	• Jaw Closed	70

CARTOON WORRIED

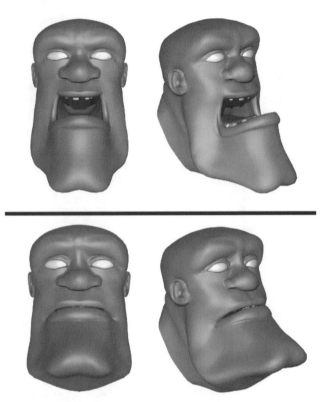

Distinguishing Features

Brows: The eyebrows may be relaxed or drawn up slightly as if sad.

Eyes: The eyes are open, with a worried pose. Most action is taking place in the mind, so the eyes are focused on nothing in particular.

Mouth: The mouth may be relaxed or squeezed together somewhat depending on the severity of the pose.

Jaw: The jaw is closed or hangs open. The mind is likely too concerned with other matters to keep the jaw shut.

Morph Target Group	Morph Target	Percentage
Brows	• Brows Middle Raised	75
Eyes	• NONE	N/A
Mouth	• Mouth Closed	75

HUMAN AFRAID

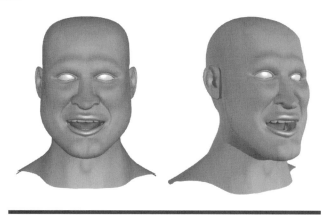

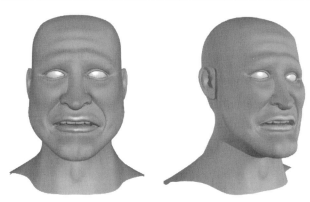

Distinguishing Features

Brows: The brows are lifted straight up and possibly drawn together in the middle.

Eyes: The eyes are open and in animation they might dart about.

Mouth: The mouth is relaxed or might be parted slightly with no strain or tightening.

Jaw: The jaw is open slightly.

Morph Target Group	Morph Target	Percentage
Brows	• Brows Middle Up	75
Eyes	• NONE	N/A
Mouth	• Frightened	70
Jaw	• Suppressed Sadness	55

CARTOON AFRAID

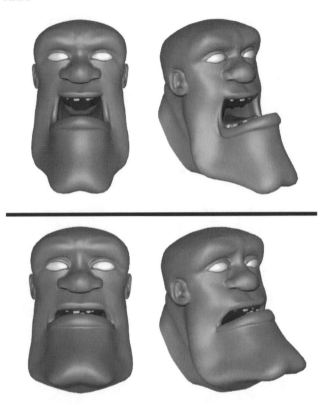

Distinguishing Features

Brows: The brows are lifted straight up and possibly drawn together in the middle.

Eyes: The eyes are open and in animation they might dart about.

Mouth: The mouth is relaxed or might be parted slightly with no strain or tightening.

Jaw: The jaw is open slightly.

Morph Target Group	Morph Target	Percentage
Brows	• Brows Middle Raised	70
Eyes	• NONE	N/A
Mouth	• Closed	65

HUMAN VERY FRIGHTENED

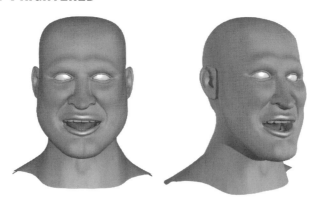

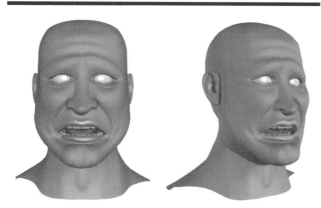

Distinguishing Features

Brows: The brows are lifted and drawn together in the middle slightly.

Eyes: The lids are open wide and the eyes stare straight ahead.

Mouth: The mouth is opened and the lower lip stretched horizontally, revealing the bottom teeth but not the upper.

Jaw: The jaw is dropped to about the halfway position.

Morph Target Group	Morph Target	Percentage
Brows	• Brows Middle Up	100
Eyes	• Eyes Wide	120
Mouth	• Cry Open	50
	• Frightened	100
Jaw	• Jaw Closed	15

CARTOON VERY FRIGHTENED

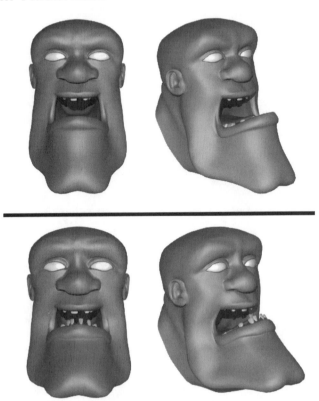

Distinguishing Features

Brows: The brows are lifted and drawn together in the middle slightly.

Eyes: The lids are open wide and the eyes stare straight ahead.

Mouth: The mouth is opened and the lower lip stretched horizontally, revealing the bottom teeth but not the upper.

Jaw: The jaw is dropped to about the halfway position.

Morph Target Group	Morph Target	Percentage
Brows	• Brows Middle Raised	70
Eyes	• NONE	N/A
Mouth	• Frightened	100

HUMAN TERROR

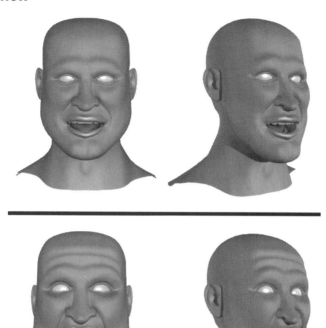

Distinguishing Features

Brows: The brows are raised as high as they will go, causing deep furrows in the forehead.

Eyes: The eyes are opened as wide as possible.

Mouth: The mouth is opened as wide as possible. The cheeks are stretched taut and pulled in toward the teeth somewhat.

Jaw: The jaw is opened to its full extent.

Morph Target Group	Morph Target	Percentage
Brows	• Brows Arched	100
	• Brows Middle Up	100
Eyes	• Eyes Wide	100
Mouth	• Yawn	100
Jaw	• Jaw Open	120

CARTOON TERROR

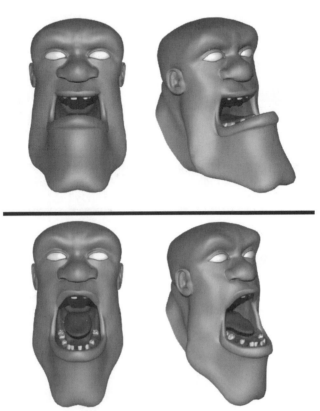

Distinguishing Features

Brows: The brows are raised as high as they will go, causing deep furrows in the forehead.

Eyes: The eyes are opened as wide as possible.

Mouth: The mouth is opened as wide as possible. The cheeks are stretched taut and pulled in toward the teeth somewhat.

Jaw: The jaw is opened to its full extent.

Morph Target Group	Morph Target	Percentage
Brows	• Brows Right Raised	100
	• Brows Left Raised	100
Eyes	• Eye Left Down	100
	• Eye Right Down	100
Mouth	• Yawn	100

HUMAN STERN

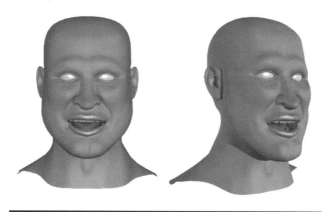

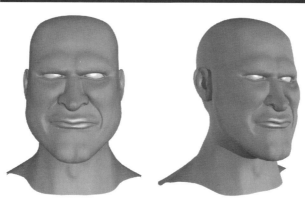

Distinguishing Features

Brows: The brows are lowered.

Eyes: The lids are lowered somewhat.

Mouth: The mouth is closed and the lips may be compressed together.

Jaw: The jaw is closed.

Morph Target Group	Morph Target	Percentage
Brows	• Brows Compressed	80
Eyes	• NONE	N/A
Mouth	• Mouth Closed	100
	• Mouth Frightened	100
Jaw	• Jaw Closed	100

CARTOON STERN

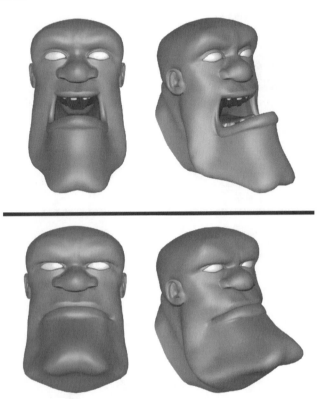

Distinguishing Features

Brows: The brows are lowered.

Eyes: The lids are lowered somewhat.

Mouth: The mouth is closed and the lips may be pressed together.

Jaw: The jaw is closed.

Morph Target Group	Morph Target	Percentage
Brows	• Brows Anger	100
Eyes	• Eye Left Down	15
	• Eye Right Down	
Mouth	• Closed	100

HUMAN ENRAGED WITH MOUTH CLOSED

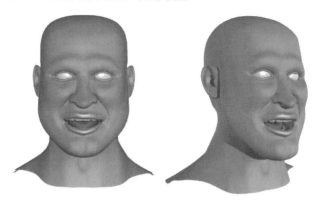

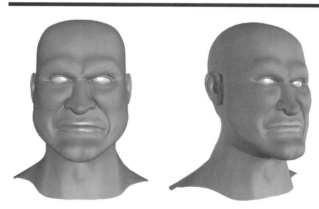

Distinguishing Features

Brows: The brows are down and drawn together in the center.

Eyes: The eyes are open wide, but may be partially obscured by the brows.

Mouth: The mouth is tightly compressed, and the corners may be drawn down slightly at the corners.

Jaw: The jaw is shut.

Morph Target Group	Morph Target	Percentage
Brows	• Brows Angry	100
	• Brows Compressed	50
Eyes	• Eye Left Down	20
	• Eye Right Down	20
Mouth	• Suppressed Sadness	60
Jaw	• Jaw Closed	100

CARTOON ENRAGED WITH MOUTH CLOSED

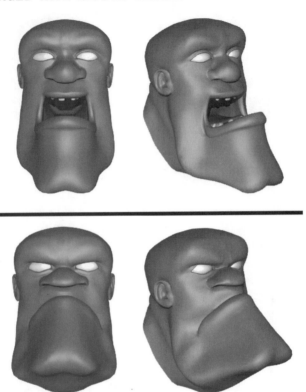

Distinguishing Features

Brows: The brows are down and together in the center.

Eyes: The eyes are open wide, but may be partially obscured by the brows.

Mouth: The mouth is tightly compressed, and the corners are drawn down.

Jaw: The jaw is shut.

Morph Target Group	Morph Target	Percentage
Brows	• Brows Anger	100
Eyes	• NONE	N/A
Mouth	• Suppressed Sadness	100

HUMAN SHOUT

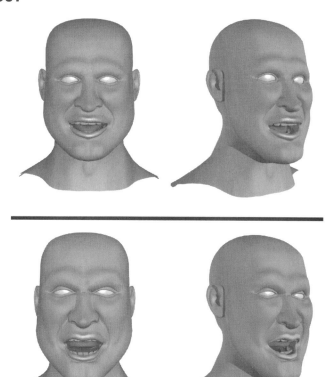

Distinguishing Features

Brows: The brows move from relaxed to raised straight up. As shouting continues, the brows might be lowered slowly.

Eyes: The eyes are either relaxed or open wide.

Mouth: The mouth is opened wide, with both upper and lower teeth showing.

Jaw: The jaw pumps open and closed, possibly to its full extent depending on the vigor of the shouting.

Morph Target Group	Morph Target	Percentage
Brows	• Brows Angry	62
Eyes	• Eye Left Down	20
	• Eye Right Down	20
Mouth	• Laughter	100
	• Surprise	120
	• Yawn	70
Jaw	• Jaw Open	60

CARTOON SHOUT

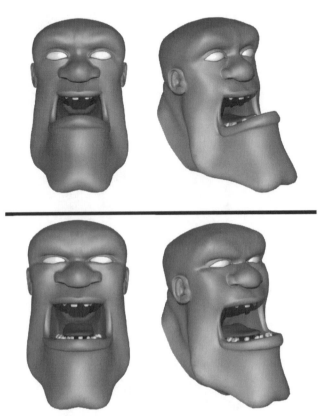

Distinguishing Features

Brows: The brows move from relaxed to raised straight up. As shouting continues, the brows might be lowered slowly.

Eyes: The eyes are either relaxed or open wide.

Mouth: The mouth is opened wide, with both upper and lower teeth showing.

Jaw: The jaw pumps open and closed, possibly to its full extent depending on the vigor of the shouting.

Morph Target Group	Morph Target	Percentage
Brows	• Brows Anger	90
Eyes	• Eye Left Down	20
	• Eye Right Down	20
Mouth	• Cry Open	100
	• Laughter	85
	• Yawn	80

HUMAN ENRAGED SHOUT

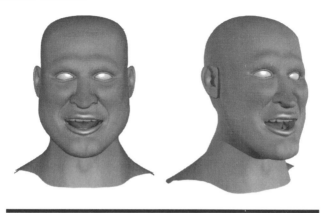

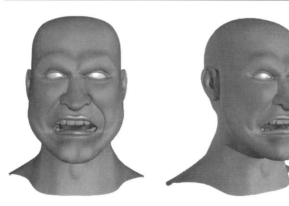

Distinguishing Features

Brows: The brows are lowered in anger.

Eyes: The eyes are opened wide.

Mouth: The mouth is opened, pulled down and back toward the ears, and tightened against the skull. The upper lip is raised, revealing the teeth.

Jaw: The jaw is opened about one-fifth of its limit. During animation it doesn't pump nearly as much as a normal shout, as the muscles seem to be locked in place.

Morph Target Group	Morph Target	Percentage
Brows	• Brows Angry	70
Eyes	• Eye Left Down	10
	• Eye Right Down	10
Mouth	• NONE	N/A
Jaw	• Jaw Closed	20

CARTOON ENRAGED SHOUT

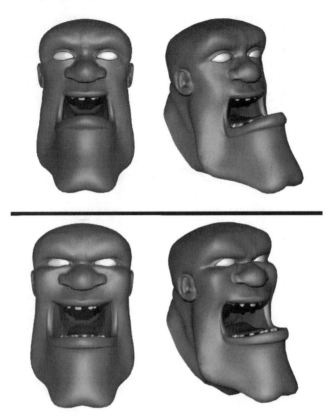

Distinguishing Features

Brows: The brows are lowered in anger.

Eyes: The eyes are opened wide.

Mouth: The mouth is opened, pulled back toward the ears, and tightened against the skull. The upper lip is raised, revealing the teeth.

Jaw: The jaw is opened wide. During animation it doesn't pump nearly as much as a normal shout, as the muscles seem to be locked in place.

Morph Target Group	Morph Target	Percentage
Brows	• Brows Anger	90
Eyes	• NONE	N/A
Mouth	• Cry Open	100
	• Laughter	62

HUMAN EXERTION

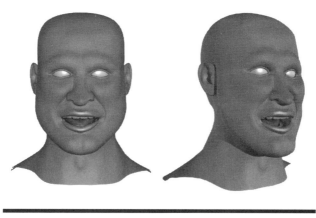

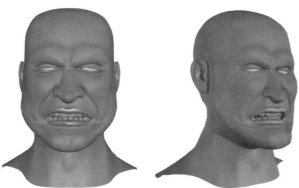

Distinguishing Features

Brows: The brows can be relaxed or lowered as if in anger, depending on the level of exertion. In animation the eyebrows can move into almost any position, as long as the mouth and jaw are correct.

Eyes: The eyes are clamped shut.

Mouth: The mouth is opened and pulled tightly against the teeth.

Jaw: The jaw is opened just so that the upper and lower teeth meet at the tips.

Morph Target Group	Morph Target	Percentage
Brows	• Brows Angry	70
Eyes	• Eye Left Down	10
	• Eye Right Down	10
Mouth	• Cry Open	80
Jaw	• Jaw Closed	20

CARTOON EXERTION

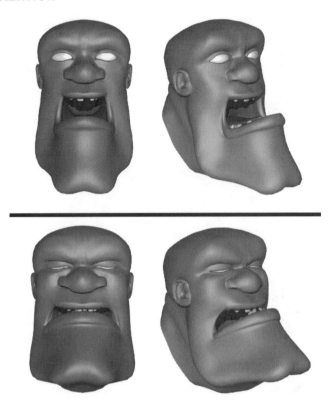

Distinguishing Features

Brows: The brows can be relaxed or lowered as if in anger, depending on the level of exertion. In animation the eyebrows can move into almost any position, as long as the mouth and jaw are correct.

Eyes: The eyes are clamped shut.

Mouth: The mouth is opened and pulled tightly against the teeth.

Jaw: The jaw is opened just so that the upper and lower teeth meet at the tips.

Morph Target Group	Morph Target	Percentage
Brows	• Brows Anger	90
Eyes	• Eye Left Down	100
	• Eye Right Down	100
Mouth	• Cry Open	100
	• Surprise	100
	• Disgust	100

HUMAN PAIN

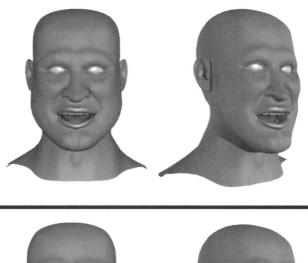

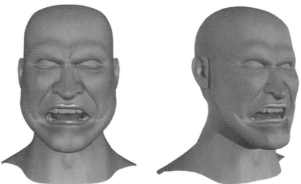

Distinguishing Features

Brows: The brows can be relaxed or lowered as if in anger, depending on the level of pain. Although pain and exertion are similar in appearance, during animation the brows will remain pressing down in pain.

Eyes: The eyes are clamped shut.

Mouth: The mouth is opened and pulled tightly against the teeth.

Jaw: The jaw is opened just so that the upper and lower teeth meet at the tips.

Morph Target Group	Morph Target	Percentage
Brows	• Brows Angry	100
	• Brows Compressed	70
Eyes	• Eye Left Down	100
	• Eye Right Down	100
Mouth	• Cry Open	90
Jaw	• Jaw Closed	15

CARTOON PAIN

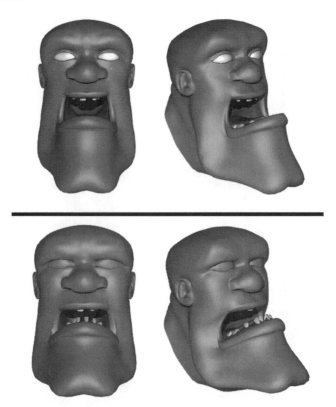

Distinguishing Features

Brows: The brows can be relaxed or lowered as if in anger, depending on the level of pain. Although pain and exertion are similar in appearance, during animation the brows will remain pressing down in pain.

Eyes: The eyes are clamped shut.

Mouth: The mouth is opened and pulled tightly against the teeth. The lower corner can be pulled down and back.

Jaw: The jaw is opened.

Morph Target Group	Morph Target	Percentage
Brows	• Brows Lowered	80
Eyes	• Eye Left Down	100
	• Eye Right Down	100
Mouth	• Surprise	100

HUMAN PAIN 2

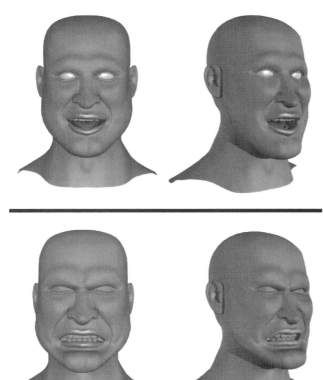

Distinguishing Features

Brows: The brows can be relaxed or lowered as if in anger.

Eyes: The eyes are open or squinting. It's even possible that one eye will be tightly shut while the other strains to open a crack.

Mouth: The mouth is closed, with the upper lip raised in a sneer. The upper lip may remain in contact with the lower lip, or may be lifted a bit to show some of the teeth.

Jaw: The jaw is closed.

Morph Target Group	Morph Target	Percentage
Brows	• Brows Angry	75
	• Brows Compressed	90
Eyes	• Eye Left Down	50
	• Eye Right Down	50
Mouth	• Repulsion	100
Jaw	• Closed	70

CARTOON PAIN 2

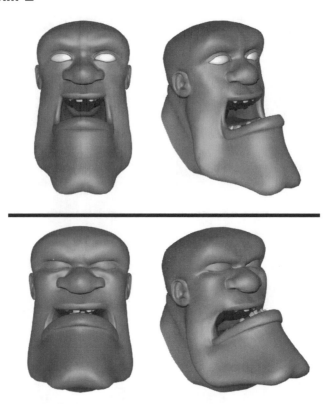

Distinguishing Features

Brows: The brows can be relaxed or lowered as if in anger.

Eyes: The eyes are open or squinting. It's even possible that one eye will be tightly shut while the other strains to open a crack.

Mouth: The mouth is closed, with the upper lip raised in a sneer. The lower corner of the mouth is pulled down and back.

Jaw: The jaw is closed.

Morph Target Group	Morph Target	Percentage
Brows	• Brows Anger	90
Eyes	• Eye Left Down	100
	• Eye Right Down	100
Mouth	• Cry Open	150
	• Surprise	100

HUMAN DISGUST

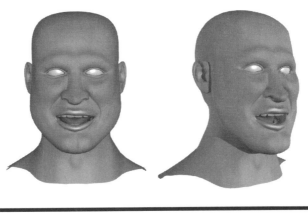

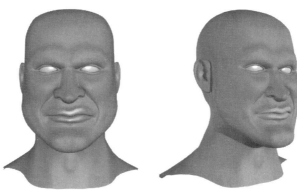

Distinguishing Features

Brows: The brows are relaxed.

Eyes: The eyes are open and relaxed.

Mouth: The mouth is closed, with one half of the upper lip pulled upward and outward in a sneer.

Jaw: The jaw is closed.

Morph Target Group	Morph Target	Percentage
Brows	• Brows Angry	80
	• Brows Compressed	70
Eyes	• Eye Left Down	20
	• Eye Right Down	20
Mouth	• Disgust	90
Jaw	• Jaw Closed	70

CARTOON DISGUST

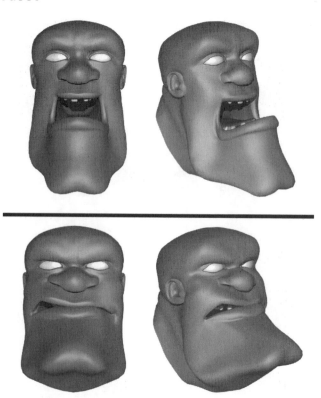

Distinguishing Features

Brows: The brows are relaxed.

Eyes: The eyes are open and relaxed.

Mouth: The mouth is closed, with one half of the upper lip pulled upward and outward in a sneer.

Jaw: The jaw is closed.

Morph Target Group	Morph Target	Percentage
Brows	• Brows Anger	90
Eyes	• NONE	N/A
Mouth	• Disgust	100

HUMAN DISDAIN

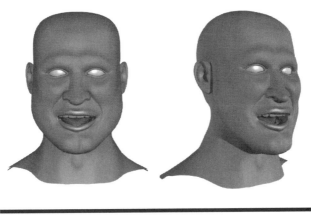

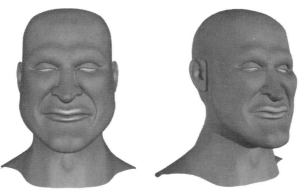

Distinguishing Features

Brows: The brows are relaxed.

Eyes: The lids are open or lowered, and the eye may look down or sideways.

Mouth: The mouth is closed, with the upper lip raised in a sneer.

Jaw: The jaw is closed.

Morph Target Group	Morph Target	Percentage
Brows	• Brows Angry	40
Eyes	• Eye Left Down	60
	• Eye Right Down	60
Mouth	• Repulsion	70
Jaw	• Jaw Closed	60

CARTOON DISDAIN

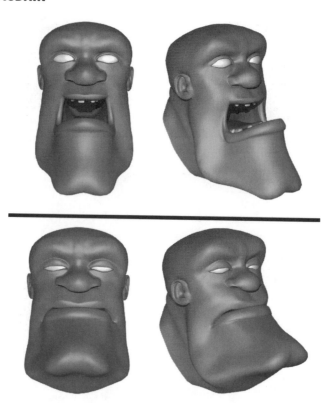

Distinguishing Features

Brows: The brows are relaxed.

Eyes: The lids are open or lowered, and the eye may look down or sideways.

Mouth: The mouth is closed, with the upper lip raised in a sneer.

Jaw: The jaw is closed.

Morph Target Group	Morph Target	Percentage
Brows	• Brows Left Raised	20
	• Brows Right Raised	20
Eyes	• Eye Left Down	50
	• Eye Right Down	50
Mouth	• Closed	100
	• Repulsion	100

HUMAN EVIL LAUGHTER

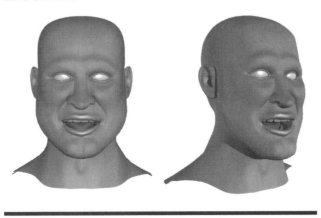

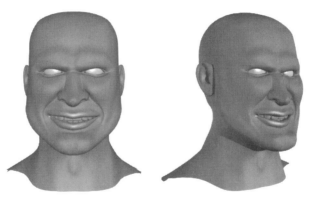

Distinguishing Features

Brows: Brows are drawn down as if in anger.

Eyes: The eyes are relaxed.

Mouth: The mouth is open, with the corners pulled back toward the ears, stretching it against the skull.

Jaw: The jaw is closed.

Morph Target Group	Morph Target	Percentage
Brows	• Brows Angry	70
	• Brows Compressed	100
Eyes	• NONE	N/A
Mouth	• Laughter	60
	• Smile Closed	70
Jaw	• Jaw Closed	80

CARTOON EVIL LAUGHTER

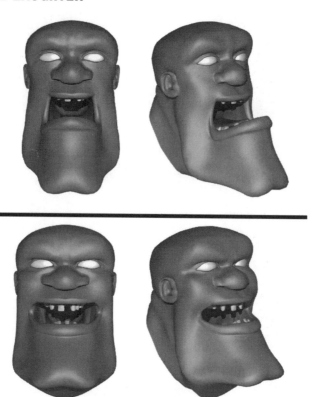

Distinguishing Features

Brows: The brows are lowered as if in anger.

Eyes: The eyes are open wide.

Mouth: The mouth is widened and pulled back towards the ears.

Jaw: The jaw is held stiffly open.

Morph Target Group	Morph Target	Percentage
Brows	• Brows Anger	80
Eyes	• NONE	N/A
Mouth	• Laughter	90
	• Smile	100
	• Smile Open	100

HUMAN INTENSE CONCENTRATION

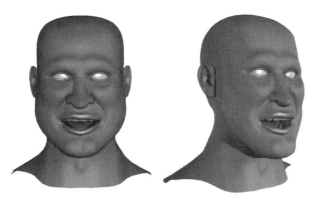

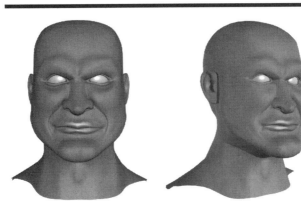

Distinguishing Features

Brows: The brows are lowered somewhat almost as if angered.

Eyes: The eyes are opened wider than normal.

Mouth: The mouth is relaxed.

Jaw: The jaw is closed.

Morph Target Group	Morph Target	Percentage
Brows	• Brows Angry	80
Eyes	• Eyes Wide	100
Mouth	• Mouth Closed	100
Jaw	• Jaw Closed	100

CARTOON INTENSE CONCENTRATION

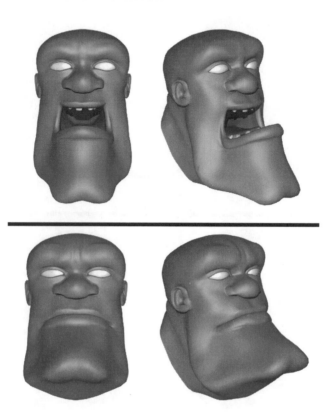

Distinguishing Features

Brows: The brows are lowered somewhat almost as if in anger, and brought together in the center. For cartoon characters, thinking is a painful process.

Eyes: The brows are lowered somewhat.

Mouth: The mouth is relaxed.

Jaw: The jaw is closed.

Morph Target Group	Morph Target	Percentage
Brows	• Brows Anger	60
	• Brows Afraid	100
Eyes	• Eye Left Down	20
	• Eye Right Down	20
Mouth	• Closed	100

HUMAN FACIAL SHRUG

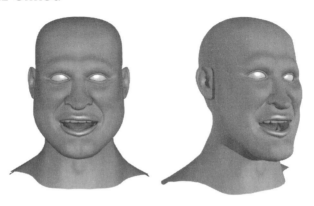

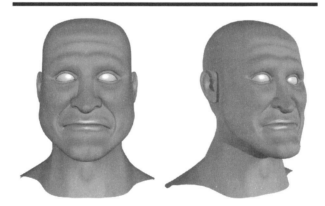

Distinguishing Features

Brows: The brows are raised straight upward to their limit.

Eyes: The eyes are open wide.

Mouth: The mouth is closed with the corners pulled down.

Jaw: The jaw may be closed, or opened fairly wide even though the mouth is closed.

Morph Target Group	Morph Target	Percentage
Brows	• Brows Arched	100
	• Brows Middle Up	90
Eyes	• Eyes Wide	100
Mouth	• Suppressed Sadness	60
Jaw	• Jaw Closed	100

CARTOON FACIAL SHRUG

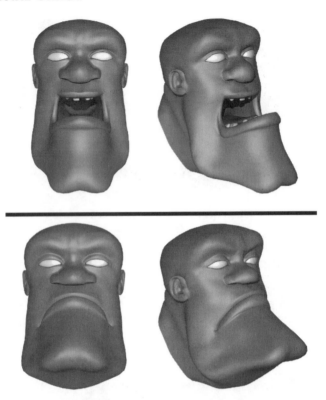

Distinguishing Features

Brows: The brows are raised straight upward to their limit.

Eyes: The eyes are open wide.

Mouth: The mouth is closed with the corners pulled down.

Jaw: The jaw may be closed, or opened fairly wide even though the mouth is closed.

Morph Target Group	Morph Target	Percentage
Brows	• Brows Left Raised	50
	• Brows Right Raised	50
Eyes	• Eye Left Down	20
	• Eye Right Down	20
Mouth	• Closed	100
	• Frown	50

HUMAN SURPRISE

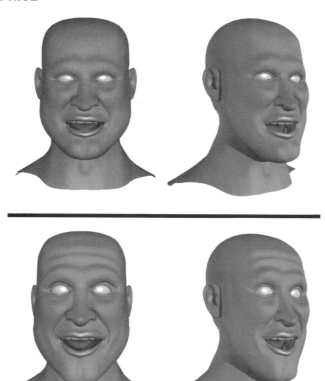

Distinguishing Features

Brows: The brows are raised high, causing wrinkles on the forehead.

Eyes: The eyes are opened wider than usual.

Mouth: The mouth is open but slack. How wide it opens depends on the severity of the surprise.

Jaw: The jaw is opened about one-third to one-half its limit.

Morph Target Group	Morph Target	Percentage
Brows	• Brows Arched	100
Eyes	• Eyes Wide	100
Mouth	• Mouth Surprise	100
Jaw	• Jaw Open	75

CARTOON SURPRISE

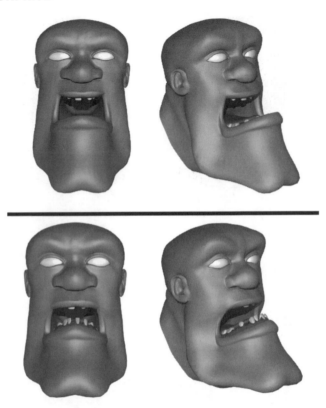

Distinguishing Features

Brows: The brows are raised high, causing wrinkles on the forehead.

Eyes: The eyes are opened wider than usual.

Mouth: The mouth is open but slack. How wide it opens depends on the severity of the surprise.

Jaw: The jaw is opened about one-third to one-half its limit.

Morph Target Group	Morph Target	Percentage
Brows	• Brows Right Raised	50
	• Brows Left Raised	50
Eyes	• NONE	N/A
Mouth	• Surprise	100

HUMAN DROWSINESS

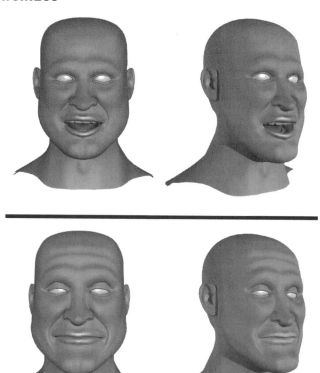

Distinguishing Features

Brows: The brows may be relaxed, or raised in an attempt to keep the lids from shutting.

Eyes: The eyelids are lowered. When animating, eye blinks may be slower in this condition.

Mouth: The mouth is relaxed. Any emotional expression will be greatly watered down.

Jaw: The jaw is closed.

Morph Target Group	Morph Target	Percentage
Brows	• Brows Arched	80
Eyes	• Eye Left Down	30
	• Eye Right Down	30
Mouth	• Mouth Smile Closed	60
	• Suppressed Sadness	60
Jaw	• Jaw Closed	70

CARTOON DROWSINESS

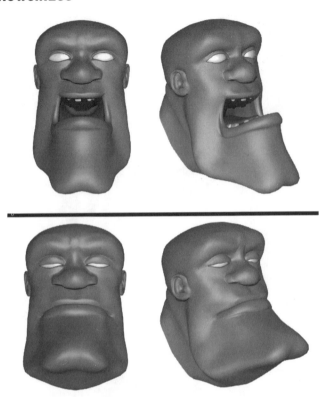

Distinguishing Features

Brows: The brows may be relaxed, or raised in an attempt to keep the lids from shutting.

Eyes: The eyelids are lowered. Eye-blinks may be slower in this condition.

Mouth: The mouth is relaxed. Any emotional expression will be greatly watered down.

Jaw: The jaw is closed.

Morph Target Group	Morph Target	Percentage
Brows	• Brows Middle Raised	50
	• Brows Right Raised	50
	• Brows Left Raised	50
Eyes	• Eye Left Down	60
	• Eye Right Down	60
Mouth	• Closed	100

HUMAN SUPPRESSED SADNESS

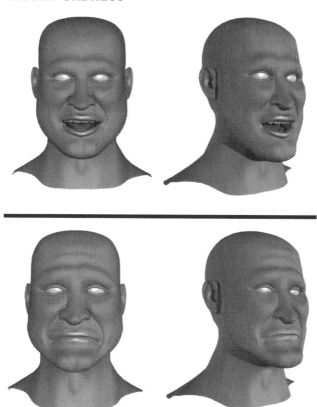

Distinguishing Features

Brows: The middle of the brow is raised.

Eyes: The eye can be open or slightly shut. Bags may appear under the eyes if the condition is prolonged.

Mouth: The lips are pressed together, and the space between the gums and lower teeth may be filled with air.

Jaw: The jaw is closed.

Morph Target Group	Morph Target	Percentage
Brows	• Brows Middle Up	70
Eyes	• Eye Left Down	25
	• Eye Right Down	25
Mouth	• Suppressed Sadness	80
Jaw	• Jaw Closed	100

CARTOON SUPPRESSED SADNESS

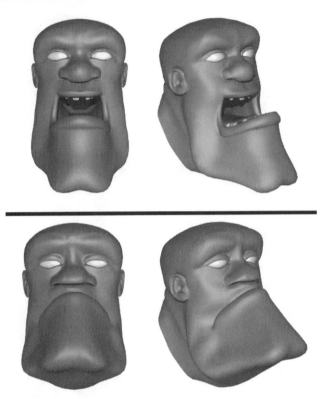

Distinguishing Features

Brows: The middle of the brow is raised.

Eyes: The eye can be open or slightly shut. Bags may appear under the eyes if the condition is prolonged.

Mouth: The lips are pressed together, and the space between the gums and lower teeth may be filled with air.

Jaw: The jaw is closed.

Morph Target Group	Morph Target	Percentage
Brows	• Brows Middle Raised	80
Eyes	• Eye Left Down	30
	• Eye Right Down	30
Mouth	• Mouth Suppressed Sadness	100

HUMAN YAWN

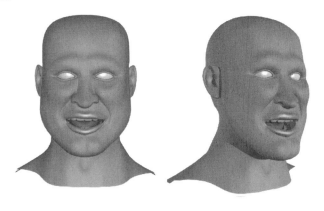

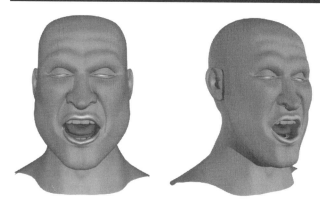

Distinguishing Features

Brows: The brows can be raised straight up, raised in the middle, or lowered.

Eyes: The eyes may be clamped shut or may be straining open.

Mouth: The mouth is open as wide as possible.

Jaw: The jaw is opened to its fullest extent.

Morph Target Group	Morph Target	Percentage
Brows	• Brows Angry	90
	• Brows Arched	100
Eyes	• Eye Left Down	50
	• Eye Right Down	50
Mouth	• Yawn	70
Jaw	• Jaw Open	120

CARTOON YAWN

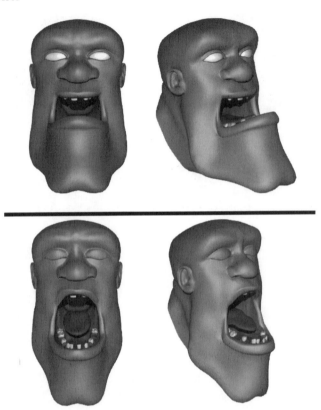

Distinguishing Features

Brows: The brows can be raised straight up, raised in the middle, or lowered.

Eyes: The eyes are clamped shut, or may be straining open.

Mouth: The mouth is open as wide as possible. Only the tips of the upper and lower teeth appear.

Jaw: The jaw is opened to its fullest extent.

Morph Target Group	Morph Target	Percentage
Brows	• Brows Middle Raised	60
Eyes	• Eye Left Down	100
	• Eye Right Down	100
Mouth	• Yawn	100

HUMAN DAZED

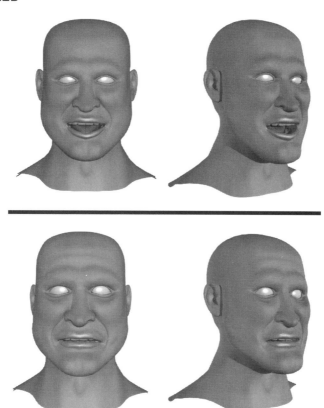

Distinguishing Features

Brows: The brows may be relaxed or raised a bit.

Eyes: The lids are opened wider than normal. The eyes stare straight ahead and unfocused. In animation they might swim about lazily.

Mouth: The mouth is relaxed.

Jaw: The jaw is closed.

Morph Target Group	Morph Target	Percentage
Brows	• Brows Arched	100
	• Brows Middle Up	90
Eyes	• Eyes Wide	100
Mouth	• Suppressed Sadness	60
	• Surprise	60
Jaw	• Jaw Closed	60

CARTOON DAZED

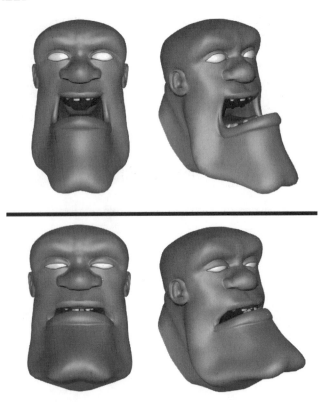

Distinguishing Features

Brows: The brows may be relaxed or raised a bit.

Eyes: The lids are opened wider than normal. The eyes stare straight ahead and are unfocused. In animation they might swim about lazily.

Mouth: The mouth is relaxed.

Jaw: The jaw is closed.

Morph Target Group	Morph Target	Percentage
Brows	• NONE	N/A
Eyes	• Eye Left Down	45
	• Eye Right Down	45
Mouth	• Closed	100
	• Frightened	40

HUMAN SLEEP

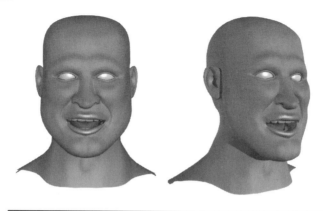

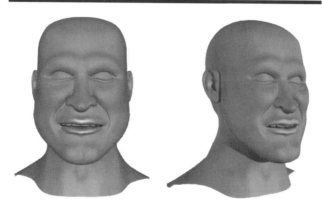

Distinguishing Features

Brows: The brows are relaxed.

Eyes: The eyes are closed.

Mouth: The mouth is either shut or slightly opened and relaxed.

Jaw: The jaw is either closed or slightly open.

Morph Target Group	Morph Target	Percentage
Brows	• NONE	N/A
Eyes	• Eye Left Down	100
	• Eye Right Down	100
Mouth	• Mouth Purse	20
Jaw	• Jaw Closed	20

CARTOON SLEEP

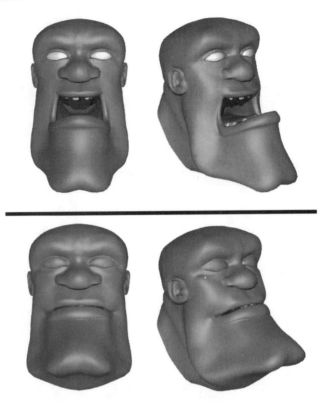

Distinguishing Features

Brows: The brows are relaxed.

Eyes: The eyes are closed.

Mouth: The mouth is either shut or slightly opened and relaxed.

Jaw: The jaw is either closed or slightly open.

Morph Target Group	Morph Target	Percentage
Brows	• NONE	N/A
Eyes	• Eye Left Down	100
	• Eye Right Down	100
Mouth	• Smile	90

HUMAN DRUNK OR TIRED LAUGHTER

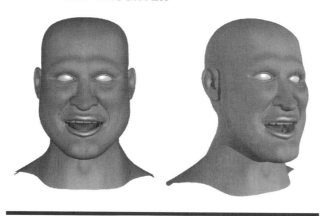

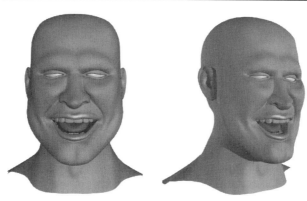

Distinguishing Features

Brows: The brows are either relaxed or raised in an attempt to raise the eyelids.

Eyes: The eyelids are drooping almost to their halfway position.

Mouth: The mouth is open and pulled back toward the ears, tightening the lips against the teeth. The cheeks bunch up and dimples appear, but these are not as severe as most other laughs.

Jaw: The jaw is open.

Morph Target Group	Morph Target	Percentage
Brows	• NONE	N/A
Eyes	• Eye Left Down	50
	• Eye Right Down	50
Mouth	• Laughter	100
Jaw	• Jaw Open	50

CARTOON DRUNK OR TIRED LAUGHTER

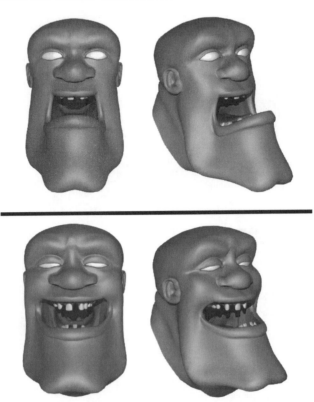

Distinguishing Features

Brows: The brows are either relaxed or raised in an attempt to raise the eyelids.

Eyes: The eyelids are drooping almost to their halfway position.

Mouth: The mouth is open and pulled back toward the ears, tightening the lips against the teeth. The cheeks bunch up and dimples appear, but these are not as severe as most other laughs.

Jaw: The jaw is open.

Morph Target Group	Morph Target	Percentage
Brows	• Brows Left Raised	100
	• Brows Right Raised	100
	• Brows Middle Raised	70
Eyes	• Eye Left Down	50
	• Eye Right Down	50
Mouth	• Laughter	75
	• Smile Open	100

HUMAN "I THINK YOU'RE NUTS" SMILE

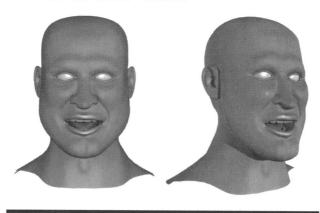

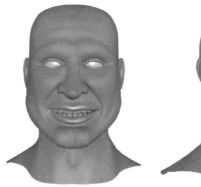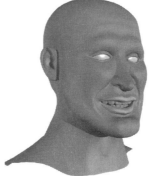

Distinguishing Features

Brows: The brows are raised straight up.

Eyes: The lids are lowered slightly.

Mouth: The mouth is opened, pulled back toward the ears, and stretched tightly against the teeth.

Jaw: The jaw is closed or slightly open.

Morph Target Group	Morph Target	Percentage
Brows	• Brows Arched	45
	• Brows Middle Up	35
Eyes	• Eye Left Down	15
	• Eye Right Down	15
Mouth	• Laughter	70
	• Smile Closed	60
Jaw	• Jaw Closed	70

CARTOON "I THINK YOU'RE NUTS" SMILE

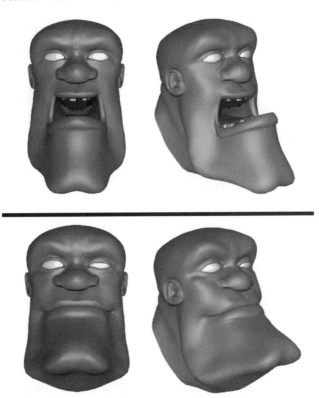

Distinguishing Features

Brows: The brows are raised straight up.

Eyes: The lids are lowered slightly.

Mouth: The mouth is opened, pulled back toward the ears, and stretched tightly against the teeth.

Jaw: The jaw is closed or slightly open.

Morph Target Group	Morph Target	Percentage
Brows	• Brows Left Raised	100
Eyes	• Eye Right Down	100
Mouth	• Smile	100

HUMAN BAD ODOR

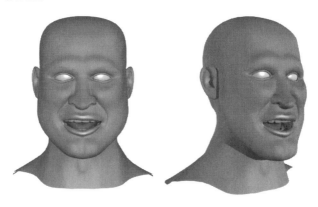

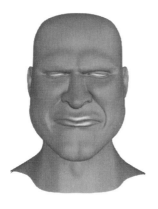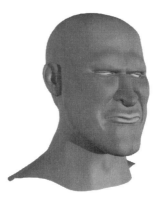

Distinguishing Features

Brows: The brows are lowered as if angered.

Eyes: The eyes are open or partly shut.

Mouth: The mouth is closed, with the upper lip raised in a sneer.

Jaw: The jaw is closed or slightly parted.

Morph Target Group	Morph Target	Percentage
Brows	• Brows Compressed	80
Eyes	• NONE	N/A
Mouth	• Crying	100
	• Closed	100
Jaw	• Jaw Closed	100

CARTOON BAD ODOR

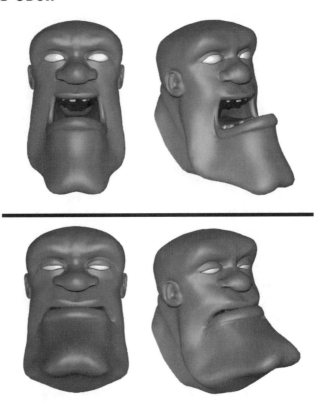

Distinguishing Features

Brows: The brows are lowered as if angered.

Eyes: The eyes are open or partly shut.

Mouth: The mouth is closed, with the upper lip raised in a sneer.

Jaw: The jaw is closed or slightly parted.

Morph Target Group	Morph Target	Percentage
Brows	• Brows Left Raised	100
Eyes	• Eye Left Down	50
	• Eye Right Down	50
Mouth	• Closed	90
	• Repulsion	100

F

Just for Fun—
Cartoon
Expressions

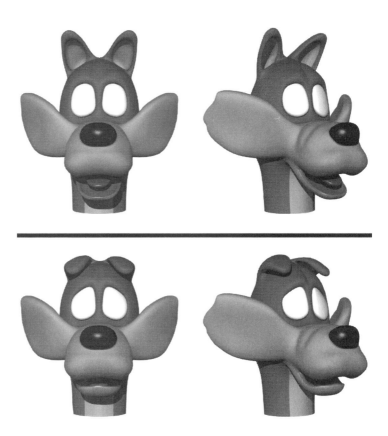

While humans and Living Toons are certainly dynamic characters, you may want to be more adventurous at times and explore the zany world of cartoon characters. Cartoon characters have the unique advantage of doing just about anything they want, meaning they can exaggerate every expression and often transform their appearance to suit the expressions. There have been a number of classic cartoon character emotions expressed over the years by Warner Brothers, Disney, and Hanna-Barbera. These expressions, along with many others, are provided in this appendix to give you a visual reference of common cartoon character expressions.

Our volunteer for this appendix is Butch that alley dog. Butch is a tough character, but like all cartoon characters he has a soft side. In Figure F.1 below you'll find an image showing the neutral pose for Butch's head.

This is the starting point for this character's facial animation. All of the expressions listed in this appendix started with this pose. When you are examining the facial expressions, you'll find the neutral pose at the top of each image, with the actual pose underneath so you can see where the changes have occurred.

The first several expressions are ones that parallel human expression. The last group of expressions cover the zany world of cartoon character expression, where anything can happen and does. Many of the examples shown are geared specifically towards a cartoon animal. I hope you find these examples useful.

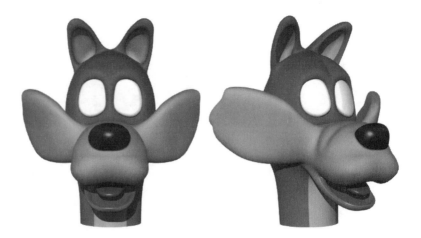

FIGURE *Butch's neutral pose.*
F.1

AFRAID

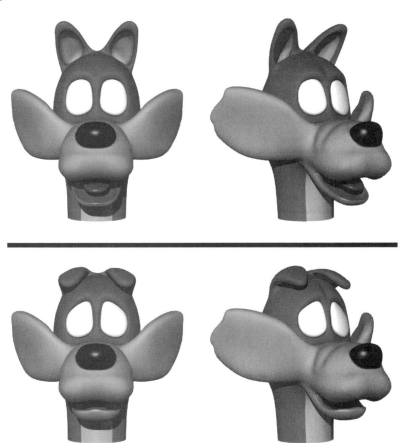

Distinguishing Features

Ears: The ears droop forward over the brow.

Brows: The brows are drawn toward the center.

Eyes: No change.

Whiskers: No change.

Mouth: The mouth is slightly open with the lower lip curled inward and the tongue resting against the lower gum.

ANGER

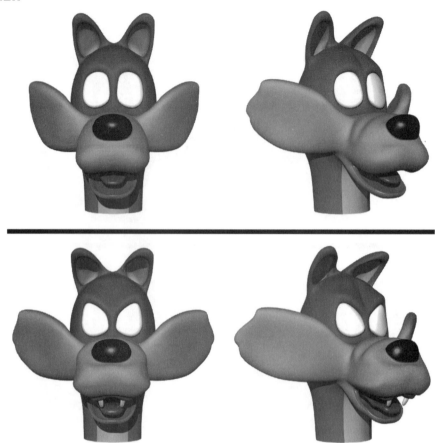

Distinguishing Features

Ears: The ears are bent forward slightly.

Brows: The inner portion of brow is drawn down toward the nose.

Eyes: No change.

Whiskers: The whiskers move forward a bit.

Mouth: The upper lip pulled up in snarl. The nose is crumpled, creating wrinkles along the muzzle. The tongue curls, making it wavy. Finally, fangs appear in the gums. Cartoon characters have the ability to spontaneously generate body parts that enhance an expression. In this case, the fangs help to make him appear more frightening.

ASLEEP

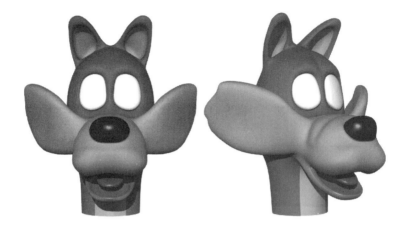

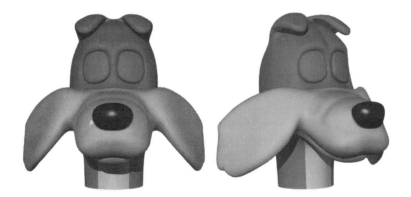

Distinguishing Features

Ears: The ears flop forward over the brow.

Brows: No change.

Eyes: The eyelids are lowered 100%, showing an eyelid seam.

Whiskers: The whiskers droop down in a relaxed position.

Mouth: The mouth is closed and relaxed.

CRYING

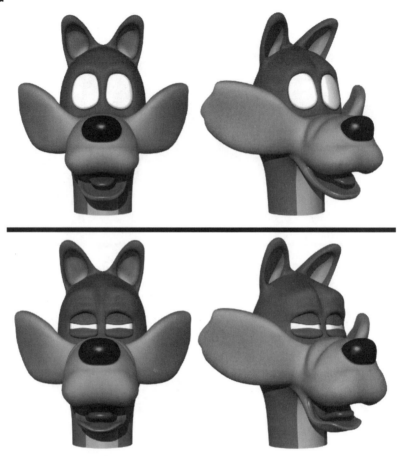

Distinguishing Features

Ears: No change.

Brows: The brow is pushed forward.

Eyes: The eyes are compressed, with the upper and lower eyelids nearly meeting in the middle.

Whiskers: No change.

Mouth: The jaw and tongue are curled and drawn back, while the nose and top of the muzzle are pulled up slightly.

DOOM

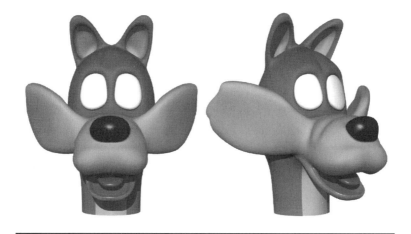

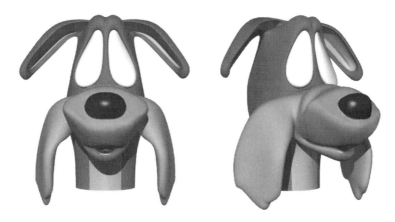

Distinguishing Features

Ears: The ears are rotated out to the side, drooped down, and stretched out.

Brows: The brows are drawn up and in toward the center, with the brow rising above the top of the head. The top of the head is compressed inward with the brow.

Eyes: The eyes are stretched upward and inward.

Whiskers: The whiskers droop down completely.

Mouth: The mouth is partially closed. The upper lip is tightened and pulled up, and the lower lip is drawn to a point, with the top of the tongue is curled to a point.

Common Uses

This is a great expression to use when your character sees its impending doom. For example, just before the piano drops on its head or possibly when it has run off the end of a cliff and is about to fall.

DUH?

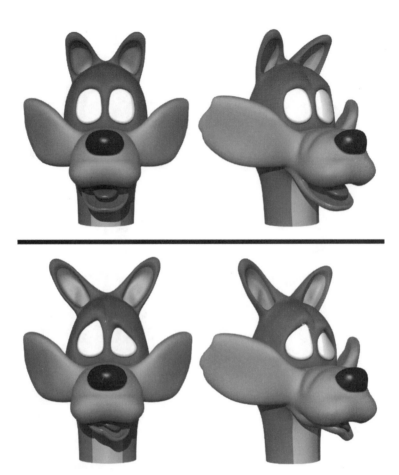

Distinguishing Features

Ears: The ears are spread wide and remain upright.

Brows: The brows are asymmetrically drawn in toward the center, with one lowered.

Eyes: The eyes are deformed asymmetrically, one squinting more than the other.

Whiskers: No change.

Mouth: The mouth is closed on one side and drooped downward on the other.

Common Uses

This is your basic confused look. It's commonly used for those characters that are less than bright. A good use would be when the character presented with a decision can't answer.

FALSE SMILE

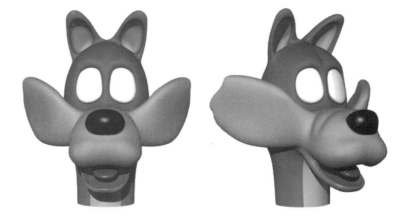

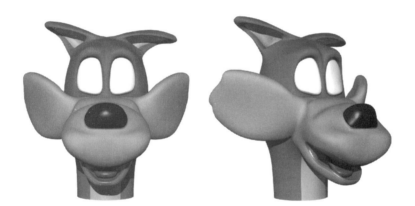

Distinguishing Features

Ears: The ears are rotated sideways and lowered to nearly parallel with the top of the head.

Brows: The brows are raised straight up so they are parallel with the top of the head.

Eyes: The inner, lower corners of the eyes are drawn down toward the muzzle.

Whiskers: No change.

Mouth: The corners of the mouth are drawn up in a smile, and the rest of the mouth, betraying a lack of sincerity, is rippled.

HAPPY

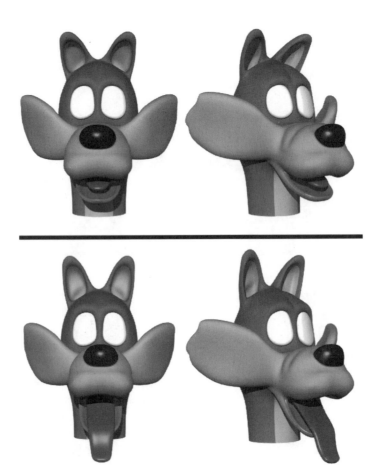

Distinguishing Features

Ears: No change.

Brows: The brows are raised slightly.

Eyes: No change.

Whiskers: No change.

Mouth: The mouth is dropped open and the tongue hangs out.

LAUGHTER

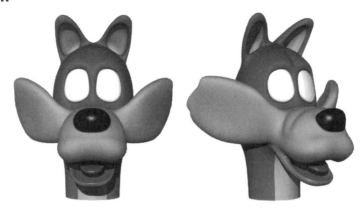

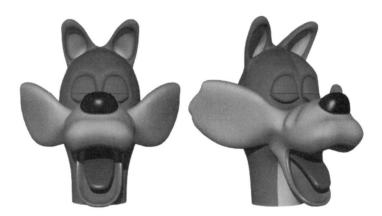

Distinguishing Features

Eyes: No change.

Brows: No change.

Eyes: The eyes are closed showing a seam where the eyelids meet in the middle. The cheeks are pushed up against the lower portion of the eye.

Whiskers: No change.

Mouth: The mouth is open wide with the upper muzzle being raised. The tongue hovers above the lower gums.

PAIN

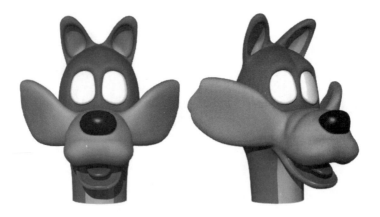

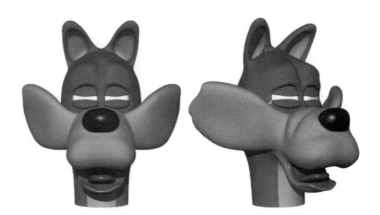

Distinguishing Features

Ears: No change.

Brows: The brow raised and pushed forward.

Eyes: The eyes are squeezed vertically, and the lids are partly shut, showing a gap in the middle.

Whiskers: No change.

Mouth: The muzzle is crumpled with the lower lip and tongue curled upward at the tip.

SAD

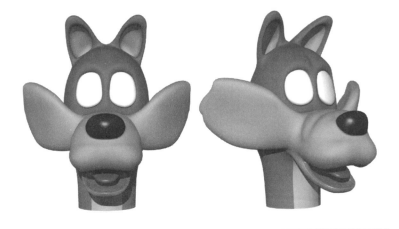

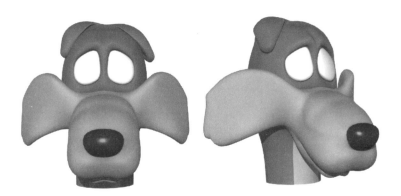

Distinguishing Features

Ears: The ears droop down and lay flat against the side of the head.

Brows: The brows are drawn up in the center and slightly forward.

Eyes: No change.

Whiskers: The whiskers droop down.

Mouth: The jaw is closed, leaving only a slight gap. The muzzle droops downward and the lower lip is pulled down on either side.

SATISFACTION

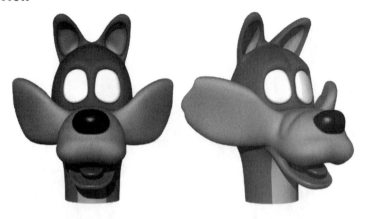

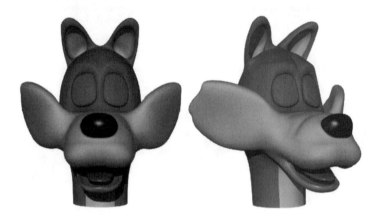

Distinguishing Features

Ears: The eyes are completely closed showing no seams.

Brows: The brows are lifted slightly.

Eyes: No change.

Whiskers: No change.

Mouth: No change.

SLEEPY

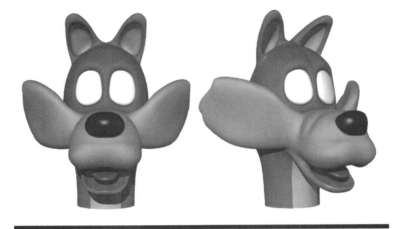

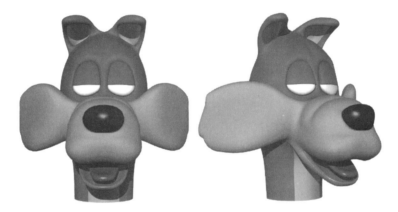

Distinguishing Features

Ears: The ears are drooped over the brow slightly.

Brows: No change.

Eyes: The upper eyelids are pulled down leaving only a small gap. There are no lower eyelids present.

Whiskers: The whiskers are drooped downward at the tips.

Mouth: The muzzle is puffed up slightly.

SNEER

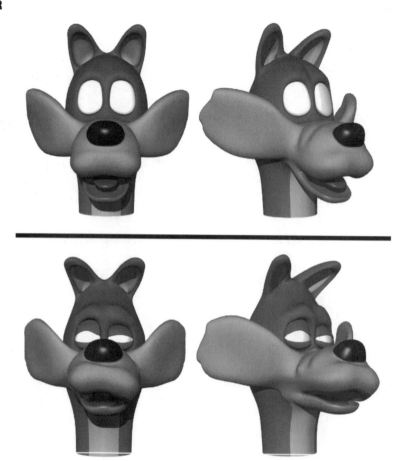

Distinguishing Features

Ears: The ears are rotated outward and downward slightly. The top of the head is tapered to a rounded point.

Brows: The brows are lowered dramatically and pushed forward. One is lowered more than the other.

Eyes: The eyes are closed, leaving only a small gap between the eyelids. The upper eyelid of the larger eye is pulled upward in the middle.

Whiskers: The whiskers are rotated down slightly at the tips.

Mouth: The upper muzzle is compressed and raised up slightly on the side of with the larger eye. The lower jaw is pulled upward to become parallel with the muzzle and the tongue rests flat on the lower gums.

SNOBBISH

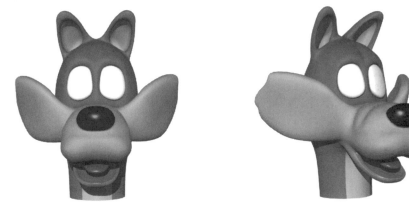

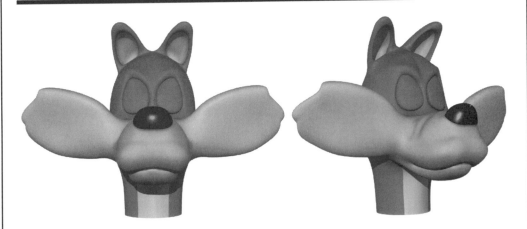

Distinguishing Features

Ears: No change.

Brows: The brows are raised on the outside of the eyes.

Eyes: The eyes are closed completely, showing no eyelid seam.

Whiskers: The whiskers are rotated forward to become parallel with one another.

Mouth: The mouth is closed with the muzzle curled upward at the tip.

YAWN

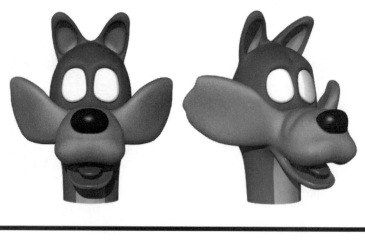

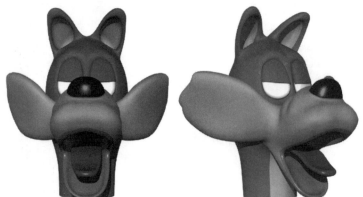

Distinguishing Features

Ears: No change.

Brows: No change.

Eyes: The upper lids of the eyes are lowered halfway down the eye. There is no lower eyelid visible.

Whiskers: No change.

Mouth: The upper muzzle is rotated upward and the mouth is wide open. The tongue remains in the middle of the mouth and curls slightly at the tip.

YELL

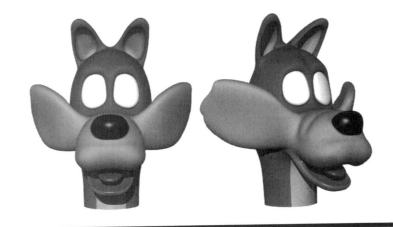

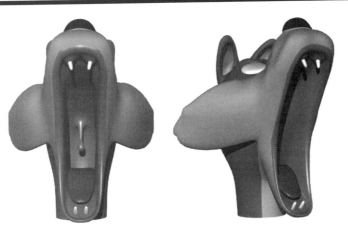

Distinguishing Features

Ears: No change.

Brows: No change.

Eyes: No change.

Whiskers: The whiskers are folded back against the head.

Mouth: The head is rotated backward significantly. The upper muzzle is rotated upward significantly. The lower jaw is dropped all the way down and fangs appear in the upper and lower gums. The tongue lies flat on the lower gums.

ACCORDION

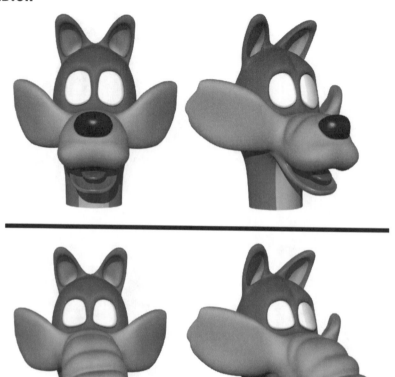

Distinguishing Features

Ears: No change.

Brows: No change.

Eyes: No change.

Whiskers: No change.

Mouth: The muzzle is stretched forward and drooped downward. The mouth is closed and multiple creases are present on the top of the muzzle, creating the accordion appearance.

Common Uses

This is a great animated expression, where the nose recoils like an accordion. This is commonly used when the character runs into an immovable object like a wall or cliff. It's also used when the character is hit in the face with an object that doesn't stick.

ANGUISH

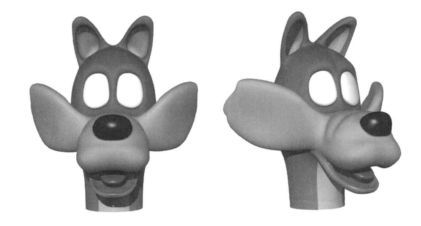

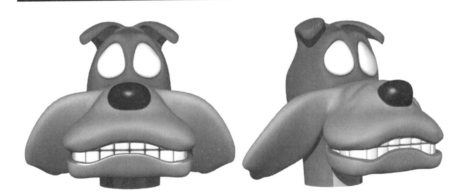

Distinguishing Features

Ears: The ears are drooped outward and down toward the brow.

Brows: The brows are raised inward to become parallel with the top of the head.

Eyes: The eyes are shaped like teardrops.

Whiskers: The whiskers are drooped downward.

Mouth: The sides of the mouth are pulled outward severely to form a square jaw. The lips are lowered and the gums are parted and lowered on either side, exposing rows of teeth.

WATCH THE BIRDIE

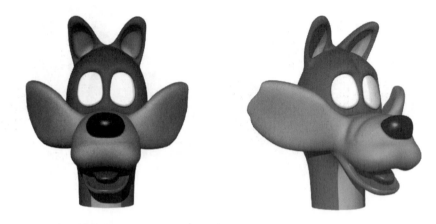

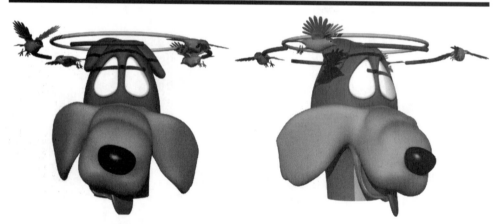

Distinguishing Features

Ears: The ears are lowered so they lay flat on the sides of the head.

Brows: The brows are pulled upward and inward until they are parallel with the head.

Eyes: The eyes are shaped like long teardrops.

Whiskers: The whiskers droop down to the sides of the head.

Mouth: The muzzle is drooped downward with the jaw open slightly, letting the tongue hang out.

Special: Little birds are added, flying in circles around the top of the head. The birds are accompanied by circular lines that also rotate around the top of the head.

Common Uses

This is a very common expression for cartoon characters. It's one of the more unique, since it has supporting cast members and is heavily animated. The common uses for Watch the Birdie are situations where the character is hit on the head with a smaller object that doesn't knock him unconscious, such as brick, rock, or anvil. Typically Spelunker expression precedes Watch the Birdie.

CLANG

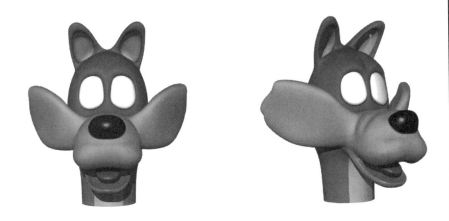

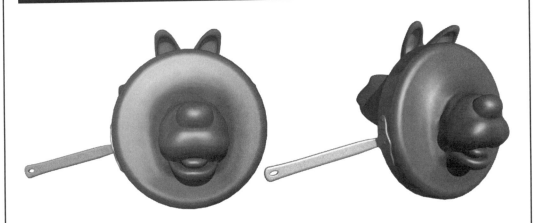

Distinguishing Features

Ears: No change.

Brows: No change.

Eyes: No change.

Whiskers: No change.

Mouth: The impact object is molded around the muzzle of the character, taking on the shape of the muzzle.

Common Uses

The Clang expression is used when an object sticks to the face of your character, taking on the shape of its face. This expression is often used when the character is hit with a frying pan, pie pan, or in many cases an object like a baseball bat. Whatever the object, it takes on the shape of the character's face. The Clang expression is typically followed by Watch the Birdie.

HUBBA-HUBBA

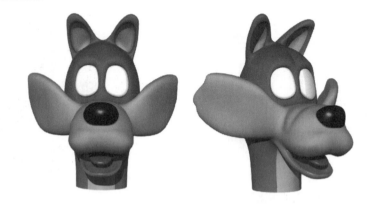

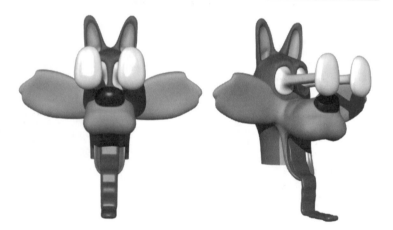

Distinguishing Features

Ears: The ears stand straight up and are stretched upward a bit.

Brows: The brows are moved forward a bit.

Eyes: The eyes pop out of the head and hang over the end of the muzzle.

Whiskers: The whiskers stand straight out to the sides of the muzzle.

Mouth: The lower jaw drops all the way down and the tongue rolls out like a carpet for a king.

Common Uses

This is a fun expression that is used to express extreme attraction. This can be used for a number of situations. While it's commonly used when your character sees an attractive character of the opposite six, it can also be used to express lust for an object such as money. It could be used when your character opens the door to a vault of money or possibly when it enters an Egyptian burial chamber full of gold.

IMPACT

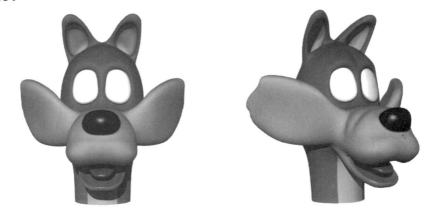

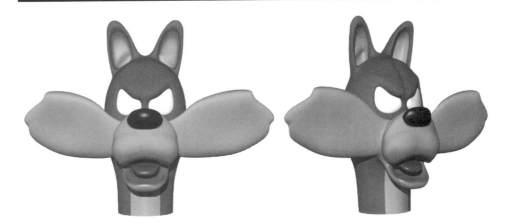

Distinguishing Features

Ears: The ears stand straight up and are stretched upward a bit.

Brows: The center of the brows are pushed downward to the center of the eye.

Eyes: Only changed by the brow movement.

Whiskers: The whiskers stand straight out to the sides of the muzzle.

Mouth: The muzzle is pushed flat against the head.

Common Uses

This expression is used in similar cased to Clang, but the object doesn't stick to the face. It's used when the impact is less severe. For example, your character is hit in the face with a board, falls flat on its face, or runs into a wall. It's a great expression to use when a door has been slammed in the face.

GRIN

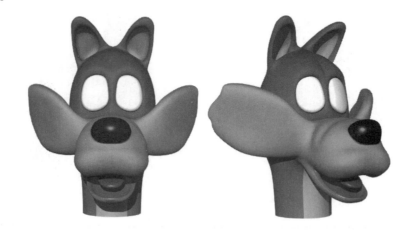

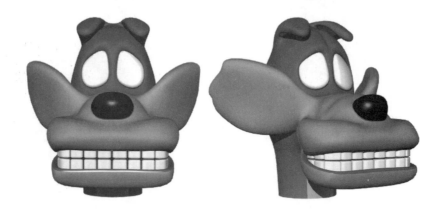

Distinguishing Features

Ears: The ears drooped forward over the brow.

Brows: The outside edge of the brow is lowered slightly.

Eyes: The eyes are shaped like teardrops.

Whiskers: The whiskers are pulled upward at the tips.

Mouth: The sides of the mouth are pulled outward severely to form a square jaw. The lips are parted exposing a wide gap that shows rows of teeth.

Common Uses

Cartoon characters are very flexible and develop features on the fly to accentuate expressions. Grin is a perfect example of this. The character has developed a full set of teeth to facilitate the Grin expression. This expression is used when it has irritated a larger character and is trying to weasel out of it with a grin.

LOVE

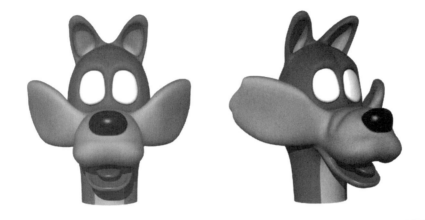

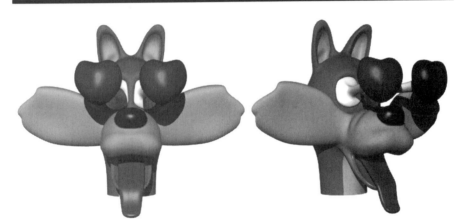

Distinguishing Features

Ears: The ears are raised upward.

Brows: No change.

Eyes: The eyes are pulled out over the muzzle and shaped like hearts.

Whiskers: The whiskers are pulled upward at the tips.

Mouth: The lower jaw is dropped downward and the tongue hangs out of the mouth, lying against the lower gums.

PUMMELED

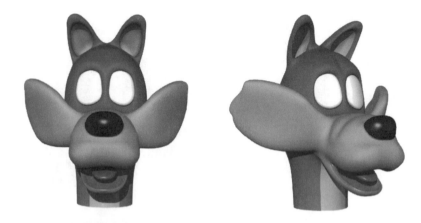

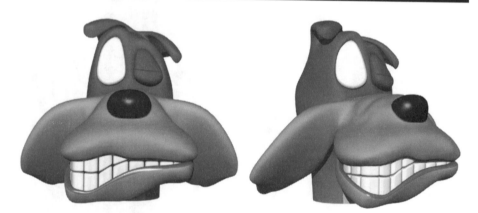

Distinguishing Features

Ears: The ears are drooped over the sides of the head.

Brows: The brows are raised with one passing the top of the head.

Eyes: The high-brow eye is unchanged while the lower-brow eye is closed with a seam in the middle where the eyelids meet. The smaller eye is also puffed outward to appear swollen.

Whiskers: The whiskers are rotated forward and drooped down against the sides of the head.

Mouth: The sides of the mouth are pulled outward severely to form a square jaw. The lips are parted exposing a wide gap that shows rows of teeth—the gap is widest on one side tapering to a small gap on the opposite side. The largest gap is on the same side as the larger eye. The jaw is lowered on the side with the greatest gap.

BLINDS

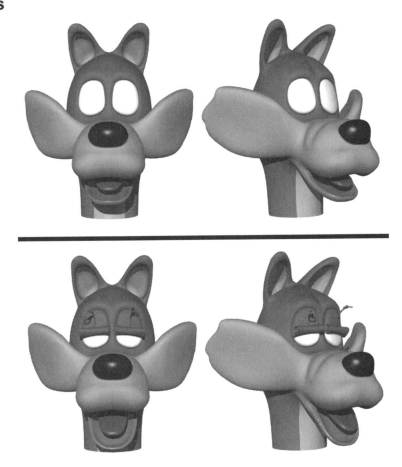

Distinguishing Features

Ears: No change.

Brows: The brow is pulled forward slightly.

Eyes: The upper eyelids are closed two-thirds of the way down the eye and curled at the tip. A string and ring are attached to the eyelid to create the appearance of blinds.

Whiskers: No change.

Mouth: The lower jaw is dropped open and the tongue hovers above the lower gums.

Common Uses

This expression is usually the result of another character's pulling your character's eyelids down like shutters. It's the cartoon equivalent of poking someone in the eyes.

SPELUNKER

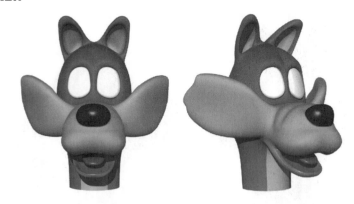

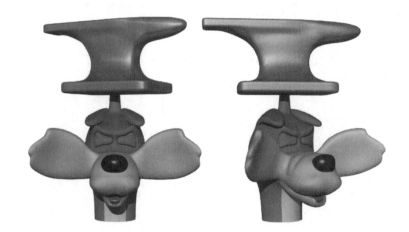

Distinguishing Features

Ears: The ears lie flat on the brow. A large bump is raised between the ears where the object that struck the character sits.

Brows: The brows are compressed downward in the middle.

Eyes: The eyes are closed showing a seam where the eyelids meet.

Whiskers: The whiskers are rotated forward, curling past the parallel point.

Mouth: The mouth is nearly closed and the lower jaw is curled inward with the tongue curled inward as well.

Special: An object sits atop the bump between the ears.

Common Uses

The Spelunker is the moment of impact, when an object of significant weight has been dropped on the character's head. This expression usually precedes Watch the Birdie.

STAR STRUCK

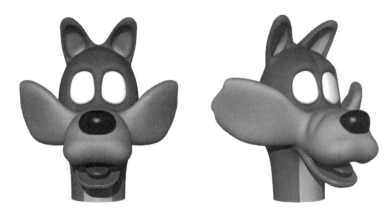

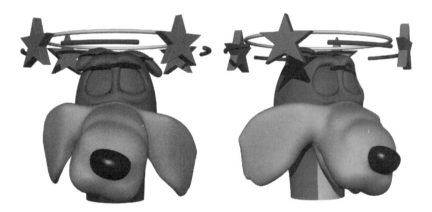

Distinguishing Features

Ears: The ears lie flat on the sides of the head and the top of the head is compressed flat.

Brows: The brows are pushed forward.

Eyes: The eyes are closed with no visible eyelid seam, and there are puffy bags below the eyes.

Whiskers: The whiskers droop against the sides of the head.

Mouth: The mouth is closed and the muzzle droops downward.

Special: Little stars are added, flying in circles around the top of the head. The stars are accompanied by circular lines that also rotate around the top of the head.

Common Uses

Star Struck is very similar to Watch the Birdie. It involves supporting cast members rotating around the character's head while it is unconscious. While Watch the Birdie is used when a small object is dropped on their head, Star Struck is used when large objects like pianos and safes are dropped on the character's head, knocking the character out.

TRAIN WHISTLE

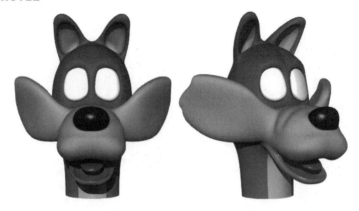

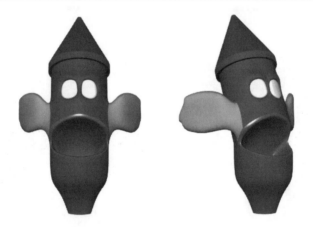

Distinguishing Features

Ears: The ears are removed.

Brows: The brows remain unchanged.

Eyes: No change.

Whiskers: The whiskers are rotated backward.

Mouth: The mouth is turned into a gaping wedge.

Special: The head is shaped like a train whistle, cylindrical with a cone top.

Common Uses

This is a severe morphing expression where the character's head takes on the shape of a train whistle. This is often used to express having eaten something hot such as chili or hot liquid.

TRUMPET

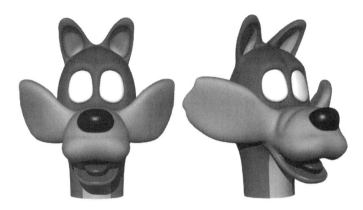

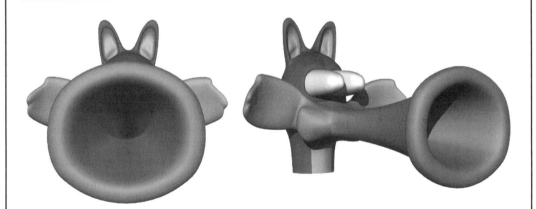

Distinguishing Features

Ears: The ears stand straight up.

Brows: No change.

Eyes: The eyes bug out of the head and stop at the end of the cheeks.

Whiskers: The whiskers stand straight out to the sides of the head and are curled forward at the tips.

Mouth: The cheeks are puffed full of air and the muzzle is stretched outward and shaped like a horn.

Common Uses

The Trumpet expression is often used to express a loud yell, calling another character, or warning it of danger. It is sometimes used to express lust, typically as a transitional expression preceding Hubba-Hubba.

WHISTLE

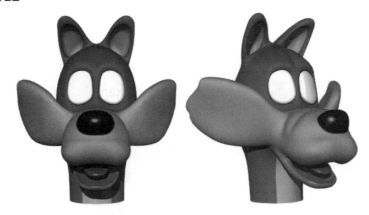

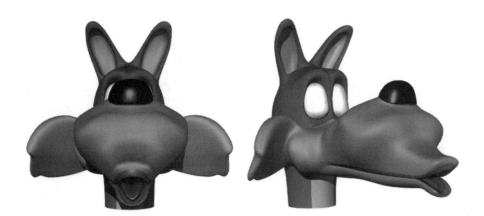

Distinguishing Features

Ears: The ears stand upward and are stretched a bit.

Brows: The brows are raised upward and forward over the eyes until they are parallel with the top of the head.

Eyes: No change.

Whiskers: The whiskers are rotated forward until the tips curl around the cheeks.

Mouth: The cheeks are puffed full of air and the muzzle is stretched outward, tapering larger at the tip. The mouth is closed, and the lips are pulled forward and parted.

Common Uses

This is a common expression used in the early days of cartoon animation to express interests in a good-looking character walking by. It's the equivalent of the construction worker's catcall. It can also be used to express interest in other things such as money. It's not as severe as the lust of the Hubba-Hubba expression, though it often precedes it.

ABOUT THE CD

Included with this book is a companion CD that contains a variety of support materials for each chapter. The support materials are provided in common formats that are compatible with all computers and 3D programs. Below you'll find a detailed description of the contents on the companion CD-ROM.

Here's what you'll find on the CD:

Chapter 1

Movies

jawmovement.mov: An example of jaw movement
jawrotation.mov: An example of jaw rotation
mandiblemove.mov: An example of Mandible motion
mandiblerotation.mov: An example of Mandible rotation
noselock.mov: An example of nose lock
supraorbital.mov: An example of Supraorbital motion

Chapter 2

DXF Models

A female skull, head modeling template
A male skull, head modeling template

Chapter 3

Movies

QuickTime movies demonstrating movement of the following muscles: Corrugator, Depressor, Frontalis, Levator, Masseter, Mentalis, Obicularis Oris, Obicularis Oculi, Platysma, Triangularis and Zygomaticus

Chapter 4

Movie

An animation of Papagaio demonstrating facial expression and emotion

Chapter 5

Movies

Kuckles1.mov: The first pass at lip-synching Knuckles
KucklesFix.mov: The improved Knuckles animation

Sound File

Knuckles.wav: Knuckles dialog

Chapter 6

Movies   2TargetMorph.mov: An example of weighted morphing
Ptest1.mov: The first pass at lip-synching Guido
Guidofinal.mov: The second pass at lip-synching Guido

Sound File   Youwant.wav: Guido's dialog

Chapter 7

Movie Files: Sweet.mov
Sweetanm2.mov
SweetFIX.mov

Sound Files: Sweet2.wav

Expression Templates   Modeling templates for forming facial expressions

Phoneme Templates   Modeling templates for forming the basic phonemes

Figures   Color copies of the figures for Chapters 1-7 and Appendices A-F

Hardware/ Software Requirements

You'll need a QuickTime player for viewing the included QuickTime Movies. If you don't have a QuickTime player you can download one from http://www.apple.com/quicktime/. You'll also need a sound player capable of playing WAV files to listen to the dialog examples.

To view the color figures and modeling templates found on the companion CD-ROM you'll need an image viewer capable of viewing JPG files.

Index